A DAY O

To help us to live

Daily readings for your comfort compiled by

Thomas Bartram

A Day of Grace

Compiled by Thomas Bartram

GRACE PUBLISHERS

A DAY OF GRACE

GRACE PUBLISHERS
Mulberry Court, Stour Road, Christchurch, Dorset BH23 1PS. (UK)
Tel: 01202 476868. Fax: 01202 480559

Here is a book you will want to read, a book to give to friends and family, a book to read at home and anywhere. It can be read at any time – beside the fire, in the train or at the bedside. It is a book to turn to as an old friend at the beginning or end of the day.

The compiler invites you to share with him some of the literary treasures that have brought him pleasure over a lifetime. It is a book for busy people. It offers a thought for practical guidance, every day of the year.

Why affirmations? In the stressful hour they may prove a source of strength and security. Some are spiritual vitamins to re-vitalise and sustain a weary body or tired brain.

This book introduces readers to writers of past and present generations. Some record deep personal experience, others moments of ecstasy and illumination.

There is something for everyone. Whether you are young or old, married or single, housewife or career girl, you should find a daily support within easy reach.

Are you wrestling with some distressing misfortune? Herein, you will find testimonies of men and women who have won through to a life of fulfilment. All record a life of achievement and purpose, yet throughout these pages runs the golden thread of Grace, source of all true wisdom that illuminates the unseen dimension of the universe.

For Valerie and Irene

ACKNOWLEDGEMENTS

The Compiler is grateful for permission given by owners of copyright. Where no credit is given, it is assumed the quotation is traditional. Extracts have been included for which it has not been possible to contact owners of copyright. The Compiler sincerely requests the goodwill of such owners and that their generous permission may be granted.

The Compiler acknowledges with sincere thanks the expertise and helpful advice from Mr Tony Purvis and his team at GreenShires Creative Colour Ltd., Leicester. It is a privilege to include extracts from the widely-read *Christophers News Notes, New York*. I am specially grateful to my dear friend Garth Henrichs for extracts from his "Sunshine", at one time one of the most popular magazines in the USA. Also, Valerie Collin and Irene Lonsdale for holding down a busy office with their usual sang-froid and efficiency at Grace Publishers.

© 1998 by Thomas Bartram.
First published in 1998 by
Grace Publishers, Mulberry Court, Christchurch, Dorset, BH23 1PS.
Phototypeset and printed in Great Britain by
GreenShires Creative Colour Ltd, 164 Barkby Road, Leicester, LE4 9LF
and bound by
F. F. Allsopp & Company Ltd, Union Road, Nottingham NG3 1FU.

ISBN 0-9515984-7-3

Cover Photograph:
Coton Manor Gardens, Ravensthorpe, Northamptonshire,
by Clive Nichols, 69 Albert Road, Caversham Heights, Reading RG4 7AW.

"We bless Thee for our creation"

The Book of Common Prayer

For Your Good Cheer

GRACE . . . what a lovely word . . . music to the soul . . . balm to the tired mind . . . gentle therapy for mind and body.

This is an anthology for family and friends. It is the hope of the compiler that the reader will embark on a fascinating voyage of discovery in which unfound gold and hidden beauties shine.

As a nation we are becoming more disturbed, tense, irritated, upset and insecure about many things. Atomic physics has unleashed tremendous energy. New, and more terrible diseases appear on the medical scene. Environmental hazards threaten our peace of mind. Thoughtful men and women confess an anxious foreboding when contemplating the future of the planet under modern science. All seek re-assurance on the future of this changing world.

Are you the magnet that attracts health and joy, or one that brings into its orbit depression and gloom? Do you look for a richer and more satisfying life? You want to move forward without losing the certainty and stability of yesterday? This book may prepare your mind for change. Happiness is something positive.

If you are ambitious, you will require the will to win. Maybe you seek recovery from a debilitating illness. You will need the faith that one day you will be restored to a sound mind and body. Develop a lively expectation of sure and certain recovery. There is such a thing as "the winning feeling".

Do not be surprised if the goal towards which you move comes in the guise of defeat. Everyone experiences unwelcome reverses at some time in life. Before every major achievement there may come a series of disappointing setbacks destroying confidence in your ultimate success. Fear robs us of our ability to make positive decisions.

One thing is certain. We cannot think in terms of fulfilment and successful living if our thought patterns rotate around failure, want, and bitterness of spirit. We have been born to learn and to enjoy earth's generous amenities. Enthusiasm and love of life is the natural response of a heart in harmony with the Creator of it all.

This present moment . . . are you having a rough time? Problems that defy solution? It is possible to stay calm in the face of irritation. Maybe life is so dark you cannot see the stars! Never once since the world began has the sun ever stopped shining.

"There are nettles everywhere," wrote Elizabeth Barrett Browning, "But smooth green grasses are more common still . . . The blue of heaven is larger than the cloud."

Every thought and emotion has a direct effect upon the physical constituents of the body. Organic disturbance may follow prolonged stress. There are times when one needs the help an affirmation may give. When we invite into our lives the love of God we stand a better chance of avoiding destructive cellular disease.

"Those only are happy," wrote John Stuart Mill, "who have their minds fixed on some object other than their own happiness, on the happiness of others, on the improvement of mankind, even on some art or pursuit followed not as a means, but as itself an ideal end. Aiming thus at something else, we find happiness by the way."

The following pages will help us to meet our daily responsibilities. When depressed and vitality is low they brace the mind with thoughts of courage and enthusiasm. Here, is practical guidance and spiritual refreshment for each day of the year. Why not set aside a few minutes each day to be still! There is strength in silence, solace in solitude, treasure in contentment.

Feel yourself on the threshold of a new life. Expect serenity and a sense of well being. Regard this book as a starting point of a new journey.

January 1st

NEW EVERY MORNING IS THE LOVE

New every morning is the love
Our wakening and uprising prove;
Through sleep and darkness safely brought,
Restored to life and power and thought.

New mercies each returning day
Hover around us while we pray;
New perils passed, new sins forgiven,
New thoughts of God, new hopes of heaven.

If on our daily course our mind
Be set to hallow all we find,
New treasures still of countless price
God will provide for sacrifice.

Old friends, old scenes, will lovelier be,
As more of heaven in each we see;
Some softening gleam of love and prayer
Shall dawn on every cross and care.

The trivial round, the common task,
Will furnish all we need to ask,
Room to deny ourselves, a road
To bring us daily nearer God.

Only, O Lord, in thy dear love,
Fit us for perfect rest above;
And help us, this and every day,
to live more nearly as we pray.

JOHN KEBLE.

January 2nd

I START TO WORK ON MY HANDICAPS.
I AM TRANSFORMED BY THE RENEWING OF MY MIND.
EVERY DAY I GET BETTER AND BETTER.

AT A New Year's Eve party I felt odd, taut, peculiar. I went to a hospital and suffered a stroke.

Medically speaking, I had suffered a coronary thrombosis, a cerebral embolism and complete aphasia.

My body was paralysed. I could hear the doctors and nurses talking, but I could not even make a sign.

They thought I was "goner". Even if I lived, they said, I would be permanently handicapped—crippled and without speech. I heard this horrible prediction—understood it with cruel clarity, yet could not protest.

I prayed as I had never prayed before, but have many times since. I believed, with unquestioning faith, that He had a purpose for my life and humbly asked Him for guidance.

One day seemingly from nowhere at all, there came to my mind this message from the Bible: Be ye transformed by the renewing of your mind. (Romans 12:2.)

I knew that He would continue to comfort and counsel me and would lend me a helping hand only when I helped myself. And first, in "renewing" my mind, I must overcome fear—fear of talking, moving, living, fear of another stroke.

I started to work on my handicaps. I kept at it; trying, trying. Improvement came gradually. My first comprehensive words were "Thank God."

In six weeks I shuffled out of the hospital with a distorted face and body. Once home, I wanted to stay there, hidden.

Although aware of what a spectacle I presented, I compelled myself to go out, to walk, to shop. In the grocery, with my wide-staring eyes, slap-hell gait, and uncontrollable voice noises, I had to point as best I could to what I wanted.

In my second year I was able to hold a pencil and copy, and in the third I could write my thoughts. When it seemed I had no more patience, prayer brought me the mental and physical strength to carry on.

After six long years I now show no physical evidence of a cerebral accident.

Hamilton Cameron, M.D.
Sincere thanks to the author whose address we are unable to trace.

January 3rd

> DROP THY STILL DEWS OF QUIETNESS . . . TILL ALL OUR STRIVINGS CEASE . . . TAKE FROM OUR LIVES THE STRAIN AND STRESS . . . AND MAY OUR ORDERED LIVES CONFESS THE BEAUTY OF THY PEACE.
>
> *John Greenleaf Whittier.*

LET us see what grace is: what strength it has, and how, by healing the will, it brings interior and exterior peace to man.

With these words, Marcello turned his eyes on the calm, translucent water which reflected as in a mirror the stars and beauty of the heavens, and seemed another heaven sown with lovely constellations. Pointing towards it, he continued: The water we see before us, which looks like another starry sky, partly helps us to understand what grace is. For as the image of the heavens, mirrored in the water, makes the lake look like the sky itself, so grace, when it comes to the soul and is enthroned in it, does not merely give it the semblance, but truly brings to it a likeness of God and His qualities, and transforms it into a very heaven as far as a creature can be so transformed without losing its substance. Grace is a quality, although created, that differs from any creature we see or that is created by the forces of nature, being neither air, nor smoke, nor born of any element; and the heavens themselves yield it precedence in the order of birth and sublimity of origin . . . For grace rises above and surpasses them all, being, as it were, a portrait of God's most special attributes, imitating and recalling closely that which pertains solely to Him.

Thus grace is like a deity or living image of Christ, which enters the soul and deifies it and is truly the soul of the soul.

Luis De Leon,
Spanish poet 1527–91.

January 4th

ONE OF THE MOST BEAUTIFUL COMPENSATIONS OF MY LIFE IS THAT WHEN I SINCERELY TRY TO HELP ANOTHER I CANNOT DO SO WITHOUT HELPING MYSELF.

LOVE is a gift of God. It is far more precious than any material thing one could ever hope to possess. It can't be purchased, for along with all of the best things in life, it is free. Its magic can change a dreary world into a heaven on earth. Its radiance is beyond human power of description. It is not restricted by race, creed or public opinion and has nothing to do with physical appearance, for "beauty is in the eye of the beholder."

There is no fault or shortcoming that love cannot overcome with charity and understanding. It does not imprison, but rather, in loving, one is set free. There is no limit to what love can accomplish, for its depth finds qualities that would otherwise remain undiscovered. It is the most beautiful, the most absorbing, and the most rewarding thing in life and by far the most important. For love is truly a gift of God.

Dorothy B. Elfstrom.

January 5th

EVERY DAY I SEE THE GOOD IN EVERYTHING AND LEARN TO PASS THE PRAISE.

"YOU'RE a wonderful little wife, and I don't know what I would do without you."

And as he spoke, he put his arms tenderly about her and kissed her, and she forgot all her cares in that moment. And, forgetting it all, she sang as she washed the dishes, and the song was heard next door, and a woman there caught the refrain and sang also, and the two homes were happier because the man had told his wife that sweet old story—the story of love.

As she sang, the errand boy, calling for an order, heard her song, and went out whistling on his journey; and the world heard the whistle, and one man, hearing it, thought, "Here is a lad who loves his work—a lad happy and contented. I resolve to love my work!"

So, because the man praised his wife, the song came from her heart, and it travelled on and on.

Democracy in Action.

January 6th

THIS, TOO, WILL PASS ... THERE'S ALWAYS ANOTHER BEND IN THE ROAD.

DURING the war, I flew lonely reconnaissance missions deep into Germany week after week. Under this stress I became strange and alien to myself: my handwriting became crabbed and illegible, I drank and gambled night after night, I could read nothing more substantial than the scandal sheets, and music, one of my chief joys, became boring and meaningless. One night, on my way to the briefing room, I even seriously considered trying to break my ankle—to avoid being sent out on another flight.

I was on the verge of a breakdown when the fighting ended. Then for weeks I slept, daydreamed and drifted through my duties. Meanwhile, deep inside, where the wellsprings of joy and health reside, a healing and regrowth must have been taking place. For gradually I began to read books again, my handwriting ceased to look like that of a crippled old man, and one day, hearing a familiar Mozart aria on a nearby radio, I suddenly felt a flood of good feeling wash through me.

I had the eerie sensation that all at once I was in the presence of a long-lost friend—myself. "It's me!" I thought in amazement, "I'm back!"

Spontaneous recoveries from emotional ailments are vastly more common than most of us realise. What does it? The mind itself.

A decade or so ago, most psychiatrists thought that an ill mind had little chance to cure itself; their thinking was still focused on the mind's frailties. Today that's changing. Many psychiatrists now stress that the human mind, like the body, has a whole battery of weapons to heal its own ills.

Without denying the value of psychiatry for the severely disturbed, the new viewpoint suggests that millions of people with emotional problems have the resources to heal themselves.

Morton Hunt,
in "Family Weekly".

May every day of this New year
From January to December,
Bring you, as you journey on,
Something lovely to remember.
Rita F. Snowden.

January 7th

WORDS OF LOVE TELL HOW WE FEEL . . . I SEEK AN OPPORTUNITY TO COMMUNICATE MY DEEPEST FEELING WHILE THERE IS STILL TIME . . . I LOVE YOU.

MY FATHER was a very reserved Canadian of English origin. Though he was a sensitive, loving parent, he wasn't a man to express his deepest feelings. Dad died almost 20 years ago, but often since, I've felt a twinge of yearning . . . I didn't remember him ever saying "I love you".

Recently, my son asked me to show him how to letter a title on the folder for a school project. "Oh, I wish your grandfather were here," I exclaimed, shaking my head. "He had an unusual way of lettering his blue-prints. He even showed me how simple it was to do. But I've forgotten the trick of it."

For hours afterward I racked my brain, trying to remember how Dad formed those simple distinctive letters; but all I could summon up was a nostalgic image of him bending over his drawing board.

The next day my brother called unexpectedly. He handed me a worn, folded envelope. "I was helping Mother sort through some of Dad's old papers, and we found this. Looks like something Dad must have done for you. We thought you'd like to have it."

When I unfolded the envelope, I felt a shiver of excitement. On it before me, in Dad's special lettering, was a complete alphabet, the very one I'd wanted to show my son.

It was like a message from heaven.

But even more thrilling was the notation at the bottom in my father's familiar hand—"This what you want, Dot?" And, alongside it, framed in a diamond, three words, words that were a long time in the coming, but not too late to warm me for the rest of my life.

"I love you."

DOROTHY CORSON.
Sincere thanks to the author whose address we are unable to trace.

MIDDLESEX, *Houses in Gentlemen's Row, Enfield.*
Photograph by A. F. Kersting.

January 8th

ENTHUSIASM IS MY KEY TO CREATIVE LIVING . . . EXCITING NEW POSSIBILITIES OPEN UP ALL THE TIME.

ENTHUSIASM is the greatest asset in the world. It beats money and power and influence. Single-handed the enthusiast convinces and dominates where the wealth accumulated by a small army of workers would scarcely raise any interest.

Enthusiasm tramples over prejudice and opposition, spurns inaction, storms the citadel of its object, and like an avalanche overwhelms and engulfs all obstacles. It is nothing more or less than faith in action.

Faith and initiative rightly combined remove mountainous barriers and achieve the unheard of and miraculous.

Set the germ of enthusiasm afloat in your plant, in your office, or on your farm; carry it in your attitude and manner; it spreads like contagion and influences every fibre of your industry before you realize it; it means increase in production and decrease in costs; it means joy and pleasure, and satisfaction to your workers; it means life, real, virile; it means spontaneous bedrock results—the vital things that pay dividends.

Henry Chester.

January 9th

A MERRY HEART DOES GOOD LIKE MEDICINE . . . BUT A BROKEN SPIRIT DRIES UP THE BONES.
Proverbs 17:22.

"A SMILE enriches those who receive without impoverishing those who give. It happens in a flash, yet the memory of it sometimes lasts for ever! None are so rich that they can get along without it, and none so poor but are richer for its benefits. It creates happiness in the home, fosters goodwill in business, and is the countersign of friends.

A smile is rest to the weary, daylight to the discouraged, sunshine to the sad, and Nature's best antidote for trouble. Yet it cannot be bought, begged, borrowed or stolen, for it is something that is no earthly good to anybody until it is given away! For nobody needs a smile so much as those who have none left to give!"

Frank I. Fletcher.

January 10th

JOY CAN BE REAL WHEN I MAKE LIFE A SERVICE, AND HAVE A DEFINITE OBJECT OUTSIDE MYSELF AND MY OWN PERSONAL HAPPINESS.

Leo Tolstoy.

I LIKE magnifying glasses. I have written about them before. They can be both useful and fun. But I don't like the magnifying glasses people seem to apply to other things—and I mentioned some things people do — like "magnifying" the harder parts of life, or carrying the whole world on their shoulders.

Here are some more things people do. There are some who "magnify" harmless remarks they hear and turn them into harmful gossip. There are those who take little incidents and "magnify" them into sensational news, as some of our newspapers are inclined to do.

There are people who get upset about some comment made about them and "magnify" them into insults. All this is really to lose our sense of proportion. We make trivial things matter and this leads us to forget or ignore really important things.

Robert Louis Stevenson used to tell how, when he was a small boy, he found it hard to sleep because of illness. His nurse would lift him from his cot and they would go to the window, even in the middle of the night, to see other windows with lights in them. Then they would tell each other that in those houses too, there were boys and girls who were sick and who couldn't sleep.

It helps us when we remember that we are all bound up in the "bundle of life" and are not the only people in trouble. It is part of being human.

We won't see so many slights and injuries in life if we stop thinking of ourselves as if we were the centre of the universe, if we think of the feelings of others as much as we think of our own.

WILLIAM BARCLAY.
Marching On. (Arthur James Ltd).

January 11th

TOMORROW'S ACHIEVEMENTS BE WHATEVER THEY MAY . . . ARE THE FUTURE RESULTS OF GOOD READING TODAY.

GOOD books, like good friends, are few and chosen; the more select the more enjoyable; and like these are approached with diffidence, nor sought too familiarly nor too often, having the precedence only when friends tire. The most mannerly of companions, accessible at all times, in all moods, they frankly declare the author's mind, without giving offence. Like living friends they too have their voice and physiognomies, and their company is prized as old acquaintances. We seek them in our need of counsel or amusement, without impertinence or apology, sure of having our claims allowed . . . What were days without such fellowship? We were alone in the world without it . . .

Next to a friend's discourse, no morsel is more delicious than a ripe book, a book whose flavour is as refreshing at the thousandth testing as at the first. Books when friends weary, conversation flags, or nature fails to inspire.

AMOS BRONSON ALCOTT.

January 12th

IT'S NOT WHAT I GIVE, BUT WHAT I SHARE—FOR THE GIFT WITHOUT THE GIVER IS BARE.

YOU should utilize your profession and your heart as a cable to bind men together. Danger cements men; why can't other forces be used? Many tools must be implemented to destroy the false walls that separate us. Medicine is one. Medicine when enveloped in that indispensable element of the human spirit. Kindness and gentleness are daily instruments of the doctor, more than of other professions. Kindness and gentleness can be potent weapons to fight against the anger of the world.

The world is made up of persons. Internationality is only a conglomeration of individuals. All individuals yearn for something human. This flings a special challenge to you, as there is no more intimate person-to-person relationship than that of the doctor and his patient. Bring the talents of your degree, and the spirituality of your heart, to distant valleys, and take back with you a rich, rich reward.

Dedicate some of your life to others. Your dedication will not be a sacrifice. It will be an exhilarating experience because it is intense effort applied towards a meaningful end.

The late DR. THOMAS DOOLEY.
In a letter to a young doctor just qualified.

January 13th

**DON'T LOOK FOR THE FLAWS AS YOU GO THROUGH LIFE,
BUT IF BY CHANCE YOU FIND THEM,
'TIS WISE AND KIND TO BE RATHER BLIND,
AND LOOK FOR THE VIRTUES BEHIND THEM!**

I WAS rushing around one morning, as usual, in a hurry to get the chores done, when my small son said, "Mummy, I like your pretty dress."

It was just a blue thing, with flowers. Quite ordinary. In fact, I hadn't even noticed it as I dressed, so I replied absently. "I'm glad you like it. Now eat up your breakfast, like a good boy."

The next thing, my little daughter began blowing bubbles into her milk, and then squealing with laughter as they burst onto her nose—aided and abetted by her brother of course.

I almost screamed in my morning irritation. "Stop that!" Then I snapped, "Now eat your food quickly, or mummy will be very cross."

During the morning, I passed off questions about the opening flowers, birds building their nests, a fly on the table, the cobwebs in the fence, a pebble, next door's cat, and a thousand other things.

I was hurrying to prepare lunch, when my son came running indoors, to say, "Mummy! Mummy come and see! My plant's got a flower!"

"Has it dear?" I replied. "I can't come now. Mummy's busy. We'll look later." He knew, and I knew, that later would probably never come.

But, suddenly, I did notice something—he had turned away from me, and now sat on the kitchen stool, staring at the wall. All the joy had gone from his little face, and I realized what I'd been doing.

There are few things, so humbling as a child's delight in the little, perfect things God has made. All the time I'd been bothering myself with everyday, unimportant things, when I should have been showing my children the wonder of God's world. They'd been asking, and asking me to show them, and to share with them, and I'd been too busy to see it.

It's a mistake I won't make again.

AUTHOR UNKNOWN.

January 14th

"A POOR LIFE THIS IF, FULL OF CARE, WE HAVE NO TIME
TO STAND AND STARE."
W. H. Davies.

LET me speak simply of common things
Of a clean, starched shirt
Of twin wedding rings
Of a child asleep in his own small bed
Of a fluffy cloud floating overhead.

Let me be grateful for everyday things
For the food at my table
For the joy music brings
For a star at my window winking at me
For a cooling swim in a salty sea.

When I cry aloud from the world's harsh stings
Let me think of my treasures of little things.
Let my spirit soar; let my heart take wings
Joy and peace fill my storehouse of everyday things.

A Housewife's Prayer by Phyllis Welchenthal.

January 15th

I PASS BY THE THINGS I CAN NO LONGER ENJOY, AND
ENJOY TO THE FULL THE THINGS THAT ARE STILL MINE.

I KNOW of no pleasure greater than a good ride, particularly if it's in a country that I know—the feel and smell of the horse, and the leather, the fresh air, and the scents of plough and hedgerow, the exercise and companionship; and from time to time, a pause on the top of a hill when my companion looks at a view, and I imagine it as I used to see it years ago. "Can you see the sea from here today?" "Yes, there's a good deal of cloud over us here, but the sun is shining through, and you can just see the horizon with the high cliff on its left." I remember that picture.

I thought that kind of recollection would cause me pain or regret. Perhaps it did at first, but long since I have learned to take comfort from it, and to get real pleasure out of it. Adjustment to blindness is very much a matter of passing by the things you can no longer enjoy, and enjoying to the full the many things that are still yours.

LORD FRASER OF LONSDALE.
From "Whereas I Was Blind".
Reproduced by permission of Hodder & Stoughton Ltd.

January 16th

I'LL SMILE AND PRETEND I'M CALM . . . EVERY SECOND I GET CALMER AND CALMER . . . NOBODY CAN ROB ME OF MY CALM.

AS THE boss hovers over your desk, your body undergoes physiological changes—adaptations dating back to our cave-dwelling ancestors. "The heart-beat quickens and the blood pressure rises," writes Barbara Archer. "Hormones pour into the blood, alerting various organs and sending sugar to the muscles and brain. The digestive process turns off so attention can be directed fully to the threat. Red cells flow into arteries to help the body take in additional oxygen.

Your body is getting ready to relieve the pressure you are under by fight or flight. Up to this point your reactions have been automatic.

What next? You must decide if the fight/flight reaction is suitable for your present circumstances. "The fight-or-flight response is often appropriate," says Dr Herbert Benson, "and should not be thought of as always harmful."

But, he cautions, "we are not using it as we believe our ancestors used it. That is, we do not always run, nor do we fight. Flight—running out of the office—isn't going to help much.

But there is another option—to learn to stay with the stress situation. Or, as psychiatrist Thomas Fogarty puts it, "Seek a balance that realistically faces the possibilities, takes action as needed and accepts what cannot be changed."

In short, you can admit your negative feelings to yourself, accept this harassment as a "fact of life" to be temporarily endured and go on to complete the report.

Such acceptance will exact wear and tear. But it will also help you keep your job. And you may even reach a new level of professional growth and personal integration.

THE CHRISTOPHERS.

January 17th

FORGIVENESS IS THE GREATEST HEALING FORCE IN THE WORLD . . . I RETURN SYMPATHY AND COMPASSION FOR EVIL . . . I MUST BE RECONCILED TO THAT PERSON WHO HAS DONE ME WRONG.

"THERE is a girl who has done me the greatest injury that one woman can do another, yet some higher power seemed to demand that I help this girl, even against my own will and my own material interests.

"We were standing one day talking earnestly, when I felt this sense of power and began to speak 'with authority'. I was in the doorway between two rooms; she was looking out at me, when suddenly she said, 'When you had your hair shampooed, did you have a blue rinse?' I thought this was rather a prosaic interruption to a serious conversation, but I replied: 'No, why do you ask?' She answered in a puzzled kind of way: 'Because there is a blue light round your hair, and it is beautiful.' I knew she was sensing the 'healing light'; we both became silent, the vibration grew more powerful, circulating between us, and in that moment I felt the compassion welling up in my heart, the forgiveness of Christ, the at-one-ment, and I knew that she felt it too, though she did not know what she felt. She flung her arms wide, her face upturned in a kind of ecstasy, while the tears poured down her cheeks, and she stammered: 'It's wonderful . . . it's marvellous, I. . .' What was working through me, I don't know, I can only guess, but I went and put my arms round her and said: 'It's all right,' and she replied: 'I have never felt so wonderful, so happy . . .' It affected us both profoundly.

"I know that when I have learned to feel true compassion for all humanity, as in that one moment of time, I shall enter the light without fear of hesitation, for then I shall *know* the time has come."

Case No. 30. Watcher on the Hills by Raynor C. Johnson.
Reproduced by permission of Hodder & Stoughton Ltd.

January 18th

> CHOOSE THE WORDS YOU SPEAK WITH CARE,
> OR USE THEM LOOSELY, IF YOU DARE.
> WORDS ARE POWERFUL TOOLS THAT DO
> BRING BACK WHAT YOU SAY, TO YOU.
>
> *Helen B. Johnson.*

KEEP a watch on your words, my children ... For words are wonderful things ... They are sweet, like the bees fresh honey ... Like bees, they have terrible stings ... They can bless like the warm glad sunshine ... And brighten a lonely life ... They can cut in the strife of anger ... Like an open two-edged knife.

Let them pass through your lips unchallenged ... If their errand be grand and kind ... If they come to support the weary ... To comfort and help the blind ... If a bitter revengeful spirit ... Prompt the words, let them be unsaid ... They may flash through the brain like lightning ... Or fall on the heart like lead.

Keep them back, if they're cold and cruel ... Under bar and lock and seal ... The wounds they make, my children ... Are always slow to heal ... May Christ guard your lips and ever ... From the time of your early youth ... May the words that you daily utter ... Be the words of beautiful truth.

AUTHOR UNKNOWN.

January 19th

> I'LL NOT DRINK FROM PUDDLES BY THE WAY WHEN HERE
> AT HOME THE CRYSTAL FOUNTAINS PLAY.
>
> *Angelus Silesius,*
> *German physician.*

WHO walks beside a rosebud ... And does not sense its bloom ... Its lovely form and colour ... Its delicate perfume ... Who walks beneath the heavens ... And does not see the sky ... The sunrise and the sunset ... The tints that glow or die ... Who treads the rural pathway ... And never hears a bird ... Nor notes the trembling grasses ... A passing breeze has stirred ... Who dwells among his fellows ... And sees them pass his door ... Nor ever hears their heartbeats ... Is pitifully poor.

AUTHOR UNKNOWN.

January 20th

I BLOOM WHERE I AM PLANTED.

I REMEMBER so well the little bride, starry-eyed and glowing, and her handsome, happy bridegroom on their wedding day. Her adoration for her new husband, and his love for her, lighted the little chapel and the reception afterward. Everything was perfect.

Now two children and three moves later, moves that had taken them far from their Midwestern home, friends, and relatives, I wondered about their adjustment to new environments, new problems, new jobs, new homes, new churches, and the making of new friends. Would she be a frustrated, disappointed housewife . . . a self-centred, immature individual?

So I let the knocker on their front door down with a sharp rap and stood waiting for it to be answered. It was an unexpected visit. Her appearance told me I need not have worried. She was as neat and pretty as I had always remembered her. True, she was a few years older—a few grey hairs, but on her they looked good. It was soon evident that the years had added a new dimension—a well-rounded personality. She was an interesting, attractive individual. A few minutes' conversation and all my doubts and worries had disappeared.

At the offer of a cup of tea, I followed her into her neat little kitchen and there above the sink I found the answer to my questions. A simple little wooden plaque with a buttercup or two, and the words—BLOOM WHERE YOU ARE PLANTED.

LENA WILLS,
in "Sunshine" Magazine.

JUST YOU

I could sail the waters of all the world; battle the wild and blue; but I'd never find a friend to love, like the friend I've found in you. I could walk down the roads of the world, and knock on the doors forever; and never I'd find a friend like you . . . never, never, never.

I want to be friend like you, I'd count my life worth while; If I could only learn to do, so much to bring a smile. I wish that I could grow to be, in all I say and do; less like the one folks know as me, and more and more like you.

Author Unknown.

January 21st

CONSISTENT CHEERINESS AND ENTHUSIASM CAN MAKE MY DAY ... MAY EVEN CHANGE MY LIFE.

MANY years ago there was a children's magazine entitled, "Sunbeam". Young members of the family belonged to the "Sunbeam Club", but before you could become a member you had to make a pledge: "In order to promote happiness, efficiency and civic welfare, I sincerely promise that wherever I am:
"I will talk health instead of sickness.
I will talk prosperity instead of failure.
I will carry good news instead of bad news.
I will tell the cheerful tale instead of the sad tale.
I will mention blessings instead of my burdens.
I will speak of the sunshine instead of the clouds.
I will think of cheerful things, not the gloomy, and my thoughts will shine in my face.
I will praise, whenever I can, those who are putting forward an honest effort to perform their tasks creditably.
I will always remember: a merry heart doeth good life medicine."

AUTHOR UNKNOWN.

January 22nd

THINGS COULD BE WORSE. I AM DETERMINED TO STICK IT OUT. ALL WILL BE WELL.

WHEN Beethoven was stricken by this greatest curse of musicians, deafness, he continued to hear in his soul the masterworks which he conceived, and thanks to his unconquerable spirit the last great string quartets were created. Chopin, undermined by consumption, mustered enough strength to write admirable compositions, and he still appeared in public even if giving more and more space to his assisting artists in order to spare himself.

Such examples are illuminating, inspirational. They show us that few obstacles exist which cannot be surmounted where there is a divine flame, profound devotion to art, and utter confidence in the power of patience, perseverance, and faith.

THE ETUDE.

January 23rd

I THINK ABUNDANCE. I LIVE ABUNDANCE. GRACE AND PROVIDENCE FILL EVERY LACK IN MY LIFE. THE MIRACLE OF 'SUPPLY' OPERATES RIGHT HERE IN THE MIDDLE OF MY LIFE.

DURING the winter and early spring following the arrival of the 'Mormons' in the Salt Lake Valley, the vanguard group planted five thousand acres of grain to insure food not only for themselves but also for the large companies of colonists who were expected to come that summer. With irrigation the grain flourished, and prospects looked bright for an excellent crop. Then one day in the spring of 1848 news was brought from the outlying fields that great hordes of crickets were devouring the grain. Frantically the people fought to stem the tide. They tried burning the insects. They tried drowning them. They used every resource at their command, but still the crickets came, leaving behind a desert where only shortly before had been a people's hope for bread. It was a desperate situation. These colonists were in an isolated outpost, with no means of communication other than slow ox teams.

With their own strength exhausted, there was but one power to whom they could turn. They lifted their voices in prayer. Then they heard the cries of sea gulls flying in from the west. At first they thought it another foe to complete the destruction already began. But the gulls settled on the fields and commenced devouring the crickets, disgorging only to continue eating and not stopping until the grain was cleaned of them. Through the intervention of the gulls, a substantial portion of the crop was saved and the pioneers were enabled to survive the following rigorous winter.

AUTHOR UNKNOWN.

January 24th

KNOW THEN, WHATEVER CHEERFUL AND SERENE ...
SUPPORTS THE MIND, SUPPORTS THE BODY, TOO ...
HENCE THE MOST VITAL MOVEMENT MORTALS FEEL ...
IS HOPE; THE BALM AND LIFE-BLOOD OF THE SOUL.

... FROM all this we get the great fact we are scientifically demonstrating today—that the various mental states, emotions, and passions have their peculiar effects upon the body, and each induces in turn, if indulged in to any great extent, its own peculiar forms of disease, and these in time become chronic.

Just a word or two in regard to their mode of operation. If a person is dominated for a moment by, say a passion of anger, there is set up in the physical organism what we might justly term a bodily thunder-storm, which has the effect of souring, or rather of corroding, the normal, healthy, and life-giving secretions of the glands, so that instead of performing their natural functions they become poisonous and destructive.

If this goes on to any great extent, by virtue of their cumulative influences, they give rise to a particular form of disease, which in turn becomes chronic. So the emotion opposite to this, that of kindliness, love, benevolence, good-will, tends to stimulate a healthy, purifying, and life-giving flow of all the bodily secretions. All the channels of the body seem free and open; the life forces go bounding through them. And these very forces, set into a bounding activity, will in time counteract the poisonous and disease-giving effects of their opposite.

A physician goes to see a patient. He gives no medicine this morning. Yet the very fact of his going makes the patient better. He has carried with him the spirit of health; he has carried brightness of tone and disposition; he has carried hope into the sick bedroom; he has left it there. In fact, the very hope and good cheer he has carried with him has taken hold of and has had a subtle but powerful influence upon the mind of the patient. This mental condition imparted by the physician has in turn its effects upon the patient's body, and so through the instrumentality of this mental suggestion the healing goes on.

RALPH WALDO TRINE.
"In Tune with the Infinite"

January 25th

WHEN, THROUGH MYSELF, A LITTLE MORE HOPE AND HELP, A LITTLE MORE HEALTH AND HEALING COMES INTO THE WORLD, THEN MY LIFE HAS MEANING.

THE JOY of giving should be learnt, and practised, early rather than late, for it is a type of joy which is constructive, both to the giver and to the receiver. If it is left too late there may be little remaining in life in which to construct. Indeed, many leave giving until life ceases and the gifts, of whatever sort, are no longer theirs to give.

Like many doctors my hobby has been gardening. In addition to its providing complete mental distraction it possesses the inestimable advantages of fresh air, early rising and sound sleep. I probably owe my love of it and much of my knowledge of gardening technique to my forbears and my early upbringing.

I suppose I have made most of the mistakes that gardeners are prone to make when they begin: planting too thickly; planting established 'subjects' (as some catalogues call plants and trees) rather than young ones; dotting things about instead of massing them; leaving out of the reckoning that the sun can kill as cruelly as the frost; and seeking to acquire every known specimen instead of specializing in those that say "thank you" when grown in my particular soil and in my particular aspect—acquisitiveness has been one of my besetting sins . . .

Since Nature's way with the plant is much the same as with the human being, gardening has also, I think, confirmed me in the lesson which clinical observation of my fellows has taught me—that you cannot, unless you sacrifice their dignity and their satisfaction, live other folk's lives for them. You can keep the ring for them so that they get a good chance of success, you can teach them the rules, you can even be a "sparring partner", but it is their fight, not yours.

Life has taught me that living has been worthwhile.

LORD HORDER.
What Life has Taught Me.
_{Sincere thanks to the author whose address we are unable to trace.}

SISSINGHURST CASTLE GARDEN.
Famous garden created by the late V. Sackville-West and Sir Harold Nicolson, between the surviving parts of an Elizabethan mansion.
Photograph by Kenneth Scowen.

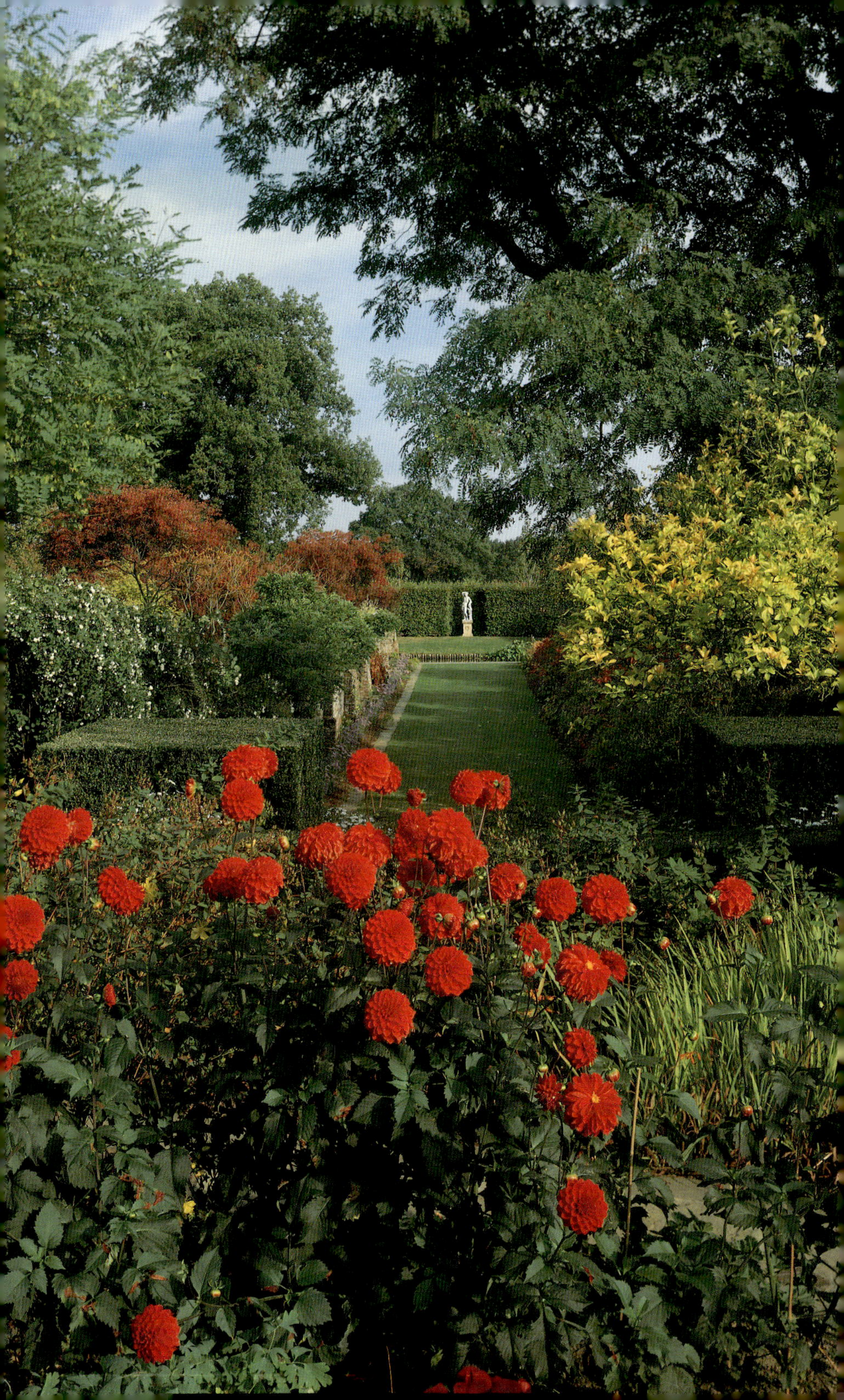

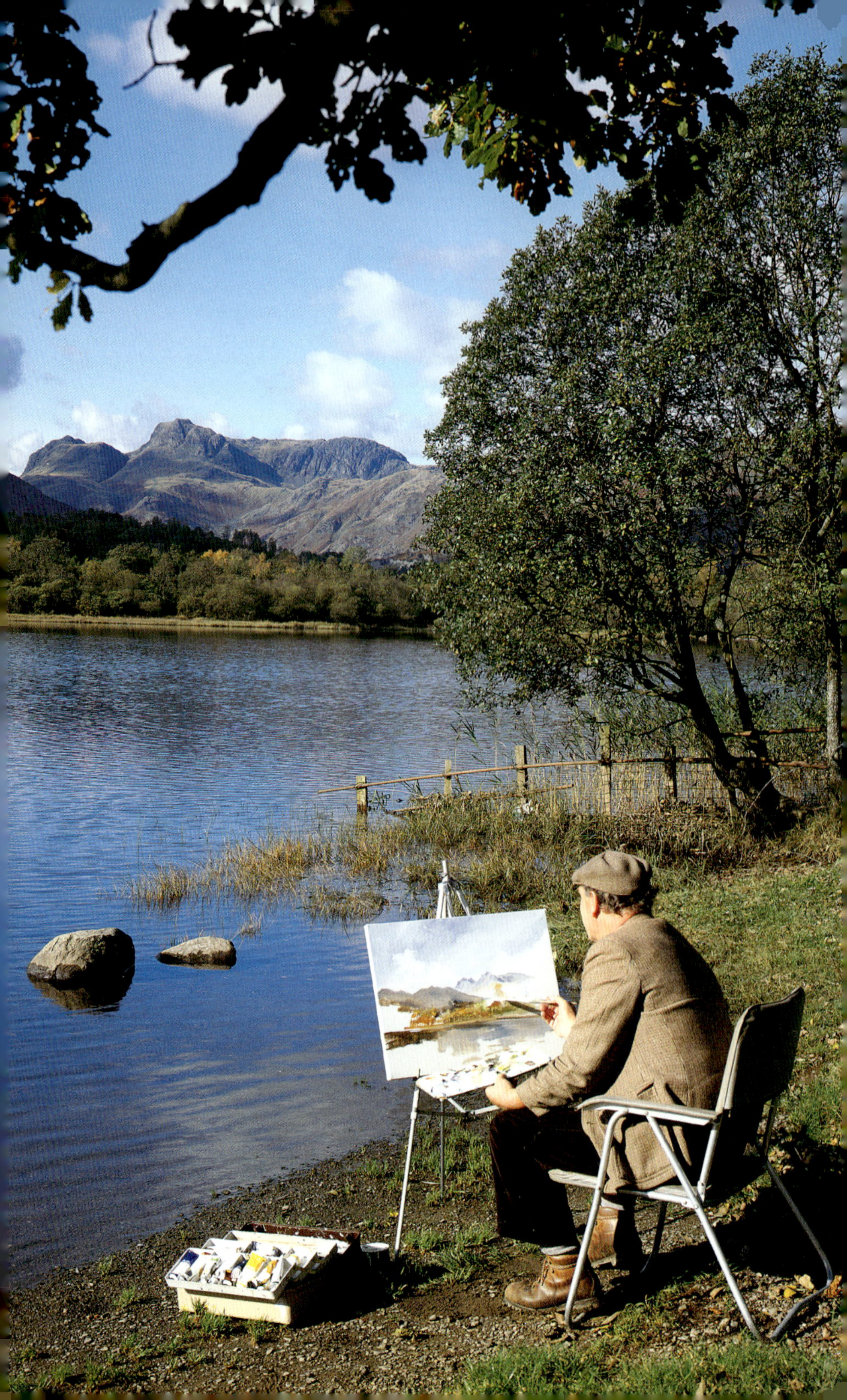

Ode on Solitude

Happy the man whose wish and care
    A few paternal acres bound,
Content to breath his native air,
        In his own ground.

Whose herds with milk, whose fields with bread,
    Whose flocks supply him with attire,
Whose trees in summer yield him shade,
        In winter fire.

Blest, who can unconcern'dly find
    Hours, days, and years slide soft away,
In health of body, peace of mind,
        Quiet by day.

Sound sleep by night; study and ease,
    Together mixt; sweet recreation;
And Innocence, which most does please
        With meditation.

Thus let me live, unseen, unknown,
    Thus unlamented let me die,
Steal from the world, and not a stone
        Tell where I lie.

Alexander Pope.

An artist captures the majesty of The Langdales from Elter Water, Cumbria. Photograph by Andy Williams.

January 26th

LET ME COUNT THE WAYS THAT I LOVE MY HUSBAND/WIFE.

HOW do I love thee? Let me count the ways.
I love thee to the depth and breadth and height
My soul can reach, when feeling out of sight
For the ends of Being and ideal Grace,
I love thee to the level of every day's
Most quiet need, by sun and candle-light.
I love thee freely, as men strive for Right;
I love thee purely, as they turn from Praise.
I love thee with the passion put to use
In my old griefs, and with my childhood's faith,
I love thee with a love I seemed to lose
With my lost saints,—I love thee with the breath,
Smiles, tears, of all my life!—and, if God choose,
I shall but love thee better after death.

ELIZABETH BARRETT BROWNING.
English poet. (1806–61).
Born near Durham. Fell from her pony when young and injured her spine, invaliding her for life. Friendship led to a secret marriage with the poet Robert Browning, during which her best work was written.

January 27th

I AM LEARNING, IN WHATSOEVER CONDITION I AM, TO BE CONTENT.

(Phil. 4:11)

SWEET are the thoughts that savour of content . . . The quiet mind is richer than a crown . . . Sweet are the nights in careless rapture spent . . . The poor estate scorns fortune's angry frown . . . Such sweet content, such minds, such sleep, such bliss . . . Beggars enjoy, which princes oft do miss.

The homely house that harbours quiet rest . . . The cottage that affords no pride nor care . . . The mean that 'grees with country music best . . . The sweet consort of mirth and music's fare . . . Obscured life sets down a type of bliss . . . A mind content both crown and kingdom is.

ROBERT GREEN.
British poet.

January 28th

I KEEP MY HEART IN PEACE. I ALLOW NOTHING TO DISTURB IT. ALL THINGS HAVE A PURPOSE. ALL THINGS HAVE AN END. I REGRET NONE OF MY PAST EXPERIENCES. I REJOICE IN ALL CIRCUMSTANCES FOR BETTER OR WORSE. DEEP WITHIN ME IS THE CERTAINTY THAT ALL WILL BE WELL.

KEKHLYUDOV remembered how at Kuzminskoye he had meditated on his life and tried to solve the questions, what he ought to do, and how he ought to do it; and he remembered how he had become perplexed in these questions and had been unable to decide them, so many were the considerations involved in each. He now put to himself the same questions, and was astonished how simple it all was. It was simple because he now took no thought of what would happen to himself—that no longer even interested him—he was thinking only of what he ought to do. And strangely enough, while he was not considering his own needs, he knew without any doubt what he ought to do for others . . .

The black cloud had moved on till it stood right above him. Lightning lit up the whole courtyard and the thunder sounded directly overhead. The birds had all ceased singing, the leaves began to rustle, and the first flaws of the storm-wind reached the steps where he sat . . . Kedhlyudov went into the house. "Yes, yes," he thought. "The work which is carried out by our life, the whole work, the whole meaning of this work is dark to me, and cannot be made intelligible . . . Why should my friend die, and I be left alive? . . . Why was Katyusha born?

Why did this war come about? Of what use was my subsequent dissolute life? To understand all this, to understand the whole work of the Master is not in my power. But to do his will as written in my conscience, that is in my power, and that I KNOW without a doubt. And when I do this, then undoubtedly I am at peace."

TOLSTOY,

Author of War and Peace and Anna Karenina. Pursued farming, education, writing and a simple mode of life. Was possessed by an inner conflict in 1862 until he married his wife, sixteen years younger. He developed a philosophy of living close to nature, even while residing on his prosperous estate at Yasnaya Polyanna.

January 29th

IF I DON'T GET THE TASKS I LIKE—
I'LL LIKE THE TASKS I GET.

MY father, a secondary-school headmaster, bidding my mother good-bye on the front steps of our home one morning, said to her: "Tell Harry that he can cut the grass today, if he feels like it." Then, after walking a few steps down the street, he called, "Tell Harry he had better feel like it."

That afternoon, although like any teen-ager I had other plans, I cut the grass and, chuckling over my father's remark, found that the job was not too bad. Before I had finished I really liked it. I never dreamed, however, that 60 years afterwards I would be hearing the echo of my father's wise counsel: *If you don't get the tasks you like, like the tasks you get.*

I could not escape from that, even in school. I hated mathematics. When I reached the university I longed for the day when no more of the miserable stuff would be required of me. Meanwhile, the compulsory courses confronted me—that grass had to be cut. Then my father's advice clicked: I had better feel like it. Believe it or not, when the compulsory courses in mathematics were finished, I chose others, right up to differential calculus.

Any layman who supposes that a minister on Tuesday morning starts preparing his Sunday sermon because he spontaneously feels like it should guess again. Preparing a good sermon is hard work, and far too many preachers think up all sorts of excuses for not tackling it. They know that sermonic grass has to be cut, but they will wait till they feel like it. Endless times on Tuesday morning, facing another sermon's preparation, I have heard the echo of my father's voice: "Tell Harry he had better feel like it."

This counsel has helped me especially in dealing with drudgery. No matter how thrilling the high spots in any vocation may be—and I have found the ministry full of them—any calling is like an iceberg, its peak visible but most of it under water, invisible routine, uninspiring details, drudgery.

Now that I have come to three-score years and 15 and face old age, I still hear my father saying about growing old, "Tell Harry he had better feel like it."

HARRY EMERSON FOSDICK.
Sincere thanks to the author who we have been unable to trace.

January 30th

> NATURE'S EVERY DAY IS A NEW BEGINNING ...
> HER EVERY MORN IS THE WORLD MADE NEW ...
> SHE IS A REWARDER OF THOSE WHO LOVE HER.

WHEN an Indian child is born, the elders tell the parents, "This child is lent to you by the Creator. This child is not your own. So take care of him. Bring him up right. Teach him about the Great Spirit. Teach him to be kind, generous, brave and courageous."

If the child lives in sorrow or suffering, it is possible that the Great Spirit will take him back. When the child grows up to manhood and to middle age, he is the same person the Great Spirit lent to us. And he may grow up to be an elder among us.

In our language we call the earth: "Mother Earth". We are fed from Mother Earth, we are kept alive by her and depend on her. We are part of Mother Earth, and she is part of us.

The forest is beautiful because of its diversity. There are all kinds of flowers. There are tall trees and small shrubs—straight trees, crooked trees, leaning trees, young trees and old trees. There are trees of all colours. When the storms come and the strong winds blow, it is not against one lonely tree but against many trees. The trees stand together. The forest is beautiful because it grows in harmony with Nature and according to the plan of the Great Creator.

In addition to the books that we read in the libraries, we should also read Nature's library. Mankind can be like a beautiful forest of people if we grow according to the plan of the Creator.

CHIEF JOHN SNOW,
... of the Stoney Indians, Alberta.

January 31st

TRUE MUSIC AND RHYTHM FIND THEIR WAY INTO THE SECRET PLACES OF THE SOUL.
Plato.

THE world of violins and flutes, of horns and cellos, of fugues, scherzos and gavottes, obeyed laws which were so beautiful and so clear that all music seemed to speak of God. My body was not listening, it was praying. My spirit no longer had bounds, and if tears came to my eyes, I did not feel them running down because they were outside me. I wept with gratitude every time the orchestra began to sing. A world of sounds for a blind man, what sudden grace! No more need to get one's bearings. No more need to wait. The inner world made concrete.

I loved Mozart so much; I loved Beethoven so much that in the end they made me what I am. They moulded my emotions and guided my thoughts. Is there anything in me which I did not, one day, receive from them? I doubt it.

Today, music for me hangs from a golden nail called Bach. But it is not my tastes which have changed but my relationships. As a child I lived with Mozart, Beethoven, Schumann, Berlioz, Wagner and Dvorak, because they were the ones I met every week. Before becoming the word of a man, even if the man is Mozart, all music is music. A kind of geometry, but one of inner space. Sentences, but freed from meaning. Without any doubt, of all the things man has made, music is the least human. When I heard it I was all there, with my troubles and my joys, yet it was not myself exactly. It was better than I, bigger and more sure.

For a blind person music is nourishment, as beauty is for those who see. He needs to receive it, to have it administered at intervals like food. Otherwise a void is created inside him and causes him pain.

JACQUES LUSSEYRAN,
"And There Was Light" (Heinemann).
The heroic experiences of a blind man.
Reprinted by permission of the Peters Fraser & Dunlop Group Ltd.

OUR acts return to us again. Liberal giving means liberal receiving. "There is that which scattereth and yet increaseth, and there is that which witholdeth more than is mete but it tendeth to poverty." "With what measure ye mete, it shall be measured to you again" is a profound teaching, and is founded upon the belief of eternal justice.   *Joseph Bibby.*

"WITH WHAT MEASURE YOU METE..."

Edmund J. Sullivan. *Bibby's Annual.*

February 1st

> I LIVE EACH DAY AS IF IT WERE THE FIRST I HAVE EVER SEEN. I RESPOND TO ITS GLOW BY DAY, ITS SMILE BY NIGHT. WITHIN ME STIRS A DEEPENING REVERENCE FOR LIFE IN WHATEVER FORM I FIND IT.

ONE of the deeply important events of my life was meeting Dr. Albert Schweitzer at Lamberene. I spent days and evenings with him and was moved at finding that his phrase "reverence for life", was not just words he put together well, but was, in fact, a concept which illumined every minute of his day and night. He respected the little stream of ants that travelled across the papers on his desk, and he considered a garden a miracle. When I saw my wife creating an arrangement for our table from zucchini, carrots, cauliflower, and parsley from our garden, I remembered the phrase "reverence for life". The beauty of the form and colour of the fruits of the earth, which are ours every day, struck me as a blessing we take too much for granted.

My organic garden has not only been a source of delicious, healthful eating for my family and me, but a joy and an inspiration.

EDDIE ALBERT,
In "Natural Food and Farming", Atlanta, Texas.

February 2nd

> EVERYTHING WHICH HAS PRAISE FROM THE WORLD IS UNNOTICED IN HEAVEN. EVERYTHING WHICH IS UNNOTICED BY THE WORLD IS KEPT IN HEAVEN.
> *Inayat Hazrat Khan.*

IT IS ten years ago since Private Harry Gaines was wounded in the invasion and admitted to Worcester Royal Infirmary with wounds in both legs and the right arm.

He tells of the kindness of a German prisoner in a Red Cross hospital in Normandy when he fell wounded. "He carried me for 70 yards to the beach, then looked down at me, smiled, put a cigarette into my mouth, lit it, and put his lighter in my pocket. Then he took off his white shirt, tore it into shreds and dressed my wounds. Having done this, he kissed me, with tears in his eyes, and then walked away to attend to other wounded."

February 3rd

ORDER IS A POWER IN MY LIFE.

WHAT comfort, what strength, what economy there is in order—material order, intellectual order, moral order. To know where one is going and what one wishes—this is order; to keep one's word and one's engagements—again order; to have everything ready under one's hand, to be able to dispose of all one's forces, and to have all one's means of whatever kind under command—still order; to discipline one's habits, one's efforts, one's wishes; to organize one's life, to distribute one's time—all this belongs to and is included in the word order. Order means light and peace, inward liberty and free command over oneself. Order is power.

Henri-Frédérique Amiel (1821–81).

February 4th

TODAY IS MY GREAT DAY

THE happiest man I know acts on the seeming belief that each day is the most important in his life, that there never was and never will be another day quite so rich in possibilities for enjoyment.

For example, luncheon for him, no matter how busy the day, is an *event*, not a hasty gulping of food between worried snatches of conversation about some crisis at the office. The fact that there may be a thousand tomorrows when luncheons can be enjoyed under more auspicious circumstances has no part in my friend's philosophy. Today is today—this day, this hour. Luncheon *now* is luncheon *now*, hence an occasion out of which it behoves him to squeeze the last drop of relaxation and enjoyment.

So my friend makes a ceremony of it. He discusses the menu in detail with the waiter, he orders carefully, he smiles in pleasurable anticipation as he awaits his food, and then he proceeds to enjoy it slowly and with relish. The food may be simple and inexpensive—a cheese sandwich and a salad, perhaps—but this man contrives, somehow, to make it all appear an occasion of special importance. And thus it is with everything he does: he takes each hour as it comes and enjoys it.

How often have I, for one, found myself letting the "transient hour" slip by, my mind foolishly anticipating another hour, much bigger and better, in some misty day ahead. How often have you, too, found yourself forgetting that *today is your great day?*

James D. Wool.
Sunshine Magazine.

February 5th

I LEARN TO DELAY THE IMPACT OF NEGATIVE EMOTIONS ... I AM THE MASTER OF MY THOUGHTS.

IF ONE holds himself in the thought of poverty, he will be poor. And the chances are that he will remain in poverty. If he holds himself, whatever present conditions may be, continually in the thought of prosperity and good health, he sets into operation forces that will sooner or later bring him into those conditions.

The law of attraction works unceasingly throughout the universe, and the one great and never-changing fact in connection with this is, that like attracts like.

RALPH WALDO TRINE.
"In Tune with the Infinite".

February 6th

SOW A THOUGHT, AND YOU REAP AN ACT, SOW AN ACT, AND YOU REAP A HABIT; SOW A HABIT, AND YOU REAP A CHARACTER SOW A CHARACTER, AND YOU REAP A DESTINY.

Author Unknown.

PROGRESS, however, of the best kind, is comparatively slow. Great results cannot be achieved at once; and we must be satisfied to advance in life as we walk, step by step. De Maistre says that "to know how to wait is the great secret of success". We must sow before we can reap, and often have to wait long, content meanwhile to look patiently forward in hope; the fruit best worth waiting for often ripening the slowest. But "time and patience," says the Eastern proverb, "change the mulberry leaf to satin."

Labourers for the public good especially, have to work long and patiently, often uncheered by the prospect of immediate recompense or result. The seeds they sow sometimes lie hidden under the winter's snow, and before the spring comes the husbandman may have gone to his rest. It is not every public worker who, like Rowland Hill, sees his great idea bring forth fruit in his lifetime. Adam Smith sowed the seeds of a great social amelioration in that dingy old University of Glasgow where he so long laboured, and laid the foundations of his Wealth of Nations; but seventy years passed before his work bore substantial fruits, nor indeed are they all gathered in yet.

SAMUEL SMILES.
"Self-Help".

February 7th

I FIND LIFE AN EXCITING BUSINESS, THE MOST EXCITING WHEN IT IS LIVED FOR OTHERS.
Helen Keller.

"AFTER a quarter of a century of helping people back to health, I have learnt the true meaning of this story I once read:"

A certain man was travelling on foot and came to a mountain pass. It was late in the autumn and snow began to fall as the man was climbing the steep slope. The trail was long and the man was benumbed and freezing. But, after great difficulty he reached the top, and there he found a stranger lying on the ground unconscious and near death from the bitter cold. Forgetting his discomfort the man hurried to the suffering stranger and began to massage his body and limbs vigorously and with all his strength.

Before long, the stranger showed signs of life and, after much brisk exercising, was restored to full consciousness. The amazing thing the man discovered was that by working hard to save the stranger's life, he himself had become warm and strong. He eagerly lifted up the stranger and together they descended the mountainside to safety. Which of the two received the greater blessing—he who gave the help or he who received it?

Nurse Isabella Abbott.

February 8th

MY LIFE IS SHAPED AND FASHIONED BY THE THINGS I LOVE.
Goethe.

I WONDER if the human touch, which people have, is not one of the greatest assets that you can have. You meet some people, and immediately you feel their warmth of mind and heart. You read a book, sit before the performance of a fine actor, or read a poem—and there it is—something that streams into your consciousness ...

Those who keep climbing higher in their chosen work, all have this outstanding something. The nurse in the hospital, the man who delivers your mail, the clerk behind many a shop counter, and the effective minister or public speaker. Without this human touch, hope has little on which to feed or thrive.

George M. Adams.

February 9th

> I BELIEVE IN THE SUN, EVEN IF IT DOES NOT SHINE.
> I BELIEVE IN LOVE, EVEN IF I DO NOT FEEL IT.
> I BELIEVE IN GOD, EVEN IF I DO NOT SEE HIM.
> *Written on the wall of a Warsaw Ghetto by a young unknown Jew when all seemed dark and hopeless.*

NOW we are the children of the earth; in eternity we are the children of the whole universe. Do I not feel in my own soul that I constitute a part of this mighty harmonious whole? Do I not have the consciousness that in this enormous, innumerable collection of beings in which Godhead is manifest—Supreme Force, if you prefer the term—that I constitute one link, one step between the lower orders of creation and the higher ones? If I see, clearly see, this ladder which rises from the plant to man, then why should I suppose that it stops at me, and does not lead higher and ever higher?

I know that just as nothing is ever annihilated in the universe, so I can never perish but shall always exist, and always have existed. I know that besides myself spiritual beings must exist above me, and that truth is in this universe.

TOLSTOY.
War and Peace.

February 10th

EVERY DAY I AM REBORN ... EVERY DAY I MAKE NEW WOOD.

WHEN Longfellow was well along in years, his head as white as snow, but his cheeks as red as a rose, an ardent admirer asked him how it was that he was able to keep so vigorous and to write to beautifully.

Pointing to a blossoming apple tree nearby, the poet replied: "That apple tree is very old, but I never saw prettier blossoms upon it than those which it now bears. The tree grows a little new wood each year. I suppose that it is out of that new wood that the blossoms come. Like the apple tree I try to grow a little new wood each year."

We cannot stop the flight of time, but we can keep on "growing new wood" and in that way keep on blossoming until the end.

SUNSHINE MAGAZINE.
Lichfield, Illinois, USA.

February 11th

I COMMIT MYSELF WHOLLY TO THE PRINCIPLE THAT THE SUPREME BEING HAS MADE FULL PROVISION FOR A COMPLETE, WHOLESOME SUSTENANCE OF LIFE WITHIN THE SOIL.

I BELIEVE in the soil as God's richest and most bounteous gift to man. It is the sustainer of his physical being—the embodiment of his spirit. It abounds in life in its most productive and complex form, yielding to all who wisely culture it a benevolence and benediction ascribed to the all-wise Creator of the Universe.

I sense in the soil an inherent quality so vital and powerful and yet so delicate and sensitive as to merit my best thought. For, as in the measure it is truly preserved, so shall I be sustained. From its springs all forms of life and by it all are nourished. None is exempt from dependence upon it.

Gratitude and appreciation well-up within me for such an abundant provision. I feel a deep sense of responsibility to my Maker to do my utmost in exercising proper diligence as keeper of a sacred trust and discharge of a faithful stewardship.

Creed of the Natural Food and Farming Associates,
PO Box 210, Atlanta, Texas 75551, USA.

February 12th

FROM NOW ON I WANT LEISURE FOR GOOD BOOKS AND GOOD MUSIC. I SHALL NOT NEGLECT RECREATION WITH MY HANDS. BY BEING HAPPY WITHIN MYSELF, OTHERS MAY DRAW SERENITY FROM MY PRESENCE.

ONE reason so many of us are despondent, worried, jittery, today is that we are using our heads too much and our hands too little. God gave us our hands to work with, and when a man lets them grow useless and clumsy he pays with neuroses.

Tests by neurologists show that mental ability increases as the ability to use the hands increases. And many cases of mental instability can be cured by teaching the patient how to use his hands.

Let it be gardening or pottery, wood-carving or model-making, photography, radio building, machinist's work—one could list indefinitely activities which relieve tension in human lives ... We need the sense of self-confidence, self-respect, that comes only from seeing something take complete form under our own hands.

Boris Blai.

February 13th

> I AM NOT COMPLETE IN MYSELF ... I AM A LINK IN THE CHAIN OF LIFE ... EACH DAY I BEAR SOMETHING ONWARD THAT CONTRIBUTES TO EXPERIENCE ... I MAY NEVER KNOW TO WHAT END THIS SERVES ... BUT I KNOW IT IS SOMETHING VITAL TO THE WORLD.

WHEN I was 19 I lost both my parents in a mountain accident. I had just started my three years at teachers' training college. The shock was immense. I felt as if the ground beneath my feet had given way and sent me spinning into a turmoil of emotion.

Over the time of the funeral, one friend in particular kept close to me. I could tell her everything I was feeling, and this helped.

When I returned to college the grief was still overwhelming. I had acute physical pain in my arms and legs. I felt numb—one day melted into the next. I knew I was not taking in all that was happening around me.

It took me a year and a half—perhaps more—to begin to grasp and assimilate what had happened. Halfway through my course I realised that if I was going to qualify, I would have to stop feeling so much. Gradually I pushed down most of my feelings. I put them into cold storage, labelled 'to be dealt with later'.

I qualified and spent three years teaching in a rough area of London. Then I went to teach in Papua, New Guinea, for two years. I loved it there. The people were warm-hearted and spontaneous, expressing their joys and griefs as they felt them.

When I came back to Britain and thought about that spontaneity, I knew I wasn't the person I longed to be.

Some time later I moved into a flat with a friend who lived near the school where I was teaching. A fortnight after I moved in, her mother died of cancer. I was glad that I could share that experience with her. We talked long into the night, as I tried to answer her questions about the things I had felt and learnt when my parents died. Suddenly, nearly ten years later, the physical pains came back. I began to cry and grieve again. My feelings were coming out of cold storage.

I've often asked myself, "Why did it take so long for me to unfreeze?" I don't know. But the important thing is that it has happened—and at a time when I was able to cope with it, because I had the people around me who could help me to do so.

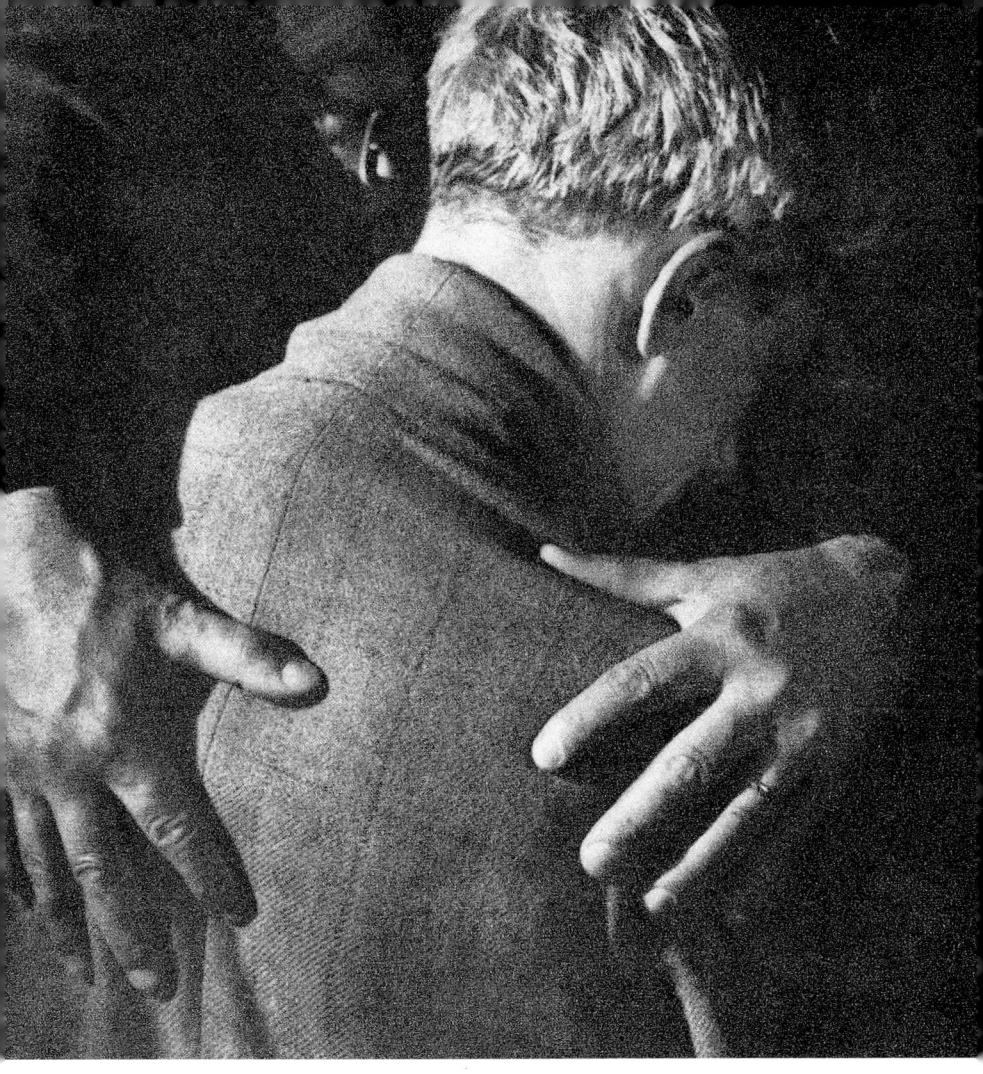

Forgiveness, by Harold Burdekin.

I know now too, that grieving is necessary, because it brings healing with it. I've come to understand that my relationship with my parents can continue to grow—and it is. I'm no longer ashamed to be grieving so long after their death. As I've let myself feel again, I've begun to learn what this experience has meant and, most important of all, I've begun to learn who I am.

AUTHOR UNKNOWN.
In New World News.
_{Sincere thanks to the unknown writer.}

February 14th

> I KNOW NOT WHERE HIS ISLANDS LIFT
> THEIR FRONDED PALMS IN AIR.
> I ONLY KNOW I CANNOT DRIFT
> BEYOND HIS LOVE AND CARE
>
> *John Greenleaf Whittier.*

YOU do not have to be clever to please me; all you have to do is want to love me. Just speak to me as you would to anyone of whom you are fond.

Are there any people you want to pray for? Say their names to me, and ask me as much as you like. I am generous, but trust me to do what I know is best ...

Tell me about your pride, your touchiness, self-centredness, meanness, and laziness. I still love you in spite of these. Do not be ashamed; there will be many saints in heaven who had the same faults as you; they prayed to me and little by little, their faults were corrected.

Do not hesitate to ask me for blessings for the body and mind, for health, memory, success; I can give anything ...

Tell me about your failures, and I will show you the cause of them. What are your worries? Who has caused you pain? Tell me about it. Forgive them, and I will bless you.

Are you afraid of anything? Have you any tormenting, unreasonable fears? Trust yourself to me. I am here. I will not leave you.

Have you no joys to tell me about? Why do you not share your happiness with me? Tell me what has happened since yesterday to cheer and comfort you. Whatever it was, however big, however small, I prepared it. Show me your gratitude and thank me.

Are temptations bearing heavily upon you? Yielding to temptations always disturbs the peace of your soul. Ask me, and I will help you overcome them.

Well, go along now. Get on with your work or play. Try to be humbler, more submissive, kinder; and come back soon and bring me a more devoted heart. Tomorrow I shall have more blessings for you.

AUTHOR UNKNOWN.

February 15th

> "DESPISE NOT ONE OF THESE LITTLE ONES ... FOR I SAY TO YOU THAT IN HEAVEN THEIR ANGELS ALWAYS BEHOLD THE FACE OF MY FATHER."
>
> *Matthew 18:10.*

WHEN 3-year-old Katy Reardon fell into the pool in her garden, she was fully clothed and *couldn't swim*. Her Dad was at work, her mum was in the kitchen and there was no one to help her. They had warned her not to go near the deep end of the pool, but on that sunny day in May 1996 she reached over to get her doll and fell in headfirst. *No one knows how long she was in the pool;* when her mother, Barbara, heard the scream, she froze in terror, then ran toward the back door. She saw Katy crying, moving toward her in dripping wet clothes, with her arms extended. When Barbara asked her what happened, she said, "I was playing and I fell into the deep end and I couldn't swim, *so I asked Jesus to help me and a hand came down out of the clouds and pulled me out of the water*". When her mother asked her <u>again,</u> she <u>repeated</u> the story several times <u>without missing a word.</u> Finally, her mother asked her, "What did the hand look like?" Katy simply replied, *"You know mum—like a cloud!"*

Today, I talked to Katy's dad on the phone and he told me that every time there's a baby-dedication in church, he sits with tears of joy as he remembers what God did for his little girl. Jesus said that our children have angels assigned to watch over them. Perhaps you think I am 'a simple soul', but I believe it with all my heart. I claim it for my children and my grandchildren and I thank God for it. Furthermore, I think <u>*you*</u> should, too!

From: The Word for Today. Daily Devotions.
United Christian Broadcasters Ltd., Hanchurch, Christian Centre,
Stoke on Trent, ST4 8RY.

February 16th

I AM NOT ALONE. I AM BEING SUPPORTED ALL THE DAY LONG THROUGHOUT THIS PILGRIM LIFE UNTIL THE EVENING COMES, WHEN THE BUSY WORLD IS HUSHED, AND MY WORK IS DONE.

Author Unknown.

PERHAPS the most arduous pilgrimage of modern times was the journey made by Sir Ernest Shackleton with his two companions across the bitter wastes of the icy Antarctic. Blinded by blizzards, frozen with cold, and weak from exposure they could do nothing but press doggedly on to fulfil their purpose. Out of that seemingly hopeless expedition came a spark of illumination which has since burned in the minds of men where heroism shines and glows. Out of that seemingly hopeless expedition came one of the greatest object lessons to those who grow weary of the way, yet who through the voice of duty cannot turn back.

Shackleton wrote: "When I look back on those days, with all their anxiety and peril, I cannot doubt that our party of three was divinely guided both over the ice and across the storm-swept sea. I know that during that long and wracking march ... it seemed to me often that we were not three but four. I said nothing to my companions on the point, but afterwards Worsley said to me: 'Boss, I had a curious feeling on the march that there was another person with us.'"

Thomas.

February 17th

LET ME BE THE FIRST TO RESPECT A PRISONER'S DIGNITY.

WHAT can I do to help? I can respect a prisoner's dignity when I write a letter. A visit to a prison may turn out to be a memorable occasion, especially when staying long enough to let you know the visited you care. A positive experience about the future may be an invigorating experience for both.

Louise Donalme, housewife, was moved by the plight of newly-released prisoners. She opened a 'half-way' house with the help of family and friends. More than a hundred men looking for work and housing stayed there for as long as 90 days in the first three years of operation. Only four returned to prison.

"I'm not a religious man," said a prisoner in jail. "I'd spent two years in another prison and had turned off all my feelings, turned off the world. But when she spoke, Mister, she's the most warm, caring person to walk the face of the earth. Her love changed the life of every prisoner."

Prisoner talking about Sister A. Brenner, in Christopher News Notes, 12 East 48th Street, New York, NY 10017.

February 18th

THE CAMEL'S HUMP IS AN UGLY LUMP, WHICH WELL YOU MAY SEE AT THE ZOO; BUT UGLIER YET IS THE HUMP WE GET, FROM HAVING TOO LITTLE TO DO.

Rudyard Kipling.

TO BE happy we must keep busy. Idleness soon becomes dreary and tiresome.

If you keep busy enough, you won't have time to think and worry about yourself.

If possible, choose work that you like and can enjoy; a job that will hold your interest and with which you can grow . . .

Hobbies are important as a means of keeping good health. They provide a complete change for mind and body which is the main purpose of recreation.

Find at least one game you like to play . . . and try to perfect yourself at it. Play should provide you with a complete change from your day's work. You should thoroughly enjoy it and it should involve a certain amount of physical activity.

GORDON BYRON.

February 19th

"FOR IT IS BY GIVING ... THAT WE RECEIVE"

PROMISE yourself ... To be strong that nothing can disturb your peace of mind ... To talk health, happiness and prosperity to every person you meet ... To make all your friends feel that there is something in them ... To look on the sunny-side of everything, and make your optimism come true ... To think only the best, to work only for the best, and to expect only the best.

To be just as enthusiastic about the success of others as you are about your own ... To forget the mistakes of the past and press on to the greater achievements of the future ... To wear a cheerful countenance at all times, and give every living creature you meet a smile ... To give so much time to the improvement of yourself that you have no time to criticize others.

AUTHOR UNKNOWN.

February 20th

I LISTEN TO GOD IN MY HEART WHEN I LISTEN TO THE SIGHTS, SOUNDS AND BEAUTY OF THE NATURAL WORLD.

I PAUSED to listen to the silence. My breath, crystallized as it passed my cheeks, drifted on a breeze gentler than a whisper. The wind vane pointed toward the South Pole. Presently the windcups ceased their gentle turning as the cold killed the breeze. My frozen breath hung like a cloud overhead.

The day was dying, the night was being born—but with great peace. Here were the imponderable processes and forces of the cosmos, harmonious and soundless. Harmony, that was it! That was what came out of the silence—gentle rhythm, the strain of a perfect chord, the music of the spheres, perhaps.

It was enough to catch that rhythm, momentarily to be myself a part of it. In that instant I could feel no doubt of man's oneness with the universe. The conviction came that that rhythm was too orderly, too harmonious, too perfect to be a product of blind chance—that, therefore, there must be purpose in the whole and that man was part of that whole and not an accidental offshoot. It was a feeling that transcended reason; that went to the heart of man's despair and found it groundless. The universe was a cosmos, not a chaos. Man was as rightfully a part of that cosmos as were the day and night.

ADMIRAL RICHARD E. BYRD,
in the frozen world of the South Pole.

February 21st

> PRAISE GOD, FROM WHOM ALL BLESSINGS FLOW;
> PRAISE HIM, ALL CREATURES HERE BELOW;
> PRAISE HIM ABOVE, YE HEAVENLY HOST;
> PRAISE FATHER, SON, AND HOLY GHOST.
> *Thomas Ken (1637-1711).*

PRAISE the Lord; ye heavens, adore him;
   Praise him, angels, in the height;
Sun and moon, rejoice before him,
   Praise him, all ye stars and light.
Praise the Lord, for he hath spoken,
   Worlds his mighty voice obeyed:
Laws, which never shall be broken,
   For their guidance he hath made.

Praise the Lord, for he is glorious;
   Never shall his promise fail:
God hath made his saints victorious;
   Sin and death shall not prevail.
Praise the God of our salvation;
   Hosts on high his power proclaim;
Heaven and earth and all creation,
   Laud and magnify his name.

Worship, honour, glory, blessing,
   Lord, we offer unto thee:
Young and old, thy praise confessing,
   In glad homage bend the knee.
As the saints in heaven adore thee,
   We would bow before thy throne;
As thine angels serve before thee,
   So on earth thy will be done.
               E. OSLER (1798–1863).

✱

February 22nd

AN OVER-RULING PROVIDENCE HOLDS ME IN THE HOLLOW OF ITS HAND. GRACE TRANSMUTES ALL MY WATER INTO WINE.

"AND when they wanted wine, the mother of Jesus saith unto Him, They have no wine" ... Alyosha heard.

"Ah, yes, I was missing that, and I didn't want to miss it, I love that passage: it's Cana of Galilee, the first miracle ... Ah, that miracle! Ah, that sweet miracle! It was not men's grief but their joy Christ visited. He worked His first miracle to help men's gladness."

DOSTOEVSKY.
Russian novelist.
From: The Brothers Karamazov

February 23rd

I ASK NOT OWNERSHIP OF LAND, NOR PILES OF STOCKS AND SHARES. I AM SATISFIED WITH WEALTH AT HAND, THOUGH HIDDEN UNAWARES.

I WAS walking along the street ... I was stopped by a decrepit old beggar. Bloodshot, tearful eyes, blue lips, coarse clothes, festering wounds ... Oh, how hideously poverty had eaten this miserable creature!

He held out to me a red, swollen, filthy hand. He groaned and mumbled for help. I began feeling in all my pockets ... No purse, no watch, not even a handkerchief ... I had taken nothing with me. And this wretched man was still waiting ... his outstretched hand feebly shook and trembled.

Confused, abashed, I warmly clasped the filthy, shaking hand ... "Don't be angry, brother; I have nothing, brother."

He stared at me with his bloodshot eyes; his blue lips smiled; and he in turn gripped my chilly fingers.

"What of it, brother?" he mumbled; "thanks for this, too. That is a gift too, brother."

I knew I too had received a gift from a brother.

IVAN TURGENEV.
Russian Novelist, 1818–83.

February 24th

I RESOLVE TO REVISE MY DIET TO WHOLEFOODS, RAW FRESH FRUIT AND VEGETABLES; AND WITH SPECIAL EMPHASIS ON HONEY.

THE ancient Greeks, in their Golden Era, put great store by honey as food, and as a prolonger of life. Hippocrates, father of medicine, prescribed honey for those who wished longer life, and ate it every day himself. Pythagoras, the great philosopher, gave a great deal of thought to the matter of natural foods for health, and devised a diet of honey, fruits, nuts, vegetables and bread which improved his health and that of his followers considerably. Pythagoras records that his followers found new energy and health in this diet, and gave particular praise to honey. He lived to be ninety, and one of his disciples, Anacreon, a devotee of honey, lived to one hundred and fifteen, and attributed his longevity to this nectar of the gods.

Democritus, considered the greatest physicist who ever lived and the founder of the atomic theory, tried many diets and finally settled on honey. At the age of one hundred and nine, he decided he had lived long enough and wished to die. He stopped eating, and the women in his household, who desired to attend the annual three-day all-feminine festival of Thesmophoria, pleaded with him not to die because that would keep them away from the festival. He agreed to postpone his death until they returned, and kept himself alive the necessary number of days by sipping honey and water.

MARC DIXON,
"Food for Life and Health".

February 25th

I LEARN THE SECRET OF ETERNAL YOUTH. I WILL WARM BOTH HANDS BEFORE THE FIRE OF LIFE, IN LOVE AND FRIENDLINESS.

ONCE there were two philosophers who were seeking to discover the secret of perpetual and eternal youth.

One of them spent his time in a laboratory poring over bulky volumes, experimenting with mystic formulae, and muttering the uncanny spells of old magicians. He buried himself in his work, and gradually shut himself away from his fellow man.

One day he was looking into a mirror, and he realized his disappointment. He became insane. For despite his spells and potions, the wrinkles had spread over his face like widening ripples on the wind-swept waters. His body was bent and withered. His skin was yellow and dry as parchment, and his eyes were weary and unspeakably aged. He had failed in his search.

The other philosopher went out into the world. He laughed with the children on the street corners. He smiled at all those he met, and they smiled back at him. Each night he slept under the guardianship of the stars, and from them he learned something of the beauty of eternity. He read the mystery in the heart of a rosebud, and his ear was tuned to the delicate calls of the songbirds. He loved everyone, and everyone loved him.

So, although his hair grew white as the hawthorn's blossoms, his blue eyes remained clear, frank, and merry. He carried his body erect, and his brow was as smooth and untroubled as a child's. The hand of time had passed over him lightly. He had discovered that the secret of perpetual youth lay deep down in his heart.

THOMAS DREIER.
English poet and writer.

February 26th

THE MIND IS THE NATURAL PROTECTOR OF THE BODY ... EVERY THOUGHT TENDS TO REPRODUCE ITSELF ... I DIRECT MY THOUGHTS INTO KINDLINESS, GRACE AND GOODWILL TO STIMULATE A LIFE-GIVING FLOW OF ALL BODY SECRETIONS.

SAYS a noted author, an able graduate of one of our greatest medical schools, and one who has studied deeply into the forces that build the body and the forces that tear it down: "The mind is the natural protector of the body ..." Every thought tends to reproduce itself, and ghastly mental pictures of disease, sensuality, and vice of all sorts, produce scrofula and leprosy of the soul, which reproduces them in the body.

Anger changes the chemical properties of the saliva to a poison dangerous to life. It is well-known that sudden and violent emotions have not only weakened the heart in a few hours, but have caused death and insanity. It has been discovered by scientists that there is a chemical difference between that sudden cold exudation of a person under a deep sense of guilt and ordinary perspiration. The state of the mind can sometimes be determined by chemical analysis of the perspiration of a criminal, which, when brought into contact with selenic acid, produces a distinctive pink colour. It is well known that fear has killed thousands of victims. On the other hand *courage is a great invigorator.*

"Anger in a mother may poison a nursing child. Rarey, the celebrated horse-tamer, said that an angry word would raise the pulse of a horse ten beats in a minute. If this is true of an animal, what can we say of its power on human beings, especially upon a child?

"Sudden mental emotion often causes vomiting. Extreme anger or fright may produce jaundice. A violent paroxysm of rage has caused apoplexy and death. Indeed, in more than one instance, a single night of mental agony has wrecked a life. Grief, long-standing jealousy, constant care and corroding anxiety sometimes tend to develop insanity. Sick thoughts and discordant moods are the natural atmosphere of disease, and crime is engendered and thrives in the miasma of the mind."

From all this we get the great fact we are scientifically demonstrating today—that the various mental states, emotions, and passions have their various peculiar effects upon the body, and each induces in turn, if indulged in to any great extent, its own peculiar forms of disease, and these may become chronic.

RALPH WALDO TRINE.
"In Tune with the Infinite".

February 27th

I WILL FORTIFY MYSELF WITH CONTENTMENT, FOR IT IS THE GATE TO MENTAL HEALTH.

WHEN I came into the country, and being seated among silent trees, and meads and hills, had all my time in my own hands, I resolved to spend it all, whatever it cost me, in search of happiness, and to satiate that burning thirst which Nature had enkindled in me from my youth. In which I was so resolute that I chose rather to live upon ten pounds a year, and to go in leather clothes, and feed upon bread and water, so that I might have all my time clearly to myself, than to keep many thousands per annum in an estate of life where my time would be devoured in care and labour.

And God was so pleased to accept that desire, that from that time to this, I have had all things plentifully provided for me, without any care at all, my very study of Felicity making me more to prosper, than all the care in the whole world. So that through his blessing I live a free and kingly life as if the world were turned into Eden.

Thomas Traherne.
English poet, 1637–74.

February 28th

I WILL SIT DOWN IN A QUIET PLACE ... OPEN ALL THE DOORS OF MY HEART ... AND LISTEN TO THE DEEPEST THING IN MY HEART ... THEN OBEY IT ... AT WHATEVER COST.

Abraham Habedi.

YOU who are letting miserable misunderstandings run on from year to year, meaning to clear them up some day; you who are keeping wretched quarrels alive because you cannot make up your mind that now is the day to sacrifice your pride and kill them; you who are passing men sullenly on the street, not speaking to them out of some spite, and yet knowing that it would fill you with shame and remorse if you heard that one of those men were dead tomorrow morning; you who are letting your neighbour starve, till you hear that he is dying of starvation; or letting your friend's heart ache for a word of appreciation or sympathy, which you mean to give him some day. If you could only know and see and feel, all of a sudden, that "the time is short", how it would break the spell! How you would go instantly and do the thing which you might never have another chance to do!

Phillip Brooks.

February 29th

IT IS FAR BETTER TO FORGIVE AND FORGET THAN TO RESENT AND REMEMBER ... LOVE REDUCES FRICTION TO A FRACTION.

WHEN he was 10, John West learned about forgiveness from his father. While playing with a tree branch, he caused his father to fall off a ladder and break his arm.

The boy's mother, Marion West, recalled that his father reassured him by saying: "Let's forget it. I'm going to be fine, and we'll cut some more branches together, later."

John learned well, according to Mrs West. When she spilt milk on him accidentally during dinner, he quickly said: "That's all right, Mama." And in an essay he wrote about forgiveness, describing it as "a sign of kindness and love."

Daily irritations and problems give us lots of chances to offer forgiveness. But families are also called on to forgive deep emotional wounds. To forgive such hurts immediately can be difficult, if not impossible. Yet it is important to try—even to be the first to extend a hand in reconciliation—so the family can avoid wasting energy on hate and revenge. Doris Donnelly said: "Forgiveness is the lynch-pin that holds a family together."

When we forgive someone we are saying to them, in essence: "I'm capable of loving you and seeing you as more than that painful thing you did." But she warns that for forgiveness to take place "you have to acknowledge the hurt and affirm the pain."

When we can feel at peace ... when we can remember the event and your stomach no longer churns "then forgiveness has taken hold." Neibhur calls forgiveness "the final form of love."

THE CHRISTOPHERS.
12 E. 48th Street, New York, NY 10017, USA.

Chipping Camden, seen through one of the arches of the medieval market hall. Photograph by Dennis Mansell.

March 1st

FOR ME, THIS DAY IS A NEW BEGINNING ... I MAKE BOLD DECISIONS ... I GO FORWARD IN THE FAITH AND CONFIDENCE THAT ALL WILL BE WELL.

WHEN the fifteenth century was swinging into the sixteenth the big names that filled the ears of men were Sultan Mohammed II, Pizarro, Cesare Borgia, Charles the Bold, Babur, Francis I. How much do you now hear of them? But here are three other names of that era: Columbus, Copernicus, Martin Luther. Any schoolchild can tell you about them. Is not that a pattern, repeated over and over again in history—the works of violence perishing, the achievements of the spirit enduring?

I dare you to be a pessimist. Plunge deep into it. Believe that all man's ideals are delusions, all his hopes mirages, that any seeming progress in the past was only a flash in the pan. Agree that we have now reached a dead end, that the dictatorships have the democracies on the run because democracy is essentially unworkable, that Christian goodness is all fantasy and fustian, and that a nuclear war will soon finish off civilization and perhaps the human race. If you are going to be a pessimist, be a real one; stop trying to be hopeful.

You can't do it. At once arguments on the other side begin shouting and will not be silenced. You are going out into a tough and stormy generation, but with hope that a victory can be won over the evil forces that threaten the world.

That kind of victory has been won so often in history that you cannot deny your faith that it can happen again. Easy-going optimism is silly; thoroughly easy-going pessimism is fatal. What we need is intelligence, faith, goodwill and courage.

I suspect that you can guess what I am going to say. Underneath the reasons I have given for keeping up an undiscouraged fight for a better world lies my religious faith. I don't believe that this universe is, as one materialist puts it, "all an affair of chance, the froth and fume of the waves on an ocean of sterile matter."

Because I believe that there is Mind behind our lives here, Meaning in them, and Destiny ahead of them, confidence and hope will not down. Such a situation as we face today, far from weakening that faith, calls it out.

I began believing in God for intellectual reasons, and I am confident that they still hold good. But today my faith is militant because the lack of it can paralyse hope and courage, and all confidence in mankind's future.

HARRY EMERSON FOSDICK.
In a letter to a friend.

March 2nd

MY NEIGHBOUR NEEDS ME. I WILL BE KINDLY AND GOOD-NATURED TO EVERYONE.

IT'S the hand we clasp with an honest grasp ... That gives us a hearty thrill .. It's the good we pour into others' lives ... That comes back our own to fill ... It's the dregs we drain from another's cup ... That makes our own seem sweet ... And the hours we give to another's need ... That make our life complete.

It's the burdens we help another bear ... That make our own seem light ... It's the danger seen for another's feet ... That shows us the path to right ... It's the good we do each passing day ... With a heart sincere and true ... In giving the world your very best ... Its best will return to you.

AUTHOR UNKNOWN.

March 3rd

"OUR LIVES ARE SONGS, GOD WRITES THE WORDS. AND WE SET THEM TO MUSIC AT LEISURE. AND THE SONG IS SAD OR THE SONG IS GLAD AS WE CHOOSE TO FASHION THE MEASURE."

EXERCISE caution in your business affairs, for the world is full of trickery. But let this not blind you to what virtue there is; many persons strive for high ideals and everywhere life is full of heroism. Be yourself. Especially do not feign affection. Neither be cynical about love; for in the face of all aridity and disenchantment, it is as perennial as the grass.

Take kindly the counsel of the years, gracefully surrendering the things of youth. Nurture strength of spirit to shield you in sudden misfortune. But do not distress yourself with the dark imaginings. *Many fears are borne of fatigue and loneliness.*

Beyond a wholesome discipline, be gentle with yourself. You are a child of the universe no less than the trees and the stars; *you have a right to be here.* And whether or not it is clear to you, no doubt the universe is unfolding as it should. Therefore be at peace with God, whatever you conceive Him to be. And whatever your labours and aspirations, in the noisy confusion of life, keep peace in your soul. With all its sham, drudgery, and broken dreams, it is still a beautiful world.

AUTHOR UNKNOWN.

March 4th

I HAVE A LARGE CAPACITY FOR ABSORBING ANNOYANCES WITHOUT BEING OVERCOME BY THEM. NOTHING HAS THE POWER TO IRRITATE ME ANYMORE. IN QUIETNESS AND IN CONFIDENCE SHALL BE MY STRENGTH.

IN THE past, when I couldn't find something, I used to keep looking for it, becoming more and more irritable, until finally I lost my temper and ended up making myself and everybody else miserable.

Later I worked for a man who combined careers in writing, public relations, and publishing, with complete self-control. For eight years I never saw him lose his temper, despite a rigid travelling schedule and constant appointments.

If our beloved "Boss" requested a letter from the file that we couldn't locate almost immediately, he would say, "Never mind; I'll dictate without it." There was never any recrimination to make you feel inefficient, so you always did your very best work for him.

Recently, while going over our tax return, I mislaid a page of figures. A few minutes' search failed to uncover it, so I started to do some filing instead of looking further. Turning back, a glance at the desk revealed the paper on the back of my time sheet!

By diverting my attention to something else I had gained perspective and the figures appeared without effort or annoyance. Happily, some of my ex-Boss's wonderful philosophy must have rubbed off on me without my knowing it. I realized that I too could follow his example and live with calm perspective as he did.

Norma S. Archer,
in "Sunshine".

March 5th

AS A SEED DIES TO GIVE BIRTH TO THE FAIR FLOWER OF TOMORROW, SO IT IS THROUGH SUFFERING THAT I REACH MATURITY.

THE thought of being thankful for your troubles may, at first, seem utterly ridiculous to you, especially being thankful for pain. When I suffered the excruciating pain of arthritis, it seemed almost ludicrous to say that I was thankful for the experience. Yet it was only when I could say to God "Gladly will I suffer any amount of pain if you will but teach me what I need to learn through it", that I could begin to reach the higher consciousness where it was possible to live objectively. Only then was I able to realize that my acceptance of the pain had enabled me to rise to the plane where I could see that my suffering need not be in vain and that "I could have good of all my pain".

Katherine Mansfield lived most of her life in pain. Not until she accepted the pain as an integral part of her life did it cease to interfere, but kept open the flow of ideas from her creative centre. She never discovered the secret of physical healing for her body, but she learned the use of suffering.

There is reward in suffering. Life can be strangely free from much trivial tediousness for one who thus accepts and uses a life of pain.

Yet there is a real temptation not to go all the way out for complete physical healing in order that one may not lose the detachment which semi-invalidism often gives. Yet the creative life pouring through a man or woman to build a symphony of words, sound, or colour, can build a symphony of radiant health within the same body if that healing power is recognised and accepted.

Dr Rebecca Beard.
"*Everyman's Goal*". Pub: Arthur James.

DUTCH TOWN SCENE.
By Cornelis Springer.
By courtesy of Christie's Images.

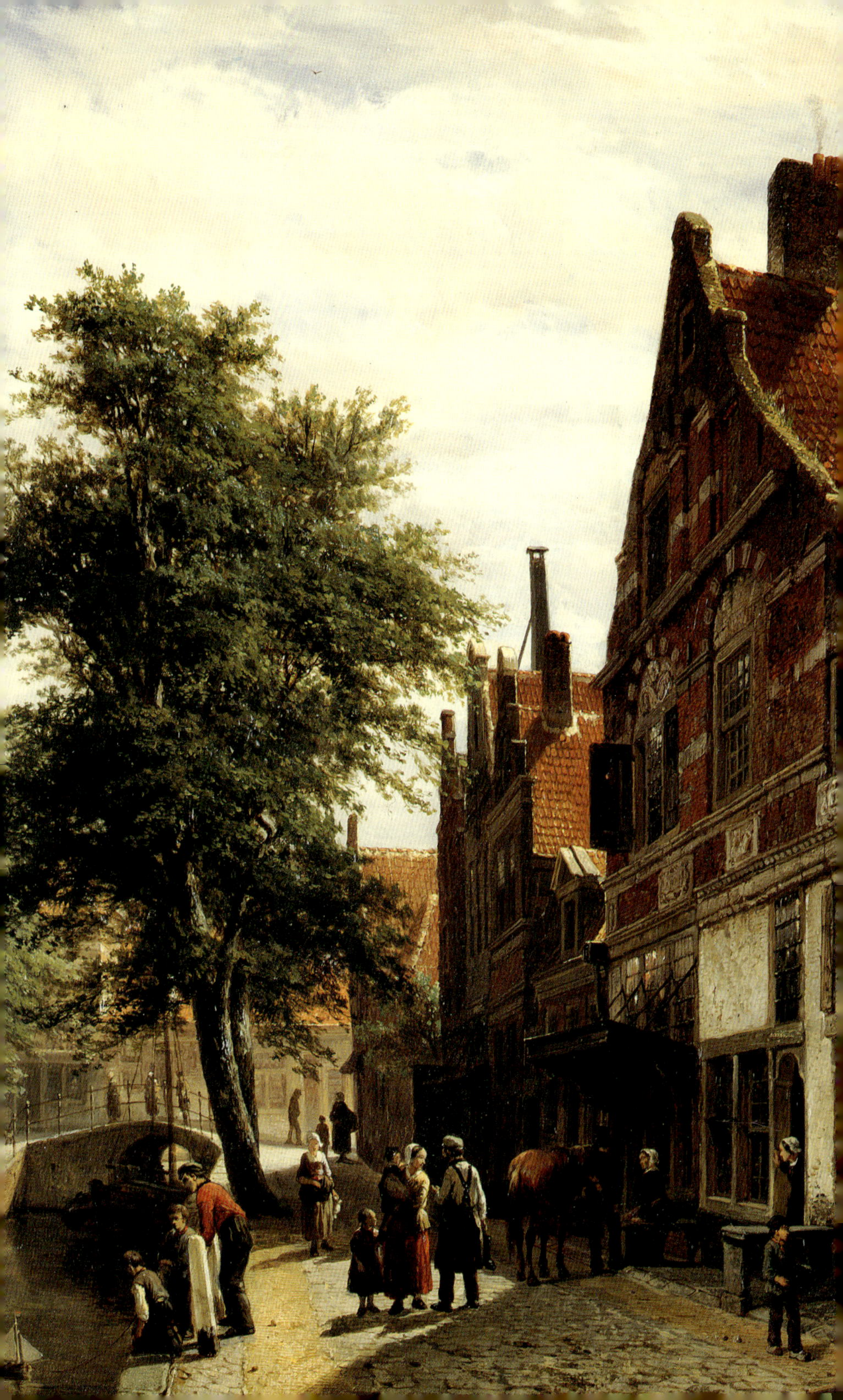

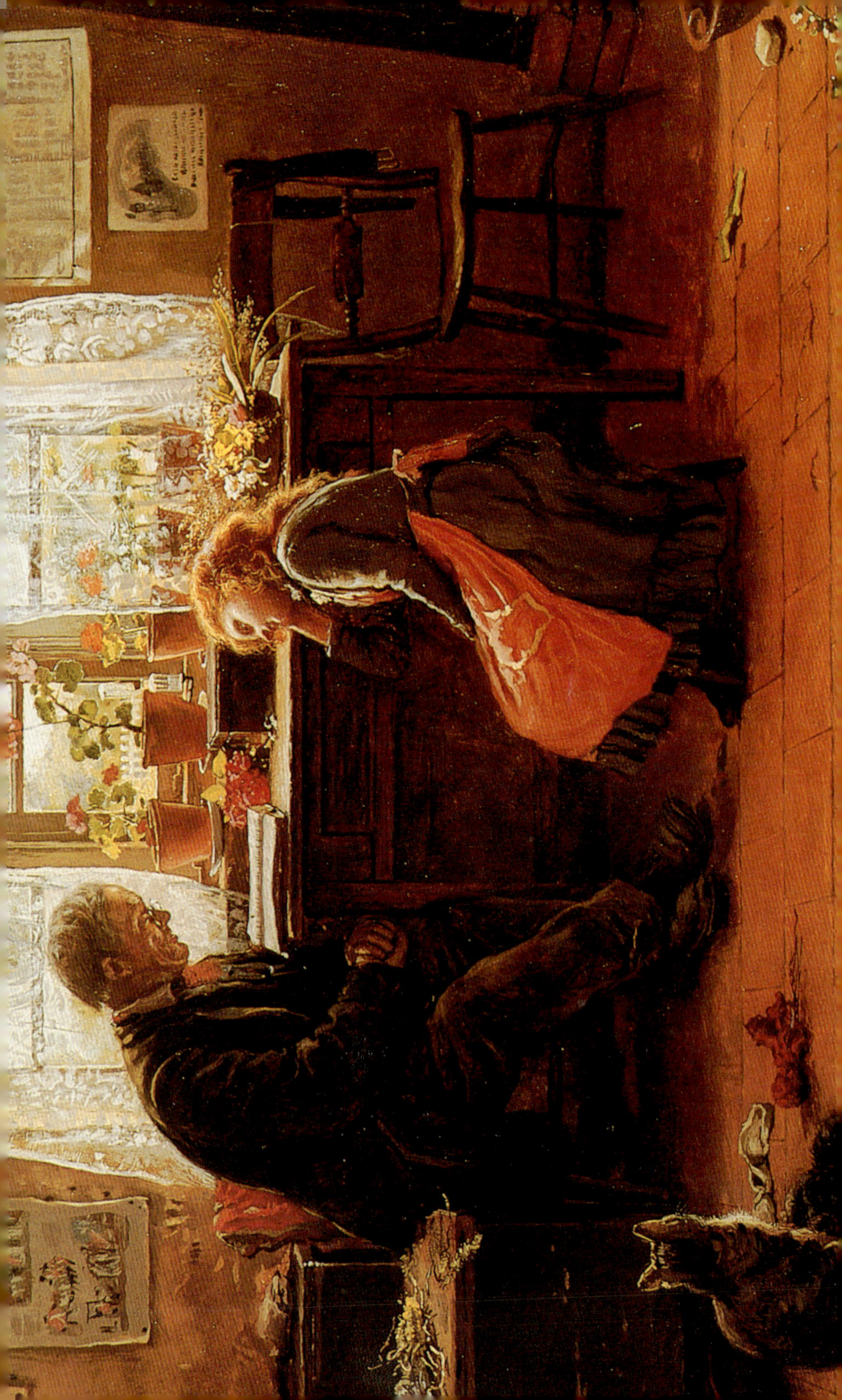

March 6th

"WHEN I REMEMBER ALL THAT WAS GOING WRONG, AND REMEMBER ALSO ALL THAT HAS GONE RIGHT, I FEEL SURE THAT WE HAVE NO NEED TO FEAR THE TEMPEST. LET IT ROAR, AND LET IT RAGE. WE SHALL COME THROUGH.

Sir Winston Churchill.

AND yet the compensations of calamity are made apparent to the misunderstanding also after long intervals of time. A fever, a mutilation, a cruel disappointment, a loss of wealth, a loss of friends seems at the moment unpaid loss and unpayable, but the sure years reveal the deep remedial force that underlies all facts.

The death of a dear friend, wife, brother, lover, which seemed nothing but privation, somewhat later assumes the aspect of a guide or genius; for it commonly operates revolutions in our way of life; terminates an epoch of infancy or of youth which was waiting to be closed, breaks up a wonted occupation or a household or style of living that allows the formation of new ones more friendly to the growth of character.

It permits or constrains the formation of new acquaintants, and the reception of new influences which prove of the first importance to the next few years. The man or woman who would have remained a sunny garden flower with no room for its roots and too much sunshine for its head, by the falling of the walls and the neglect of the gardener is made the banian of the forest yielding shade and fruit to wide neighbourhoods of men.

EMERSON,
American poet & essayist.
(1803–1882).

GRANDFATHER AT HOME.
From the painting by William H. Snape.
By courtesy of Christie's Images.

March 7th

TO LOVE SOMEONE IS TO REVEAL TO THEM THEIR VALUE AND HELP THEM DISCOVER THAT THEY ARE PRECIOUS.
Jean Vanier.

THEY called Rebecca and said to her "Will you go with this man?" And she said, "I will go".

And they sent away Rebecca their sister, and her nurse, and Abraham's servant and his men. And they blessed Rebecca saying, "You are our sister, be then the mother of thousands of millions, and let your seed possess the gate of those who hate them."

And Rebecca arose with her damsels, and they rode upon the camels and followed the man. And the servant took Rebecca and went his way.

And Isaac came by way of the well Lahai-roi; for he lived in the south country. And he went out to meditate in the fields at eventide. He lifted up his eyes and saw, and behold the camels were coming. And Rebecca lifted up her eyes, and when she saw Isaac, she lighted off the camel. For she said to the servant, "Who is this who walks in the field to meet us?" And the servant answered, "It is my master". Therefore she took a veil and covered herself.

And the servant told Isaac all the things that he had done. And Isaac brought her into his mother Sarah's tent, and took Rebecca, and she became his wife. And he loved her.

THE BIBLE.
Genesis, 24.

March 8th

I REALIZE I HAVE CREATIVE POWER WITHIN ME. A SOLUTION TO ALL MY PROBLEMS WILL EMERGE. I FACE THE FUTURE WITH COURAGE AND CERTAINTY, DAILY LEARNING HOW TO PUT 'FIRST THINGS FIRST'.

IF YOU want to enjoy one of the greatest luxuries in life, the luxury of having enough time—time to play; time to rest; time to think things through; time to get things done and know you have done them to the best of your ability, remember there is only *one* way.

Take enough time to think and plan things in the order of their importance. Your life will take on a new zest. You will add years to your life—and more life to your years.

BENJAMIN FRANKLIN, (1706–90).
American statesman. Scientist. Writer. Born in Boston of poor parents. Helped to draft the Declaration of Independence. Inventor of the lightning conductor.

March 9th

REGARDLESS OF HOW MY DAY HAS BEEN, LET MY LAST THREE WORDS BEFORE SLEEP BE, 'I LOVE YOU'.

KATHY, a social worker, and Scott, an engineer, are in their mid-20s, both rather nervously preparing for their wedding;
"What is the quality in Scott you most admire right now?" Kathy was asked. "He is always giving . . . to me, to everyone."
"And how about you, Scott, what is the quality you most love in Kathy?"
"She is a great care-giver, at home toward her family, in her professional work, with me."
Caring, giving, loving—the words seem to be near synonymous not only for Kathy and Scott, but for couples everywhere, those soon to marry.
"I love you," applied to the sometimes hard choices of married life, means think of the happiness of the other rather than your own, wondering how you can please rather than waiting to be pleased.
Love, according to Erich Fromm in "The Art of Loving," is primarily giving, not receiving, although a very high form of giving can be the act of allowing others to give to us.
The paradox is that the more we give, the more we receive, the stronger our love, the deeper our joy, the more genuinely we care for others, the more profoundly we experience peace ourselves.
Couples married many years often observe, "Marriage is not a 50-50 proposition. Each partner must give 100%." Self-forgetfulness is a sign of true love.
Someone once advised newlyweds: "Regardless of how the day has been, let the last three words before sleep be, 'I love you'."
THE CHRISTOPHERS.

I KNOW some good marriages — marriages where both people are just trying to get through their days by helping each other, being good to each other.
Erica Jong.

March 10th

> I HAVE NO MORE RIGHT TO CONSUME HAPPINESS WITHOUT PRODUCING IT THAN TO CONSUME WEALTH WITHOUT PRODUCING IT.
>
> *Bernard Shaw.*

IT IS undeniable that the great quest of humanity is happiness. But was the world created to be happy? How many are truly happy? I've studied people in all classes and conditions, and everywhere I have found, when you get below the surface, that it is mostly the insincere individual who says: "I am happy".

Nearly everybody wants something he hasn't got. As things are constructed, what he wants is money—more money than he has in his pocket. But after all, money can buy only a few things. Why should one envy the captains of industry? Their lives are made up of those vast incessant worries from which the average individual is happily spared. Worry, worry, is the great evil of life.

What do I consider the nearest approximation to happiness of which the present human nature is capable? Why, living on a farm which is one's own, far from the hectic, artificial conditions of the city—a farm where one gets directly from one's own soil what one needs to sustain life, with a garden in front and a healthy normal family to contribute to those small domestic joys which relieve a man from business strain.

THOMAS EDISON,
American inventor, born in Ohio, of Dutch Scottish parentage. Starting life as a newsboy, he later became a telegraph operator.

March 11th

> TAKE THESE MEN FOR YOUR EXAMPLE. LIKE THEM REMEMBER THAT PROSPERITY CAN ONLY BE FOR THE FREE, THAT FREEDOM IS THE SURE POSSESSION OF THOSE ALONE WHO HAVE THE COURAGE TO DEFEND IT.
>
> *Pericles.*

WE COMMEMORATE the British people's magnificent achievements in the long and desperate struggle against the Axis attempt to enslave the world.

Though long exposed to the full fury of attack, the Empire, both when alone and when fighting alongside her allies, refused to flinch from danger or modify her defiance. The British contribution to the final victory will always command the admiration, respect, and gratitude of all peoples devoted to the cause of freedom.

GENERAL DWIGHT DAVID EISENHOWER,
34th President of the USA. Supreme Commander of all the Allied armies of the West during the Second World War.

March 12th

HAPPINESS IS BEST ATTAINED BY LEARNING TO LIVE EACH DAY BY ITSELF. THE WORRIES ARE MOSTLY ABOUT YESTERDAY AND TOMORROW.

Michael Nolan.

VICTOR HUGO exclaimed, "Why was I not exiled before!" This was a score of years after Napoleon III banished him from France. Hugo had been France's most popular literary figure when the Emperor took exception to some of Hugo's political beliefs and sent him into what everybody thought would be oblivion. But during this period of "adversity" Hugo really found himself. In his exile he wrote his most successful novels, including *Les Misérables*. He returned to France more famous than when he left.

If misfortune or seeming disaster strikes you and you have no choice but to start all over again—keep Victor Hugo in mind. You, too, might be saying someday, "Why didn't this happen to me sooner!"

WHATSOEVER THINGS.

March 13th

NOT HE WHO HAS MUCH IS RICH, BUT HE WHO GIVES MUCH. THE HOARDER WHO IS ANXIOUSLY WORRIED ABOUT LOSING SOMETHING IS, PSYCHOLOGICALLY SPEAKING, THE POOR, IMPOVERISHED MAN, REGARDLESS OF HOW MUCH HE HAS. WHOEVER IS CAPABLE OF GIVING OF HIMSELF IS RICH.

Erich Fromm, psychoanalyst.

EVERY sweet has its sour; every evil its good. Every faculty which receives pleasure has a penalty put on its abuse. It is to answer for its moderation with its life. For every grain of wit there is a grain of folly. For everything you have missed, you have gained something else; and for everything you gain, you lose something. If riches increase, they are increased that use them. If the gatherer gathers too much, nature takes out of a man what she puts into his chest; swells the estate, but kills the owner. Nature hates monopolies and exceptions. The waves of the sea do not more speedily seek a level from their loftiest tossing than the varieties of condition tend to equalise themselves. There is always some levelling circumstance that puts down the overbearing, the strong, the rich, the fortunate, substantially on the same ground with all others.

RALPH WALDO EMERSON.
American poet & essayist, brilliant prose writer and friend of Thomas Carlyle.
From: "The Law of Compensation".

March 14th

I ACCEPT MYSELF ... I ACCEPT MY LIMITATIONS WHICH CAN BECOME OPPORTUNITIES ... I DO NOT WISH TO BE SOMEONE ELSE ... I CAN MAKE SOMETHING WORTHWHILE OUT OF MYSELF.

THE most stimulating successes in history have come from people who, facing some kind of limitations and handicaps, took them as part of life's game and played splendidly in spite of them. Once when Ole Bull, the great violinist, was giving a concert in Paris, his A string snapped and he transposed the composition and finished it on three strings. That is life—to have your A string snap and finish on three strings.

As soon as a man begins to accept this positive technique for handling his handicaps, they present themselves to him as opportunities always challenging, sometimes fascinating. Rebellion against your handicaps gets you nowhere. Self-pity gets you nowhere. One must have the adventurous daring to accept oneself as a bundle of possibilities and undertake the most interesting game in the world—making the most of one's best.

HARRY EMERSON FOSDICK.
Sincere thanks to the author whose address we are unable to trace.

March 15th

AS LONG AS I HAVE HOPE I HAVE A NEW POWER AND A HIDDEN ENERGY ... WHICH CARRIES ME HALF-WAY TO WHERE I WANT TO GO.

FIFTEEN-YEAR-OLD Douglas Maurer had been feeling poorly for weeks. His mother took him to the Children's Hospital. Blood tests revealed leukaemia.

Douglas bravely endured transfusions, spinal and bone marrow tests and chemotherapy. He knew the possible outcome of leukaemia, and fought to maintain hope.

A relative, wishing to cheer him up, ordered flowers at a shop near the hospital. The relative briefly explained Doug's plight to the clerk. When the flowers arrived, the boy was surprised to see a card from the clerk attached. It read:

"Douglas, I took your order. I work at Brix Florist ... I had leukaemia when I was seven years old. I'm 22 years old now. Good luck. My heart goes out to you. Sincerely, Laura Bradley."

The encouraging and loving words of a stranger gave Douglas the hope he needed.

THE CHRISTOPHERS.

March 16th

I ASKED FOR RICHES, THAT I MIGHT BE HAPPY; I WAS GIVEN POVERTY, THAT I MIGHT BE WISE. I ASKED FOR ALL THINGS, THAT I MIGHT ENJOY LIFE; I WAS GIVEN LIFE, THAT I MIGHT ENJOY ALL THINGS. I AM, AMONG ALL MEN, MOST RICHLY BLESSED.

Henry Viscardi. Man without legs.

AS THE rickety old airport bus rattled its way along the narrow road to New Delhi I was conscious of an extraordinary sense of peace. When approaching Connaught Circus through the usual tangle of burdened cyclists, ambling buffaloes, sleek cars, lean pedestrians and bouncing Sikh-propelled 'chuff-chuffs', I tried to define what I was feeling—but could only think of it as the peace of poverty.

To arrive suddenly in India fresh from the stress and tension of an affluent society induces a strong sense of liberation—freedom from some intangible but threatening power.

Here, one is aware that a man is free, at the deepest level. How impossible it is to be so, in societies where elaborately contrived pressures daily create new needs—false needs—to dilute his delight in small and simple joys.

Outside a sagging bamboo shelter at the edge of the road a graceful, dark-skinned young woman was washing her feet in water drawn from a stagnant pond with a surface of bright green scum. She looked up as we passed and met my eyes. Her smile possessed a quality rarely seen in modern Europe. It was an unforgettable moment. It recalled something I had read in Dr Radhakrishnan's essay on "Ethics" . . . 'When the soul is at peace, the greatest sorrows are borne lightly.'

Eric Fisher.
(Maidstone).

A LITTLE bit of heaven . . . Comes earthward every day . . . And you will sense its presence . . . When it comes along your way.

Katharine G. Gobell.

March 17th

LOVE IS THE VITAL FORCE, THE ESSENTIAL INGREDIENT THAT TRANSFORMS EVERY ACT OF MINE INTO A NEW, RICH, AND EXCITING EXPERIENCE.

MAN must love or perish. The great error all of us are likely to make in middle age is to forget this human law, and to revert to the conception of love in its primitive biological form alone! There is a reason for this. It is almost as if the change of life in men and women unconsciously compels us to recollect an earlier age of evolution when—as in the dayfly or the salmon—the parent organism dies soon after its mission of reproduction has been fulfilled. We naturally became depressed at this time, for the biological change we undergo revives the sense that love has been taken from our lives altogether.

Yet we may successfully move to combat our depression as a passing phase if we will remember two basic truths.

The first truth is this: Human life is *not* carried out solely on a primitive biological level. At the human stage of evolution, we do *not* die upon reaching the middle phase of life. Certain limitations develop, of course, and must be accepted. We are never again as powerful physically as we were in our twenties; at fifty, we can no longer play football or dance the whole night through. But the fact is that we normally retain sufficient virility and strength to serve us more than amply for two or three decades to come. Few of us are ever so enfeebled that we cannot pursue a normal life.

The second truth to remember is this: Our opportunities for the expression of love in its characteristically human aspects may actually increase as we grow older. If we have learned the lesson that love's task merely *begins* with the biological creation of life, we can use our years of knowledge and skill to carry it out in a broader and richer manner than ever before.

We will be conscious of the fact that in human life there is no end to the need for the arts of love, which offer innumerable channels of activity. Men and women can create, invent, produce, nurture and educate until their very last days on earth!

SMILEY BLANTON M.D.
"Love or Perish" (World's Work).
_{Our sincere thanks to owners of copyright we are unable to contact.}

Dancing class, Community Centre, Braintree, England.
Photograph by Dennis Mansell.

March 18th

IN THIS GREAT BIG WORLD OF OURS, GOD HAS MADE ENOUGH FLOWERS FOR EVERYONE TO FEEL THEIR HEALING AND UPLIFTING INFLUENCES AT HOME, IN THE OFFICE, AND EVERYWHERE.

A BUSINESSMAN I know always keeps fresh flowers on his desk, insisting they are a wise investment. In silent eloquence they exert their influence. "It is difficult to think mean or selfish thoughts in the presence of flowers," he says. "They help a gentleman to *be* gentle."

Beauty in any form has a way of encouraging our better qualities. While one man sees beauty in a flower, others find it in music or a painting. A scientist may find in his microscope beauty as exciting as a sunset is to someone else. God surrounds us with beauty, one of His great healing aids to the sick soul and the wounded spirit.

GERALD HORTON BATH,
in The Little Gazette.

All Lovely Things

All lovely things never pass . . .
A chair of Hepplewhite design,
A bowl of red Venetian glass
With traces of flower and vine,
A quaint, old street in Quaker town,
The reverent thought of saying grace,
A treasured heirloom, handed down,
Of wedding veil in rosepoint lace.

So fine, old chivalries remain
of honour, truth, integrity,
Virtues that through the years sustain
In sheer, unchanged ideality.
Life's deeply rooted tendril clings
To justify proven fine, old things.

Florence M. Taylor.

Sincere thanks to the author we have been unable to trace.

March 19th

NOTHING GREAT IS EVER ACHIEVED WITHOUT COMPASSION ... TODAY, I MAKE MY CONTRIBUTION TO THE WORLD.

THERE was once a very old man whose eyes had become dim, his ears dull of hearing, his knees trembling. When he sat at the table he could hardly hold the spoon and spilled his soup upon the clean tablecloth.

His son and his son's wife were disgusted at this, so the old grandfather at last had to sit in the corner behind the stove. They gave him his food in an earthenware bowl, and not even enough of it. He used to look toward the table with tear-filled eyes.

Once, his trembling hands could not hold the bowl, and it fell to the ground and was smashed. The young wife scolded him; but he said nothing and only sighed. Then they bought him a wooden bowl for a few pence, out of which he had to eat.

They were once sitting thus when the little grandson four years old began to gather together some bits of wood upon the ground. "What are you doing there?" asked the father. "I'm making a little trough," answered the child, "for father and mother to eat out of when I am big."

The man and his wife looked at each other for a while, and presently began to cry. They took the old grandfather to the table and henceforth always let him eat with them, and said nothing if he did spill a little.

GRIMM'S FAIRY TALES.
A Lesson in Caring.

March 20th

THE SUN MEETS NOT THE SPRINGING BUD THAT REACHES TOWARDS IT WITH HALF THE CERTAINTY THAT GOD, THE SOURCE OF ALL GOOD, COMMUNICATES HIMSELF TO THE SOUL THAT LONGS TO PARTAKE OF HIM.
William Law.

EASTER. A soft, warm breeze replaces the icy blasts of winter; the smell of rich damp earth warmed by the sun fills the air; young tender buds appear on trees that yesterday seemed barren, and tiny crocuses lift their lovely heads to the sun. The earth is responding to the touch of spring and giving of its beautiful gifts to delight the heart of man. Just as spring awakens the earth and stirs it to activity, Easter awakens the soul of man and arouses in him a divine restlessness, a desire to share his inner spiritual joy with others. It is small wonder that his heart is filled with a desire to give the message of Christ to others.

AUTHOR UNKNOWN.

March 21st

I WILL REMEMBER MY RESPONSIBILITY TO LESS FORTUNATE FRIENDS AND RELATIVES. THEY NEED MY HELP. I WILL ACT—NOW.

BRAHMS' father was a vagrant double-bass player who earned his *pfennige* by playing at dances and in garden restaurants, but throughout his life he was his son's adored idol. Once when Johannes Brahms, as a world-famous composer, returned to his native Hamburg to conduct a concert, the old gentleman insisted on playing the double-bass in the orchestra. He could not well be refused, although his technique was utterly insufficient for the intricacies of his son's *Serenade*, Op. 11. The rehearsals became a nightmare for the conductor. Eventually he could not stand it any more: he stopped, coughed rather puzzled, and thought for a moment how to explain things to father. In this very instant old Brahms' sonorous voice was heard all over the hall, "I know what you want to say, Hannes—but don't say it, better keep your big mouth shut!"

The old man refused steadfastly to take any money from his son, and it required all of Brahms' tact and delicacy to support him. At one time, when the two parted, Johannes said to father Brahms: "Believe me, Father, music in every situation is the greatest comforter. Whenever you are discouraged and feel you need something to lift you up, just take my old score of Handel's *Saul* and read it: I am sure you'll find whatever you need!"

Some time later the old man was in trouble. He remembered Johannes' words and looked through the old score. What he found was indeed the one thing he needed: his son had carefully put a bank-note between each page!

BERNARD GRUN,
"Private Lives of the Great Composers". Rider & Co.

March 22nd

IF I QUARRELS WOULD AVOID ... AND IN PEACE OF MIND REJOICE ... I MUST KEEP ANGER OUT OF MY WORDS ... AND ALSO OUT OF MY VOICE.
Author Unknown.

"ONCE I came home after school with a black eye, and, while my mother bathed it, I told her it was the other boy's fault.

"But she said it took two to make a fight, led me to the back porch, and told me to call out some insulting phrase as loud as I could. So I yelled at the top of my voice, and the hills sent back the echo.

"Then she told me to call out, 'God bless you,' and this time the echo returned, 'God bless you.' I've never forgotten that lesson."

L. B. MAYER,
Head of MGM studios.

March 23rd

I MAY TRAVEL THE WORLD IN SEARCH OF PEACE AND HAPPINESS ... BUT IF IT IS NOT IN MY HEART I SHALL FAIL TO FIND IT.

"EVERY morning, when we wake up, we have twenty-four brand-new hours to live. What a precious gift! We have the capacity to live in a way that these twenty-four hours will bring peace, joy and happiness to ourselves and others.

Peace is present right here and now, in ourselves and in everything we do and see. The question is whether or not we are in touch with it. We don't have to travel far away to enjoy the blue sky. We don't have to leave our city or even our neighbourhood to enjoy the eyes of a beautiful child. Even the air we breathe can be a source of joy.

We can smile, breathe, walk and eat our meals in a way that allows us to be in touch with the abundance of happiness that is available. We are very good at preparing to live, but not very good at living. We know how to sacrifice ten years for a diploma, and we are willing to work very hard to get a job, a car, a house, and so on. But we have difficulty remembering that we are alive in the present moment, the only moment there is for us to be alive. Every breath we take, every step we make, can be filled with peace, joy, and serenity. We need only to be awake, alive in the present moment.

... please do not wait ... to find peace. Peace and happiness are available in every moment. Peace is every step. We shall walk hand in hand. Bon voyage."

THICH NHAT HANH,
in Peace is Every Step.

March 24th

> THE CLOSING YEARS OF LIFE ARE LIKE THE END OF A MASQUERADE PARTY … WHEN THE MASKS ARE DROPPED.
> *Arthur Schopenhauer.*

TODAY I have completed sixty-four Springtimes … And now here I am, a very old woman, embarked on my sixty-fifth year. By one of those strange oddities of my destiny, I am now in much better health, much stronger, much more active, than I ever was in my youth …

I am troubled by no hankering after the days of my youth; I am no longer ambitious for fame; I desire no money except insofar as I should like to be able to leave something to my children and grandchildren … This astonishing old age … has brought me neither infirmity nor lowered vitality.

Can I still make myself useful? That one may legitimately ask and I think that I can answer 'yes'. I feel that I may be useful in a more personal, more direct way than ever before. I have, though how I do not know, acquired much wisdom. I am better equipped to bring up children …

It is quite wrong to think old age as a downward slope. One climbs higher and higher with the advancing years, and that, too, with surprising strides. How good life is when all that one loves is aswarm with life!

Letter from George Sand to a friend, July 5th, 1868.

March 25th

> I ENJOY FRESH FRUITS, GREEN VEGETABLES, AND THE WHOLESOME FOODS DIRECT FROM MOTHER EARTH. I COMPREHEND THE HYGIENIC ROLE PLAYED BY NATURAL DIET AND EFFICIENT DRAINAGE.

SIR William Lane, England's greatest abdominal surgeon, stated in a lecture at John Hopkins Medical School: "Gentlemen, I shall never die of cancer, for I am taking measures to prevent it. It is caused by poisons created in our bodies by the food we eat.

"What we should do, then, if we would avoid cancer, is to eat whole wheat bread, raw fruits and vegetables and their juices. First, that we may be better nourished and, secondly, that we may more easily eliminate waste products.

"We have been studying disease when we should have been studying diet and drainage. The world has been on the wrong track. The answer has been within ourselves all the time. Drain the body of its poisons, feed it properly, and the miracle is done. No one need have cancer who will take the trouble to avoid it."

Sir William Lane.
Distinguished physician & nutritionist.

March 26th

> WHEN ONE DOOR OF HAPPINESS CLOSES ANOTHER OPENS … BUT OFTEN WE LOOK SO LONG AT THE CLOSED DOOR THAT WE DO NOT SEE THE ONE OPENED FOR US.
> *Helen Keller (1880–1968)*

WHEN my husband died of a malignant disease, my fears were darkened by the unknown future. One sleepless night, I had decided to throw overboard the crumbling pieces of my life, when I was suddenly impelled to cry out *at once* to God for help.

In the dark outside my bedroom window, was an icy, deserted garden, a fitting parallel with my loss and fears.

Then I heard it—trilling notes to the cold, starless sky—a bird singing. My heart lifted with hope: God had heard my cry and was speaking to me through his creation.

A prayer, voiceless this time, rose in my throat. Then swelling in sound, came the feathered choir of the Dawn Chorus.

Was it the end of Winter? Food would not be abundant; the sunny days would still be few—yet, *they sang!*

My prison-door seemed to open to the unknown future and in that moment I was ready to face my new life—for it now held Hope and God had not failed me.

AUTHOR UNKNOWN.

March 27th

> ALL THAT A MAN DOES OUTWARDLY IS BUT THE EXPRESSION AND FRUITION OF HIS INMOST THOUGHT. TO BE A SUCCESSFUL GRANDFATHER HE MUST BE INTELLECTUALLY TOLERANT, EMOTIONALLY MATURE, AND ALWAYS A LITTLE KINDER THAN IS NECESSARY.
> *Author unknown.*

TO ME, a most happily-married-for-thirty-four-years Granny, the main attraction in a man is his intellect. Mere rugged "bull" strength often hides a small, mean mind, and more often than not mere glamour plus handsomeness is the outward covering of a vain fop.

But an intelligent man is a "lasting" man. Beauty perishes, muscles grow flabby, mean, evil, petty spirits ruin the body as time takes its grim toll of their wealth, or their pleasures, but the man of intellect grows even more serene, and time cannot wither him.

GRANNY,
in New Zealand Home Journal.

March 28th

> I'LL HAVE A SMILE AND PRAISE FOR ALL,
> FOR FRIENDS AND NEIGHBOURS WHEN THEY CALL,
> TO GREET THEM WITH A WORD OF CHEER,
> THEIR LIVES THE RICHER 'COS I'M HERE.
>
> *Author Unknown.*

A SMILE, resting on a foundation of sincerity, is one of the most valuable things in the world. It cheers when nothing else would make an impression. A smile is the sun that dissipates the clouds of despair. A smile has changed the whole course of a human life. It is the cheapest and most valuable gift we can make. When smiles can do so much, why are we not more liberal with them?

JOHN D. ROCKEFELLER, SR.

March 29th

> MY CROWN IS IN MY HEART, NOT MY HEAD:
> NOT DECKED WITH DIAMONDS, AND INDIAN STONES,
> NOT TO BE SEEN: MY CROWN IS CALLED CONTENT;
> A CROWN IT IS THAT SELDOM KINGS ENJOY.
>
> *Shakespeare.*

"I HAVE achieved something of high happiness in these years, something I know of pure contentment and I have learned two or three deep and simple things about life. I have learned that happiness is not to be had for the seeking, but it comes quietly to him who pauses at his difficult task and looks upward. I have learned that friendship is very simple and more than all else I have learned the lesson of being quiet, of looking out across the meadows and hills and trusting a little in God.

What I am seeking is something as simple and quiet as the hills or the trees. Just to look around me at the pleasant countryside, to enjoy a little of this passing show, to meet (and to help a little if I may) a few human beings and thus to get more nearly into the sweet kernel of human life.

My friend, you may or may not think this is a worthy object, but if you do, why, we'll exchange great words on the road, we'll look at the sky together, we'll see and hear the finest things in this world, we'll enjoy the sun. We'll live light in the spring."

DAVID GRAYSON.
American naturalist & writer.

March 30th

I AM RESOLVED TO MEET PETULANCE WITH PATIENCE, QUESTIONINGS WITH KINDNESS, HATRED WITH LOVE, EAGER ALWAYS TO DO THE KINDLY DEED THAT ALONE MAKES HUMAN LIFE TRULY HUMAN.

BY EXAMPLE and not by precept. By living, not by preaching. By doing, not by professing. By living the life, not by dogmatizing as to how it should be lived. There is no contagion equal to the contagion of life. Whatever we sow, that shall we also reap, and each thing sown produces its kind. We can kill not only by doing another bodily injury directly, but we can and we do kill by every antagonistic thought. Not only do we thus kill, but while we kill we suicide. Many a man has been made sick by having the ill thoughts of a number of people centred upon him; some have been actually killed. Put hatred into the world and we make it a literal hell. Put love into the world and heaven with all its beauties and glories becomes a reality.

Not to love is not to live, or it is to live a living death. The life that goes out in love to all is the life that is full, and rich, and continually expanding in beauty and in power. Such is the life which becomes ever more inclusive, and hence larger in its scope and influence. The larger the man or the woman, the more inclusive they are in their love and their friendships. The smaller the man or the woman, the more dwarfed and dwindling their natures, the more they pride themselves upon their "exclusiveness". Anyone—a fool or an idiot—can be exclusive. It comes easy. It takes and it signifies a large nature to be universal, to be inclusive.

Only the man or woman of a small, personal, self-centred, self-seeking is exclusive. The man or the woman of a large, royal, unself-centred nature never is. The small nature is the one that continually strives for effect. The larger nature never does. The one goes here and there in order to gain recognition, in order to attach himself to the world. The other stays at home and draws the world to him. The one loves merely himself. The other loves all the world; but in his larger love for all the world he finds himself included.

RALPH WALDO TRINE.
In Tune with the Infinite.

Down in the Forest, Essex.
Photograph by Dennis Mansell.

March 31st

WE LOVE THE THINGS WE LOVE FOR WHAT THEY ARE.
Robert Frost.

THE coppice at our back is full of birds, for it is far from the road and they nest there undisturbed year after year. Through the still night I heard the nightingales calling, calling, until I could bear it no longer and went softly out into the luminous dark.

   The little wood was manifold with sound. I heard my little brothers who move at night rustling in grass and tree. A hedgehog crossed my path with a dull squeak, the bats thrilled high to the stars, a white owl swept past me crying his haunting note, a beetle boomed suddenly in my face; and above and through it all the nightingales sang—and sang!

MICHAEL FAIRLESS,
"The Roadmender" (Duckworth)

April 1st

EVERY DAY I FIND OUT SOMETHING THAT MAKES ME GLAD ... THE MOST BEAUTIFUL THINGS IN THE WORLD CANNOT BE SEEN OR TOUCHED ... BUT JUST FELT IN THE HEART.

LETTER to Rev. Phillip Brooks from Helen Keller who as a baby of nineteen months was stricken with a severe illness which left her totally blind and deaf. Until she was nearly seven years old she lived in a world of darkness and silence, her lively intelligence unable to find an outlet.

Then Anne Sullivan came to teach her and there began that remarkable story of her development into a woman of great culture and spiritual insight. Today Helen Keller's name is known throughout the world; a triumph as much for the teacher as for the pupil.

My dear Mr Brooks, "I send you my picture as I promised, and I hope when you look at it this summer your thoughts will fly southward to your happy little friend. I used to wish I could see pictures with my hands as I do statues, but now I do not often think about it because my dear Father has filled my mind with beautiful pictures, even of things I cannot see.

"If the light were not in your eyes, dear Mr Brooks, you could understand better how happy your little Helen was when her teacher explained to her that the best and most beautiful things in the world cannot be seen or touched, but just felt in the heart. Every day I find out something that makes me glad.

"Yesterday I thought for the first time what a beautiful thing motion was, and it seemed to me that everything was trying to get near to God, does it seem that way to you? It is Sunday morning, and while I sit here in a library writing this letter you are teaching hundreds of people some of the grand and beautiful things about their heavenly Father. Are you not very, very happy? and when you are a bishop you will preach to more people and more and more will be made glad. Teacher sends her kind remembrances, and I send you with my picture my love. From your little friend."

HELEN KELLER *(11 years)*,
From "Helen Keller – Autobiography".
_{Sincere thanks to the author whose address we are unable to trace.}

April 2nd

IT IS NOT ENOUGH FOR MAN TO BEG HIS CREATOR FOR HEALTH AND LONG LIFE. HE SHOULD ALSO USE HIS INTELLIGENCE TO DISCOVER AND BRING TO LIGHT THE TREASURES GRACIOUSLY HIDDEN BY GOD IN NATURE AS A MEANS OF HEALING THE ILLS OF THIS HUMAN LIFE.
Father Kneipp

WATCHING the medicinal trees and shrubs and herbs ... seeing their properties by their forms and colours and odours, and their changes in character with the changes of the seasons, and alteration of drought and plenty—how great is the wonder and work of nature!

We note how substances are being elaborated into plants, which we, wanting their help, know how to take at the crucial moment: "Now we must draw the resin, now we must take these flowering tops", and so on. But we are not the only watchers. The bees have been waiting, and the birds, and the slugs, the ants, the herbivora—and these and many others waiting to draw from such supplies that which is applicable to their requirements.

Nature herself also waits for these to be collected from her treasury. It is for us ourselves not to pass them by. If we did nothing more than study the materia medica of ancient days we should have ample material for thought, and become cognizant of the link between that age and this. The herbs are still cultivated and still used in the East in the manner of the past.

DR. CAMERON GRUNER, M.D.
(The Canon of Medicine of Avicenna).

April 3rd

HE LOVES ME NOT BECAUSE I AM BRILLIANT, BUT BECAUSE I AM THE SHINING JEWEL IN HIS CROWN.

Anon.

MY HUSBAND is a plain looking, plain acting sort of character. I cannot remember when he said to me, "I love you". But he shows in many ways that he does. Flowers from a florist he does not buy. He takes pleasure in raising them himself. When he is rewarded for his efforts with an especially fine rose or other blossom, that flower he brings to me with his love.

When our children were small, he could be depended upon to change or burp our youngest and help with the cooking and cleaning. We worked side by side and enjoyed our family together.

In those days when money was so important to all of us, I knew on payday my husband would deposit his cash in our account—no stopping off for a "quick one" with the boys while his supper and his wife burned.

Now our family is all grown, married and gone. Our marriage has endured for almost 50 years. It has been filled with love, understanding and companionship. Although my husband is hesitant with words to express his love, his actions tell me what is in his heart.

G.L.R.

April 4th

THE WAY TO PEACE IS THE WAY TO POWER. IT BRINGS REPOSE WITHOUT LETHARGY, ACTIVITY WITHOUT EFFORT, AND JOY WITHOUT SORROW.

... THERE is no doubt whatever that after every silence I feel recuperated and have greater energy for work. The output of work during silence is much greater than when I am not silent.

The mind enjoys peace during silence which it does not without it. That is to say, the decision to be silent itself produces soothing effect on me. It lifts a burden off my mind. My experience tells me that silence soothes the nerves in a manner no drugs can. With me it also induces sleep.

I find spiritual value in it. That is the time when I can best hold communion with God.

MAHATMA GANDHI.
Harijan, October, 1939.

April 5th

I ENJOY LIFE, I ENJOY BEING WITH PEOPLE. I ENJOY MY JOB, EACH DAY GROWING MORE PERFECTLY IN HARMONY WITH ALL WHO SHARE MY WORKING HOURS.

EMPLOYERS who complain about the high incidence of absenteeism because of ailments may have themselves to blame, according to a survey of work-connected illness by Dr. Helmutt Sopp, industrial psychiatrist in Dusseldorf.

Among 100,000 cases of illness in various branches of German industry, 60 per cent could be traced to psychological factors. Often the boss was to blame—unconsciously so, of course.

Women who were sewing in a textile factory, for instance, kept getting headaches. The supervisors there were considerate and rarely said a word, but they occasionally stood behind the women to observe their work. And that was it. Without quite knowing it themselves, the women felt edgy. The behind-the-back supervision was stopped, and the headaches diminished.

Postal employees, it turned out, have the lowest absentee rate from illness at their busiest season before the Christmas and New Year holidays. Why? The Dusseldorf consultant answers: "Not because they're too busy to get ill at that season—but because suddenly everybody who works for the post office is a very important person."

The employer with the healthiest employees is the one, says Dr. Sopp, who provides them with three things: recognition, the security that comes from the feeling of being liked, and freedom to get the job done in the employee's own way.

The Bulletin, Press and Information Office, Germany.

There is an angel in the family, who, with a mysterious influence of charm, sweetness, and love, makes the accomplishment of duties less arduous, pains less bitter. The angel of the family is the woman . . . Mother, Wife, Sister . . . Woman is the caress of life, the gentleness of love.

Guiseppe Mazzini.

Photograph by Dennis Mansell

CHILDHOOD is like a mirror, which reflects in later life the images first presented to it. *(Samuel Smiles).*

April 6th

PEACE I LEAVE WITH YOU … MY PEACE I GIVE TO YOU … NOT AS THE WORLD GIVES DO I GIVE TO YOU … LET NOT YOUR HEART BE TROUBLED … NEITHER LET IT BE AFRAID.

John 14:27.

GRIEF is not an illness. It is a normal life-time experience, a process that needs to be dealt with. The process of accommodation is different for everyone, says Dr Phyllis Silverman. Abraham Lincoln takes up the theme: "In this sad world of ours, sorrow comes to all, and it often comes with bitter agony. Perfect relief is not possible except with time. You cannot now believe that you will ever feel better. But this is not true. You are sure to be happy again. Knowing this, truly believing it, will sustain you."

We are born to die. Because we are, we are also born to grieve—to mourn the loss of those who are dear to us: members of the family, friends, neighbours, teachers, co-workers, all whose lives are entwined with ours. How can we deal with the pain? It helps to recognize that the pain will diminish; that there are memories to cherish.

The great French artist, Renoir, teaches us that. He suffered so much from arthritis that it was difficult for him to paint. Once a friend said to him: "You have done enough, Renoir. Why do you continue to torture yourself?" Renoir replied: "The pain passes, but the beauty remains." So it is with grief. Grief is like a desert. There is only one way out of it—and that's to go through it.

"Grief," said the author Clare Luce, "has a great purgative value. Since God cannot fill the soul until it is emptied of all trivial concerns, a great grief is a tremendous bonfire in which all the trash of life is consumed."

THE CHRISTOPHERS.

April 7th

POSITIVE THOUGHTS ARE MY DAILY VITAMINS.

THERE'S nothing so bad that it could not be worse … There's little that time may not mend … and troubles, no matter how thickly they come ..
Most surely will come to an end.

You've stumbled—well, so have we all in our time … Don't dwell over-much on regret, for you're sorry, God knows … well, leave it at that: let past things be past, and forget.

Don't despond, don't give up, but just be yourself … The self that is highest and best … Just live every day in a sensible way … And then leave to God all the rest.

AUTHOR UNKNOWN.

April 8th

> DO ALL THE GOOD YOU CAN,
> BY ALL THE MEANS YOU CAN,
> IN ALL THE WAYS YOU CAN,
> IN ALL THE PLACES YOU CAN,
> AT ALL THE TIMES YOU CAN,
> TO ALL THE PEOPLE YOU CAN,
> AS LONG AS EVER YOU CAN.

ONE of the greatest castles in England is Arundel Castle, and one of the greatest of all the English aristocracy is the Duke of Norfolk to whom the castle belongs.

Once a certain Duke of Norfolk happened to be at the railway station, when a little Irish girl arrived off the train with a very heavy bag. She had come to be a maid-servant at the castle.

The castle is about a mile from the station and the little Irish girl was trying to persuade a porter to carry her heavy bag to the castle, for which she offered him a shilling, all the money that she had. The porter contemptuously refused. The Duke stepped forward, shabby as usual in appearance. He offered to carry her bag to the castle, took it and walked beside her along the road to the castle, talking to her.

At the end of the journey, he gratefully accepted the shilling she offered him, never allowing her to know who he was; and it was only the next day, when she met her employer, that the little Irish girl knew that the Duke of Norfolk had carried her bag from the station to the castle and that she had tipped him a shilling!

A very wonderful story of a true nobleman that tells us a good many things about this kind of man!

It is never safe to judge a man by externals.
A great man is always a thoughtful man.
There is grace in taking as well as giving.
The truly great man does not think of his place or his prestige.

It is only little people who think how great they are.

It is only unimportant people who think how important they are. There is nothing in this world which is a surer sign of a small mind than the complaint that one did not get in one's place; and there is no motive in this world that is more wrong than the desire for prestige.

In the last analysis, to the truly great man, no act of service can possibly be humiliating.

No task, if it is going to help someone else, can possibly be beneath his dignity.

WILLIAM BARCLAY.
Through the Year with Barclay.
Arthur James Ltd.

April 9th

I WILL LOVE MY PARTNER FOR LOVE'S SAKE ONLY.

IF THOU must love me, let it be for nought
Except for love's sake only. Do not say
'I love her for her smile—her look—her way
Of speaking gently,—for a trick of thought
That falls in well with mine, and certes brought
A sense of pleasant ease on such a day' –
For these things in themselves, beloved, may
Be changed, or change for thee,—and love, so wrought,
May be unwrought so. Neither love me for
Thine own dear pity's wiping my cheeks dry,—
A creature might forget to weep, who bore
Thy comfort long, and lose thy love thereby!
But love me for love's sake, that evermore
Thou mayst love on, through love's eternity.

ELIZABETH BARRETT BROWNING.

April 10th

HAPPY THE MAN, AND HAPPY HE ALONE,
HE, WHO CAN CALL TODAY HIS OWN;
HE WHO, SECURE WITHIN, CAN SAY;
"TOMORROW, DO YOUR WORST, FOR I HAVE LIVED TODAY."

Emerson.

THIS is my delight, thus to wait and watch at the wayside where shadow chases light and the rain comes in the wake of the summer.

Messengers, with tidings from unknown skies, greet me and speed along the road. My heart is glad within, and the breath of the passing breeze is sweet.

From dawn to dusk I sit here before my door, and I know that of a sudden the happy moment will arrive when I shall see.

In the meanwhile I smile and I sing all alone. In the meanwhile the air is filling with the perfume of promise.

RABINDRANATH TAGORE.
Indian poet and writer.

April 11th

> I SHALL NO LONGER BE FALTERING OR HESITANT. I REFUSE TO ALLOW TIMIDITY TO PARALYSE WHAT LATENT GIFT I MAY POSSESS. PESSIMISM GIVES PLACE TO A GROWING OPTIMISM. A CONSCIOUS SERENITY SUFFUSES MY WHOLE NERVOUS SYSTEM WITH PEACE, DISPELLING THOUGHTS OF INADEQUACY.

AT EXETER, New Hampshire, a youth was asked to address his schoolmates, but each attempt that he made was a fiasco. Here in his own bitter words is his confession: "I could not speak before the school. Many a piece did I commit to memory, and recite and rehearse in my own room, over and over again, and yet, when the day came, when my name was called, and all eyes turned to my seat, I could not raise myself from it. When the occasion was over, I went home and wept bitter tears of mortification." Later the youth determined that he would conquer his timidity, if he died in the attempt. That he succeeded admirably is indicated in the mere fact of his identity. He was Daniel Webster, often still acclaimed as the greatest orator America has ever produced.

Journal of Living.

April 12th

> THE MIND OF MAN HAS NO DEFENCE
> TO EQUAL PLAIN, OLD COMMON SENSE.
> THIS HOMELY VIRTUE DON'T DESPISE
> IF YOU'D BE HEALTHY, WEALTHY AND WISE.

IT APPEARS to me necessary to every physician to be skilled in nature and to strive to know, if he would wish to perform his duties, what man is in relation to the articles of food and drink and to his other occupations and what are the effects of each of them on everyone. Whoever does not know what effect these things produce upon a man cannot know the consequences which results from them.

Whoever pays no attention to these things, or, paying attention, does not comprehend them, how can he understand the diseases which befall man? For by every one of these things a man is affected and changed this way and that, and the whole of his life is subject to them—whether in health, convalescence or disease. Nothing else then can be more important and necessary to know than these things.

HIPPOCRATES.
Greek physician, commonly styled the Father of Medicine. Born on the island of Cos. Author of medical works and who set a high standard of medical ethics.

April 13th

HELP ME TO BE CONTENT WITH MY LOT,
AND NEVER TRY TO BE WHAT I AM NOT.

Irene Witmer

THERE are nine requisites for contented living: ... health enough to make work a pleasure ... wealth enough to support our needs ... strength enough to battle with difficulties and forsake them ... grace enough to confess our shortcomings and overcome them ... patience enough to toil until some good is accomplished ... charity enough to see some good in our neighbour ... love enough to move us to be useful and helpful to others ... faith enough to make real the things of God ... hope enough to remove all anxious fears concerning the future.

GOETHE, (1794–1842).
German poet.

April 14th

IT'S A HEAP OF SATISFACTION
WHEN A HELPING HAND I LEND:
JUST TO KNOW SOMEONE'S HAPPIER
BECAUSE I PAUSED TO BE A FRIEND.

I'M NOT much on philosophy, I don't know all the creeds; I don't know what's inside the books my next door neighbour reads. I haven't studied ancient tongues, my English isn't good; I know I've said a lot of things that a scholar never would. But this is my experience, and so I'll pass it on; the time to be a friend to man is when he's needing one.

I don't discuss religion, much—I wouldn't if I could; I know I hate to draw a line between what's bad and good. I've had to plod along through life, and learn from other men, and so I've done a lot of things I'll never do again. But then, I found along the way, the time to be a friend is when a fellow's needin' all the help that you can lend.

I'm not much on philosophy, the books I've never read; I've had to get the things I know from life that's hard indeed. I've never seen a winter through but I've had to stand alone, or seen some man without the means, and forced to make a loan. So if you have a cheer to give, or extra strength to lend—go out and help the man along who really needs a friend.

AUTHOR UNKOWN.

April 15th

> "GRATITUDE IS THE FAIREST BLOSSOM THAT SPRINGS FROM THE SOUL ... OUR HEARTS KNOW NOTHING MORE FRAGRANT".
>
> *Hosea Ballou.*

STILL later in the season, Nature's tenderness waxes stronger. It is impossible not to be fond of our Mother now; for She is so fond of us! At other periods, She does not make this impression on me, or only at rare intervals; but in these genial days of autumn, when She has perfected her harvests and accomplished every needful thing that was given Her to do, then She overflows with a blessed superfluity of love. She has leisure to caress Her children now. It is good to be alive at such times. Thank heaven for breath—yes, for mere breath—when it is made up of a heavenly breeze like this! It comes with a real kiss upon our cheeks; it would linger fondly around us if it might; but since it must be gone, it embraces us with its whole kindly heart and passes onward to embrace likewise the next thing that it meets.

A blessing is flung abroad and scattered far and wide over the earth, to be gathered up by all who choose. I recline upon the still unwithered grass and whisper to myself, "O perfect day! O beautiful world! O beneficent God!" And it is the promise of a blessed eternity; for our Creator would never have made such lovely days and have given us the deep hearts to enjoy them, above and beyond all thought, unless we were meant to be immortal. This sunshine is the golden pledge thereof. It beams through the gates of paradise and shows us glimpses far inward.

NATHANIEL HAWTHORNE.
American author (1804–1864).
In boyhood was impressed by the Puritan tradition.
Extract from "Thoughts of Autumn".

April 16th

I AM RESOLVED TO CHANGE MY DIET FROM DEAD TO LIVING FOOD. FROM NOW ON IT IS GOING TO BE FRESH FOOD—CONTAINING LIVING ELEMENTS—THE FRESHER, THE BETTER.

A BOY lay dying in a hospital in Chicago. He had undergone many operations and countless injections, and still his tubercular hip refused to heal. Finally, the doctors decided: "Send this boy home. There is nothing more we can do for him."

So the unhappy boy was sent back home to die in the serenity of the Swiss mountains. There a miracle happened. One morning the boy was having his usual breakfast of coffee, rolls and marmalade, when an old man, a family friend who had spent his life as a missionary, said to him, "If you keep on eating such dead foods, you certainly will die. Only living foods can make a living body."

"What are living foods?" asked the boy.

The gentle old man described them: "Fresh young growing things, especially green and yellow garden vegetables, saturated with earthy elements; lemons, oranges, and other tree fruits, full of sunshine and living juices." The old man knew nothing about proteins, vitamins, minerals, and the many other nutrients discoverd since. But the sick boy listened thoughtfully. And from that day on, he began to eat enormous amounts of fresh living foods. And wonder of wonders, the hip that had defied all sorts of treatment, now slowly but surely healed. Through this amazing recovery, I discovered for the first time what fresh food can do. Yes, food saved my life for I was that boy.

GAYELORD HAUSER.
"Treasury of Secrets".
Our sincere thanks to owners of copyright who we have been unable to trace.

April 17th

I HAVE BEEN A FAILURE. I HAVE MADE A MISTAKE, BUT, WHO KNOWS? MAYBE IT'S THE BEST THING THAT COULD HAPPEN TO ME.

HOW often we intend one thing and it turns into another! There is the joke about the man who invented a stove that didn't work but served excellently as a wine-cooler in summer. A New England eccentric sent a strange cargo of warming pans to the West Indies and made his fortune when the natives discovered that the pans, with their long handles, were perfect for cooking in a hot climate. Columbus aimed at India and found America. The experience has become proverbial; we aim for the goose and hit the gander.

The same thing happens with cheerful frequency in daily life. A job is lost which, if it had been taken, would have prevented the acceptance of a better one. The wrong book comes home from the library and opens a whole new field of interest. I know of a student in college who wandered into the wrong classroom and was so interested in the subject discussed there that he pursued it and made it his career. I need scarcely add that, being so absent-minded, he became a professor.

It should take the edge off disappointment to remember that half the things that go wrong surprise us by turning out all right.

ROBERT HILLYER,
in "This Week".

April 18th

THERE IS ONLY ONE WAY UNDER HEAVEN FOR ME TO GET THE BEST OF ANY ARGUMENT—THAT IS, TO AVOID IT. A MAN CONVINCED AGAINST HIS WILL IS OF THE SAME OPINION STILL.

Dale Carnegie.

A MAN was walking in the countryside with his grandson when they came across a small land turtle. The boy picked up his find, examined it and tried to pry open the shell with a stick. The turtle promptly pulled in its head.

"That will never get you anywhere," the grandfather remarked. "Let me show you."

They returned to the house, and the man put the turtle on the warm hearth. A few minutes later the turtle stuck out its head and feet and started crawling toward the boy.

"Never try to force a fellow into anything," was the grandfather's observation, "Just warm him up with a little kindness and he'll respond."

THE CHRISTOPHERS.

April 19th

THERE IS A DESTINY THAT MAKES US BROTHERS: NONE GOES HIS WAY ALONE. ALL THAT WE SEND INTO THE LIVES OF OTHERS COMES BACK INTO OUR OWN.
Author Unknown.

THE lonely person must look for the causes within himself, for in loneliness he admits defeat. Very seldom can you blame anyone but yourself for that condition. If you care enough, you can find a remedy. Focus the searchlight within and determine whether you are too self-centred, too sensitive, too timid. You cannot live unto yourself or for yourself alone, and the sooner you realize this truth, the better it will be.

We can make it easy for people to approach us; we can circulate with the kind of people we want to know. The more circles of interest we have, the happier we are, so make yourself proficient in something—golf, tennis, swimming—anything that appeals to you. Store your mind with interesting information, clever anecdotes or jokes, and with a little practice you can become the centre of attraction in any group.

Choose a hobby that you can share with others. For instance, just mention casually in a crowd that you have some valuable old stamps to swap, or some rare plants to give away, and watch people surround you.

Notice and act on the little things that give pleasure to others. Surprise someone with flowers you grew, or fruit you canned, an inexpensive gadget you discovered, or even a brief note of cheer or appreciation. Nothing accomplishes as much as a little attention, and wins friends quicker than simple words of approval. Little things do count, especially these unstudied gestures of friendship.

HAZEL GEST,
in "Sunshine Magazine", Litchfield, Illinois, U.S.A.

Be with us at our table when we dine . . . For all life's mercies, Lord, are Thine . . . Grant us Thy blessings on our daily bread . . . And over all our lives Thy radiance shed.

Anonymous.

KITTY'S BREAKFAST
by Emily Farmer, (1826-1905).
Victoria & Albert Museum, London,
Bridgeman Art Library, London & New York.

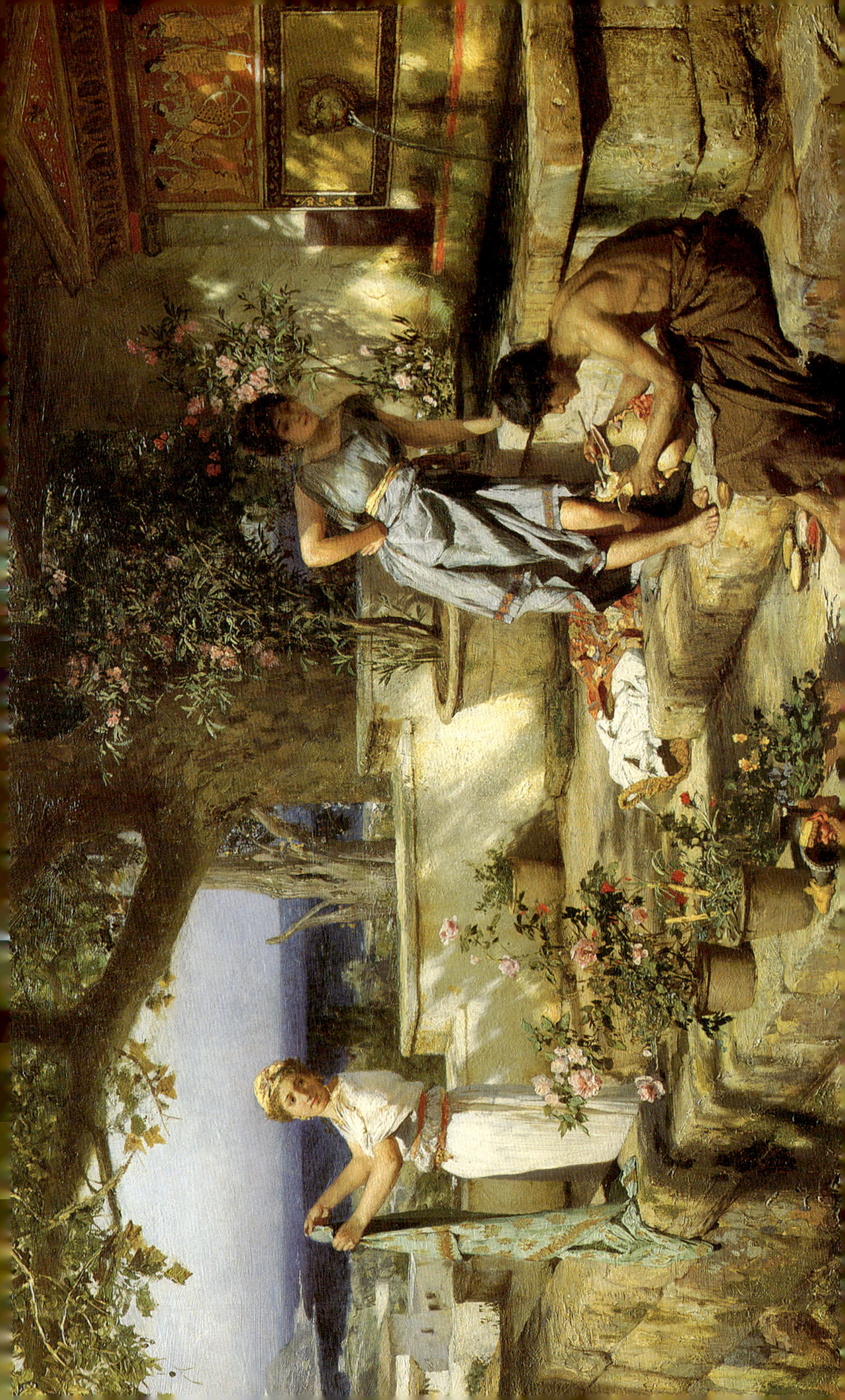

April 20th

I AM RESOLVED TO EAT LESS PROCESSED FOOD AND MORE FRESH RAW VEGETABLES, FRUITS AND NUTS, REBUILDING MY BODY AND FILLING ME WITH HEALTH AND STRENGTH.

FOOD and drink are necessary to keep the organism in the right condition, so that the vital force can manifest and operate through it to the best advantage. To this end food is needed to build up and to repair the tissues of the body. It also serves to a certain extent as fuel material, which is transmuted into animal heat and vital energy.

Furthermore, just as coal has to come in touch with fire before it can be transmuted into heat, so the life force is needed to "burn up" or to "explode" the fuel materials. When "life" has departed even large amounts of sugars, fats, proteins, tonics and stimulants are not able to produce one spark of vital energy in the body.

On the contrary, digestion and assimilation of food and drink and elimination of waste materials require the expenditure of considerable amounts of vital energy. Therefore all food taken in excess of the actual needs of the body wastes vital force instead of giving it.

If these facts were more generally known and appreciated, people would not habitually over-eat under the mistaken idea that their vitality increases in proportion to the amount of food they consume; neither would they believe that they can derive strength from poisonous stimulants and tonics. They would not be so much afraid of fasting in acute diseases and healing crises and would avail themselves more frequently of this most effective means of purification. They would no longer believe themselves in danger of dying if they were to miss a few meals ...

The greatest artist living cannot draw harmonious sounds from the strings of the finest Stradivarius if the body of the violin be filled with dust and rubbish.

Dr Henry Lindlahr.
From: Natural Therapeutics—Philosophy—Vol 1. Pub: C.W. Daniel Company Ltd., 1, Church Path, Saffron Walden, Essex, CB10 1JP, England.

AT THE WELL.
By Hendrik Siemiradski, (1843-1902).
By Courtesy of Christie's Images.

April 21st
LAUGHTER IS THE BEST MEDICINE.

PAIN is among the maladies for which laughter is a good medicine. After a good dose of laughter, it's harder to feel pain.

In a study conducted by Rosemary Cogan of Texas Tech University students were tested to determine their normal pain threshold level. Pain was created by means of a blood pressure cuff, which was inflated until the subject indicated discomfort. After this initial testing, one group of students was treated to 20 minutes of Lily Tomlin's comedy. Another group heard a 20-minute relaxation induction tape. A third group heard a lecture on ethics, while a fourth group received no treatment. Afterwards, the subjects' pain threshold was retested. Only the group that had the chance to enjoy some laughter showed any decrease in sensitivity to pain. Relaxation, a proven pain reducer in other studies, had no effect in this case. The use of relaxation to reduce pain typically required special training. Laughter, however, seems to be an innate analgesic.

Journal of Behavioural Medicine, Vol. 10. Pp. 139–144.

April 22nd

SICK THOUGHTS AND DISCORDANT MOODS ARE THE NATURAL ATMOSPHERE OF DISEASE. I INTEND TO STIMULATE THE LIFE-GIVING POWER OF MY INTERNAL SECRETIONS BY EMOTIONS OF GOOD-WILL, SERENITY, AND CHEERFULNESS.

ALL negative emotions such as hate and anger, distress and deep melancholy create poisonous secretions in the glands of the body. It has, for instance, long been known that the venom of the cobra is far more poisonous when the creature is excited.

Just as negative reactions and emotions have a destructive effect, a positive attitude to life releases reserves of energy and vitality that are practically unlimited.

Only by ordering our lives in harmony with the laws of nature are we able to build up true health. This we can do by introducing into our daily living positive health-building factors, and by turning away from the disease-producing habits and ingrained prejudices of so-called civilized living.

EBBA WAERLAND.
"Rebuilding Health"

April 23rd

I EXTEND THE SPIRIT OF FORGIVENESS TO ALL WHO HAVE WRONGED ME ... INSTEAD OF CRITICISM I SEND OUT THOUGHTS OF RECONCILIATION AND FRIENDLINESS.

LIFE isn't long—a mother's song ... And then another's smile ... Then romping feet, and then the sweet ... Remembrances awhile ... From gold to gray, from dawn to day ... And then the twilight hours ... Life is too brief to hunt for grief ... For thorns among the flowers.
If hurt today by what men say ... If wounded by a friend ... O, let tonight put all things right ... Let trouble have an end ... Life is too short to let report ... Or rumour long annoy ... Today has had so much so glad ... We need it all for joy.
God's world, God's word, his breeze, his bird ... No hand can rob you of ... Wrong comes too late for hearts to hate ... There is so much to love ... Life isn't long, just time for song ... And love, and things sublime ... Be not concerned with thoughts that burned ... Good friends, there isn't time.

AUTHOR UNKNOWN.

April 24th

MY GOD IS OVER ALL, AND THROUGH ALL, AND IN ALL ... IN HIM I LIVE, AND MOVE AND HAVE MY BEING.

The Bible

ALSO in this He showed me a little thing, a hazel nut in the palm of my hand. It was as round as a ball. I looked upon it with the eye of my understanding and thought, "What may this be?" And it was answered thus: "It is all that is made." And I marvelled how it might last, for I thought it might suddenly have fallen to naught or littleness. And I was answered in my understanding: "It lasts, and ever shall last, because God loves it." And so everything has its being by the love of God.

In this little thing, I saw three properties. First, that God MADE it. The second, that God LOVES it. The third, that God PRESERVES it.

JULIAN OF NORWICH.
("Revelations of Divine Love").
Pre-Reformation mystic and writer, her life spanning 14th and 15th centuries.
From "Revelations of Divine Love", described by Donald Attwater as "the tenderest and most beautiful exposition in the English language of God's loving dealings with man."

April 25th

THE QUALITY OF MY BLOOD AND TISSUE REFLECTS THE KIND OF FOOD I EAT. IN FUTURE, NATURAL UNPROCESSED FOODS—WHOLEFOODS—SHALL BE MY PHYSICIAN, INVIGORATING MY BODY AND SUSTAINING MY MIND.

MAN is made up of what he eats. The constituents of his food are those of which his body is composed. His foodstuffs, derived from the vegetable and animal kingdoms, consist, for the most part, of matter that was formerly living.

Man cannot himself build up living tissue from materials which have in themselves no necessary connection with living protoplasm. This, plants do for him. Out of the earth and air, and under the influence of the sun, they transmute certain inorganic substances—mineral salts, water and carbon dioxide—into organic foodstuffs suited to his use ...

Man is, indeed, created out of the earth; and according as earth provides, by way of plant and animal life, the materials needed by his body, so is that body well, ill or indifferently made and sustained.

Sir Robert McCarrison.

Distinguished physician and nutritionist. Original research into deficiency diseases. Writes: "The newer knowledge of nutrition is the greatest advance in medicine since the days of Lister ... when physicians, medical officers of health, and the lay public learn to apply the principles which this newer knowledge of nutrition has to impart ... then will this knowledge do for medicine which asepsis has done for surgery."

April 26th

I WILL STOP WORRYING . . . I WILL LET GO MY PROBLEM . . . I WILL TRUST THE POWER WITHIN.

THERE is something in your mind beyond the conscious brain – that can solve your problem if quiescent you remain . . . If you struggle – round and round your troubled thoughts will spin – never getting anywhere . . . so trust the power within – to find the right solution and to work the whole thing out. Stop worrying, stop wondering. Get off the roundabout.

Shelve your problem for the moment. Try and let it be. Tomorrow or the next day you will wake and you will see – the answer to the question and the road ahead will run – straight and clear and prove to be the best for everyone . . . Worry is destructive – but your battle you will win – if you pray for guidance and you trust the power within.

PATIENCE STRONG.
Copyright.

April 27th

IF THERE WERE NO GRIEF TO HOLLOW OUT OUR HEARTS . . . WHERE WOULD THERE BE ROOM FOR JOY? . . . I AM LEARNING TO WALK ALONE.

A DEEP hush was in the church; only the soft voice of the minister could be heard. Outside the windows slanted the gentle rain. Inside, the air was heavy with the perfume of flowers. My heart was leaden and my body was numb. It is never quite possible to be ready for separations. My husband was gone; only his body remained. I listened to the minister's words, trying to find comfort.

Then, incredibly, it happened. Far away through the rain I heard the robin's song. He sang through the rain, despite the rain. He put his whole small heart into that song, and a voice within me repeated his message just as clearly as if it had been spoken in words; "Do not grieve; there will be happiness and song for both of you, beyond the tears."

All at once the crushing burden seemed lighter. A moment later when the congregation sang the final hymn, I found that I could raise my heart to the Creator in song, just as the robin had done.

Later, when I spoke of this to others, no one else had heard the robin sing. Perhaps I dreamed it, I don't know. It doesn't matter. I can hear it still, whenever I need the faith and courage to go on.

MRS LAURA KOHR.

April 28th

I NO LONGER REBEL AT MY HANDICAPS. I ACCEPT MYSELF. I BELIEVE THAT GREAT LIVING STARTS WITH A PICTURE HELD IN MY IMAGINATION, OF WHAT I WOULD LIKE SOME DAY TO DO OR BE. I INTEND TO BUILD A PERSONALITY UNMOVED BY LIMITATION OR CIRCUMSTANCE, MAKING THE MOST OF MY BEST.

LOOK at John Keats: orphaned in early childhood, pressed by poverty, lacerated by the cruelty of his literary critics, disappointed in love, stricken by tuberculosis, and finally shoved off the scene by death at twenty-six. But with all his ill-fortune, Keats's life was not driven by circumstance. From that day when, a youth, he picked up a copy of Spencer's *Faërie Queene* and knew beyond doubt that he, too, was born to be a poet, Keats's life was drawn by a masterful purpose which gave him a lasting place among the world's renowned. "I think," he once said, "that I shall be among the English poets after my death." He got that picture in his imagination, and to him it was like the heart of Robert the Bruce to the fighting Scots.

Hold a picture of yourself long and steadily enough in your mind's eye and you will be drawn towards it. Picture yourself vividly as winning and that alone will contribute immeasurably to success. Do not picture yourself as anything and you will drift like a derelict.

HARRY EMERSON FOSDICK.
"Building a Personality". Condensed from "Physical Culture".

April 29th

O NEVER HARM THE DREAMING WORLD, THE WORLD OF GREEN, THE WORLD OF LEAVES, BUT LET ITS MILLION LEAVES UNFOLD THE ADORATION OF THE TREES.
Kathleen Raine.

IF YOU stand very still in the heart of a wood, you will hear many things, the snap of a twig, and the wind in the trees, and the whirr of invisible wings ... if you stand very still in the turmoil of life and you wait for the voice from within ... you'll be led down the quiet ways of wisdom and peace ... and a mad world of chaos and din ... if you stand very still and you hold your faith, you will get all the help you ask, you will draw from the silence the things that you need, hope and courage, and strength for your task.

MOLLY JONES.

April 30th

ALL THINGS WORK TOGETHER FOR GOOD TO THOSE WHO LOVE GOD.

OUT of evil, much good has come to me. By keeping quiet, repressing nothing, remaining attentive, and, hand in hand with that, by accepting reality—taking things as they are, and not as I wanted them to be—by doing all this, rare knowledge has come to me, and rare powers as well, such as I could never have imagined before. I always thought that, when we accept things, they overpower us in one way or another. Now this is not true at all, and it is only by accepting them that one can define an attitude toward them. So now I intend playing the game of life, being receptive to whatever comes to me, good and bad, sun and shadow that are for ever shifting, and, in this way, also accepting my own nature with its positive and negative sides. Thus everything becomes more alive to me. What a fool I was! How I tried to force everything to go according to my idea.

A Patient's Letter to Jung.
From: "The Secret of the Golden Flower", as explained by Richard Wilhelm, with a European Commentary by C. G. Jung and translated into English by Cary F. Baynes, (Kegan Paul)

In the reign of James the First two companies were formed to colonise America. One company obtained a charter to occupy the southern part of the country, named Virginia; and another the northern part. This company sailed from Plymouth, and its followers were known as the Pilgrim Fathers (seen above as they landed). They sought also religious liberty.

*Thatched cottages surround the village church, Cavendish, Suffolk.
Photograph by Dennis Mansell.*

May 1st

FOR ME TO EXIST IS TO BLESS.
LIFE IS A BENEDICTION OF JOY.

MAGNIFICENT weather. The morning seems bathed in happy peace, and a heavenly fragrance rises from mountain and shore; it is as though a benediction were laid upon us ... One might believe oneself in a church—a vast temple in which every being and every natural beauty has its place. I dare not breathe for fear of putting the dream to flight—a dream traversed by angels ...

In these heavenly moments the cry of Pauline rises to one's lips. 'I feel! I believe! I see!' All the miseries, the cares, the vexations of life, are forgotten; the universal joy absorbs us; we enter into the divine order, and into the blessedness of the Lord. Labour and tears, sin, pain, and death have passed away.

To exist is to bless; life is happiness. In this sublime pause of things all dissonances have disappeared. It is as though creation were but one vast symphony, glorifying the God of goodness with an inexhaustible wealth of praise and harmony.

We question no longer whether it is so or not. We have ourselves become notes in the great concert; and the soul breaks the silence of ecstasy only to vibrate in unison with the eternal joy.

HENRI FREDERIC AMIEL.
Swiss philosopher (1821–1881).

Let us come before his presence with thanksgiving

O BE joyful in the Lord all ye lands. Serve the Lord with gladness, and come before his presence with a song.

Be ye sure that the Lord he is God. It is he who has made us, and not we ourselves. We are his people, and the sheep of his pasture.

O go your way into his gates with thanksgiving, and into his courts with praise. Be thankful unto him, and speak good for his name.

For the Lord is gracious. His mercy is everlasting: and his truth endureth from generation to generation.

Psalm 100.

May 2nd

LOVE TOUCHES LIFE-SPRINGS OF THE NATURAL AND SPIRITUAL KINGDOMS … LOVING CASTS A SPELL BETWEEN A GARDENER AND HIS FLOWERS.

YEARS ago Luther Burbank resolved to experiment with the cactus of the western desert in an effort to encourage the cactus to remove its thorn. In the book, The Autobiography of a Yogi, you may find the story told by one of the eastern gurus who came to visit Burbank to learn of his experiments. He relates how Burbank studied the cactus as it grew natively in order to give it the most favourable conditions in which to grow. When he did everything his technical studies had taught him he went one more step—he talked to the plants and loved them.

He promised them his care and protection. He told them he understood why they had developed the thorn as a protective device, but he assured them that he was going to raise them under such perfect conditions that they would not need the thorn and would gradually discard it.

The greenhouses were so constructed that the currents of air would not blow through causing the leaves of the plants to brush one against the other and so disturb them and cause them to feel that something was about to harm them.

Little by little, through generation after generation, the thorn disappeared. Today the edible cactus grows on the western plains, a boon to man and beast, for it contains a liquid which can be used for drink in an emergency. It can now be broken open as it never could have been when covered with its sharp, protecting thorns.

George Washington Carver once said that anything would give up its secret if you loved it enough.

Dr Rebecca Beard.
From: Everyman's Goal. Pub: Arthur James Ltd., 70 Cross Oak Road, Berkhamsted, Herts HP4 3HZ.

✳

May 3rd

I PRACTISE SERENITY … NATURE'S HEALING FORCES INVIGORATE MY MIND AND BODY WITH ALL THE ELEMENTS ESSENTIAL TO PERFECT HEALTH.

SELF PITY in its vibratory nature and in its effect upon body, mind and soul, closely resembles the ravages of tuberculosis. It is psychological phthisis. A person affected by this phase of emotional self indulgence presents the miserable, haggard, negative appearance of a consumptive. The victim of self pity assumes that he is being unjustly dealt with by Providence, by fortune and by his fellowmen. He considers himself a martyr, enduring undeserved hardships, privations and injustice. This results in resentment, gloom and depression. It effectually kills cheerfulness, ambition and virile initiative …

A well known ancient legend strikingly illustrates the foolishness of self pity. The people of a certain country had become very much dissatisfied with their sufferings. Each one believed his own cross was much larger and heavier than that of his neighbour. An angel of God appeared among them in human form and told them to bring their crosses and deposit them in one great heap, when everyone would be allowed to select a burden which he deemed lighter than his own. The people rejoiced at this good fortune, discarded their crosses and proceeded to choose what they thought were lighter ones. However, their happiness at the change was not of long duration. One after another they returned, confessing dejectedly that the new cross was heavier and more painful to carry than the old one and asking to be allowed to take up again the old accustomed burden which a wise Providence had adjusted to each one's needs and powers of endurance.

Dr Henry Lindlahr.
From: Natural Therapeutics—Practice—Vol 2. C.W. Daniel Company Ltd., 1 Church Path, Saffron Walden, Essex CB10 1JP, England.

May 4th

> I'LL HAVE A SMILE FOR ONE AND ALL; FOR
> FRIENDS AND STRANGERS WHEN THEY CALL
> I'LL GREET THEM WITH A WORD OF CHEER;
> KIND AND GRACIOUS AND SINCERE.
>
> *Patience Strong.*

MORE than 100,000 spectators taught themselves an unforgettable lesson when they jammed the Los Angeles Coliseum one evening. They had gathered to watch a mighty pageant honouring the city's war heroes. After a mock battle scene had driven home the seeming helplessness of the human individual, silence fell. Only the voice of the master of ceremonies could be heard.

He began in a clear, resonant voice; "Perhaps you sometimes say to yourself, 'My job isn't important because it is such a little job.' But you are wrong. The most obscure person can be very important. Let me show you what I mean," he said, raising his hand for a signal.

The giant searchlights, bathing every corner of the great Coliseum, were shut off, transforming the daylight splendour of the arena into total darkness.

Then the speaker struck a match, and in the blackness the tiny flame could be seen by all.

"Now you can see the importance of one little light," said the master of ceremonies. "Suppose we *all* strike a light".

Instantly matches were struck all over the stadium until nearly 100,000 pinpoints illuminated the summer night. Everyone gasped with surprise. Quickly and effectively they comprehended that it is within the power of each single individual to "light a candle" instead of "curse the darkness."

THE CHRISTOPHERS.

May 5th

> TALK HEALTH. THE DREARY NEVER-ENDING TALE
> OF MORTAL MALADIES IS WORN AND STALE;
> YOU CANNOT CHARM, OR INTEREST, OR PLEASE
> BY HARPING ON THAT MINOR CHORD DISEASE.
> SAY YOU ARE WELL, AND ALL IS WELL WITH YOU,
> AND GOD SHALL HEAR YOUR WORDS AND MAKE THEM
> TRUE.
>
> *Ella Wheeler Willcox.*

THERE is a chronic pessimism developed by so many men and women in later life. They view the world with anxiety and alarm, and take every opportunity to insist that it is going to the dogs. Such people merely project their personal feelings of inadequacy on to external events. I knew a woman in her early forties, for example, who always greeted her friends with some such exclamation as: "Isn't it awful what is happening in Europe!" or perhaps: "Did you read that terrible story in the papers this morning?"

She was a successful interior decorator and an attractive woman; but she had been twice divorced and obviously had little hope left of achieving a happy marital relationship. She might still have done so had she come to grips with her own inner problem. Instead, she worried constantly about such things as social justice and economic exploitation, but took no action, and was always in a turmoil about one public cause or another.

... Mental attitudes and behaviour patterns like these cause a vast amount of misery in the world. Individuals so afflicted dissipate most of their energies in sterile pursuits, spend a good proportion of their lives under a pall of gloom. Even worse, they inflict untold injury upon those associated with them. The chronically ill woman, for example, often imposes severe emotional and financial burdens upon her family. One of the most sorrowful aspects is that younger lives may be permanently warped as a consequence.

Yet much of this appalling waste can be avoided if we seize the gift of love properly and shape it to our human purposes. Too many of us assume that love will be automatically denied to us as we enter upon the later years. This is a fallacy we must learn to correct.

Smiley Blanton MD.
"Love or Perish" (The World's Work).

_{Our sincere thanks to owners of copyright we have been unable to trace.}

May 6th

BE STILL AND KNOW THAT I AM GOD.
Psalm 46:10.

AS A physician, I have seen men, after all other therapy has failed, lifted out of disease and melancholy by the serene effort of prayer. It is the only power in the world that seems to overcome the so-called 'laws of nature': occasions on which prayer has dramatically done this have been termed 'miracles', but a constant, quieter miracle takes place hourly in the hearts of men and women who have discovered that prayer supplies them with a steady flow of sustaining power in their daily lives. Only in prayer do we achieve that complete and harmonious assembly of body, mind and spirit, which gives the frail human reed its unshakeable strength.

If you make a habit of sincere prayer, your life will be altered. Prayer stamps with an indelible mark our actions and demeanour; a tranquillity of bearing, a facial and bodily repose are observed in those whose inner lives are thus enriched. Within the depth of consciousness a flame kindles. A man sees himself. He discovers his selfishness, his silly pride, his fears, his greed, his blunders; he discovers a sense of moral obligation and intellectual humility, and this begins a journey of the soul towards the realm of grace.

Dr. Alexis Carrel.
Nobel Prizewinner. Scientist who worked in the famous Rockefeller Institute of Medical Research. Hailed as the physiologist of the century. Born in France, 1873. Book, "Man the Unknown" is regarded as a medical classic.

May 7th

MY LIFE HAS A PURPOSE ON THIS EARTH. I BELIEVE I HAVE SOMETHING TO GIVE WHICH CANNOT OTHERWISE BE GIVEN.

IF ONLY one knew the essential qualities of Charm, one might be able to cultivate it. But nobody does. It is indefinable ... A quiet but very definite sense of humour gives it a sense of proportion, not only where the heart solely is concerned, but also the head. It is unassertive. It wins all its battles without seemingly waging warfare. It never self-advertises; it never engulfs; it never seeks to pose. It is more potent at the quieter end of the social drawing-room. It is the most enchanting company *à deux* or *à trois*, but it is never the life and soul of any large party. That is why it endures to the very end and is ageless. Most of those who possess it, possess it unknowingly. It exudes from them unconsciously. Once they are aware of it, they lose it. It must come naturally or not at all.

RICHARD KING.

May 8th

WHEN I LIE DOWN, I SHALL NOT BE AFRAID. YES, I SHALL LIE DOWN, AND MY SLEEP SHALL BE SWEET.
Proverbs 3:24.

WHEN shall I enjoy a solid peace, a peace never to be disturbed and always secure, a peace both within and without, a peace every way assured? ...

As long as we carry about this frail body, we cannot be without sin, nor live without weariness and sorrow. We would fain be at rest from all misery; but because we have lost innocence by sin, we have also lost true blessedness.

We must therefore maintain patience, and wait for the mercy of God until iniquity pass away; and this mortality be swallowed up of life.

Peace shall come in the day which is known to the Lord; and it will not be day or night such as is at present, but everlasting light, infinite brightness, steadfast peace, and secure rest ... because after the winter comes spring, after night the day returns, and after a storm there follows a great calm.

THOMAS À KEMPIS, *(1380–1471).*
German monk. Born near Dusseldorf. Entered the Augustinian monastery of Zwolle. His Immitation of Christ is perhaps the best-known devotional book ever written.

May 9th

THIS IS MY LOVELY DAY ... NOTHING CAN SPOIL IT ...
I AM GLAD TO BE ALIVE.

I STOPPED for a fast breakfast at a small restaurant. Seated beside me at the counter was a young woman who smiled at me when I unfolded my newspaper.

My mind said to me, "She's a flirt." But my mouth said, "Hi."

"It's a beautiful morning," she replied. "Why do you look so mad?"

I straightened up at that and said in my best voice, "Do I know you?"

"No," she said, "but you looked so unhappy I felt sorry for you."

"Good reason, too," I snapped. "Nothing but bad news in the morning's paper."

"Why let that spoil your day?" She smiled again and continued, "Think of all the good news papers never print."

I had to return that smile.

"I've finished my breakfast," she said as she rose to leave. "Try to have a happy day. It's good to be alive."

"Have a happy day, too," I said.

When I paid the cashier for my breakfast, I repeated that "happy day" phrase and the cashier smiled and said, "You too, sir."

That day continued to be one wonderful day.

Tom Lavin.

In "Natural Food & Farming", Box 210, Atlanta, Texas 75551, USA.

May 10th

WHO SEEKS FOR HEAVEN ALONE TO SAVE HIS SOUL
WILL KEEP THE PATH BUT WILL NOT REACH THE GOAL;
WHILE HE WHO WALKS IN LOVE MAY WANDER FAR,
YET GOD WILL BRING HIM WHERE THE BLESSED ARE.

Henry van Dyke.

WE NEVER know how much one loves until we know how much he is willing to endure and suffer. The characters that are great must, of necessity, be characters that shall be willing, patient and strong to endure for others. To hold one's nature in the willing service of another is the divine idea of manhood, of the human character. That is the symphony of love.

Henry Ward Beecher, (1813–87).

May 11th

I AM FREED BY FAITH, STIMULATED BY HOPE, AND RE-VITALIZED BY CHEERFULNESS.

SPEAKING of those afflicted with nerve trouble, William James says they are like a bicycle of which the chain is too tight. As a result the movements of the mind are so strained that wasteful friction is the result. Their need is nervous and mental relaxation. The chain of the machine must be slackened if the friction is to be reduced, and if it is to run freely and smoothly.

The habit of cheerfulness is the best means of loosening the chain. Cheerfulness acts upon the nervous system as a lubricant acts upon the machine. Depression must be fought, but fought in a positive way. It is possible to see the bright side of things rather than the dark. This is especially so in cases where depression is due to low nervous vitality.

A writer in *The Lancet* said; "Mental influences affect the system. A cheerful spirit not only relieves pain but increases the momentum of life within the body." The simple fact is, that the great sympathetic nerves are closely connected. When one set carries bad news to the brain, the nerves which regulate the digestive organs are at once affected. Indigestion can follow, and, following that, inevitable depression.

In cases of nervous breakdown, it is not often that the victim is heard to laugh, or even smile, with any kind of radiance. For days he or she may move in and out amongst family and friends, with never a lively remark. Even when something amusing is said it leaves them passive and unmoved. Such people are afraid to let themselves go. Their first and pressing need is a kind of explosive nervous relief to break through the blocked-up passages of the nerve currents with the aid of a hearty laugh.

The habit of hearty laughter can do much in regaining a normal and healthy nervous system.

W. CHARLES LOOSMORE.
Brown scholar of Glasgow University.
From: *"Nerves and the Man"*.

A CHEERFUL heart and a smiling face
put sunshine in the darkest place.
Author Unknown.

May 12th

I MAKE A CONSCIOUS RETURN TO SIMPLICITY OF THINKING AND LIVING.

I WENT to the woods because I wished to live life deliberately, to front only the essential facts of life, and see if I could not learn what it had to teach, and not, when I came to die, discover that I had not lived.

I did not wish to live what was not life, living is so dear. Nor did I wish to practise resignation, unless it was quite necessary. I wanted to live deep, and suck out all the marrow of life, to live so sturdily as to put to rout all that was not life, to cut a broad swath and shave close, to drive life into a corner, and reduce it to its lowest terms, and, if it proved to be mean, why then to get the whole and genuine meanness of it, and publish its meanness to the world: or if it were sublime, to know it by experience, and be able to give a true account of it in my next excursion.

HENRY THOREAU.
American naturalist and writer.
From: "Walden".

May 13th

LOVE NEVER FAILS ME.

> LET me not to the marriage of true minds
>   Admit impediments. Love is not love
> Which alters when it alteration finds,
>   Or bends with the remover to remove.
> O, no! It is an ever-fixed mark,
>   That looks on tempests and is never shaken;
> It is the star to every wandering bark,
>   Whose worth's unknown, although his height be taken.
> Love's not Time's fool, though rosy lips and cheeks
>   Within his bending sickle's compass come;
> Love alters not with his brief hours and weeks,
>   But bears it out even to the edge of doom.
>   If this be error, and upon me proved,
>   I never writ, nor no man ever loved.

WILLIAM SHAKESPEARE.

May 14th

WE MAINTAIN A BALANCE IN OUR MARRIAGE THROUGH GIVE-AND-TAKE ... WE BALANCE OUT THE TOTAL AMOUNT OF EMOTIONAL SATISFACTION WE EACH REQUIRE WITH THE AMOUNT WE ARE ABLE TO GIVE.

HERE, drawn from the experience of Family Service counselling staffs, are suggestions that can help any couple to recognize and deal with the warning signals of marital imbalance:

Be alert when family circumstances change. The arrival of a baby, a change of job or a move to a new home are probably the last things most people would think of as potential threats to marriage. But they should be among the first to be considered.

Don't ignore the physical symptoms of anxiety—excessive fatigue, insomnia, depression, or a vague sense that "everything is slipping". These often signal the beginnings of marital imbalance.

Are there any unusual new groupings or "alliances" within the family? A person whose emotional needs are not being met by his spouse may turn to children or in-laws or parents for gratification.

If there is a drop in marital satisfactions during a time of stress, make every effort to adjust. The ability to tolerate periods of emotional deprivation is a hallmark of a good marriage. Giving in to the urge to "get back at" a partner tilts a marriage even further out of balance.

Cultivate the skills of patience and flexibility that help restore balance to a marriage. As one case-worker said; "Breakdowns don't happen because of differences. Thy happen because a couple cannot handle those differences."

Says Dr Beck, "If each person is able to give enough of what the other needs emotionally, the marriage works. This does not mean that *all* of a person's needs must *always* be met. Nor must the giving and getting be absolutely equal. It means that each spouse's *basic* needs must be satisfied enough of the time so that the ratio of satisfaction to frustration is tolerable to both."

In short: two people on a see-saw must constantly make adjustments if they hope to stay in equilibrium.

NORMAN LOBSENZ.

Sincere thanks to the author we have been unable to contact.

May 15th

> WHO WOULD COME TO ANOTHER'S AID
> MUST THE PRICE OF GRIEF HAVE PAID.
> WHO WOULD PLAY THE PILOT'S PART
> MUST THE WAY HAVE GOT BY HEART.
> WHO WOULD BE ANOTHER'S GUIDE
> MUST BY PAIN BE QUALIFIED.
>
> *E. Fuller Maitl.*

I AM such a little nobody, my Lord, and yet You shower so many blessings upon me. You gave me a mother who does not feel well herself but will sit by my bed all night, should I be in pain. A little brother so very cute, who scampers to my beck and call, a grandmother who buys me the little luxuries my mother cannot, and a doctor who eases my pain. You gave me, oh Lord, such sweet and understanding teachers and all those wonderful people who help me in my little projects.

How can I thank you, oh my Lord, for these my treasures? It is true I am ill most of the years of my life, but for that I am thankful, too. Because I know what pain is, I feel for others and whenever I hear or read of somebody's trouble, I say a prayer for their sake.

I know, dear Lord, you have a reason for everything, so I will not try to question why You took my daddy who was so good; who never had a vacation or drank or cursed and always worked so hard to take care of us. I will try not to question any hardship I will go through but should I sometimes fail and cry when I am in pain, please remember I am just a weak little nobody, my Lord.

What I am most thankful for is being able to have You, oh my Lord, as my truest Friend of all.

YOLANDA MARIA HOLTZEE.
Sincere thanks to the author we have been unable to contact.

He that planteth a tree is a servant of God, he provideth a kindness for many generations, and faces that he hath not seen shall bless him.

Henry van Dyke.

Light breaks through into one of the fine beechwoods, Cadman, Hampshire. Photograph by Kenneth Scowan.

May 16th

GOD MUST HAVE LOVED THE COMMON PEOPLE. HE MADE SO MANY OF THEM. IT'S MY TURN TO DO SO NOW.

Dear Madam,

I HAVE been shown in the files of the War Department a statement of the Adjutant-General of Massachusetts that you are the mother of five sons who have died gloriously on the field of battle.

I feel how weak and fruitless must be any words of mine which should attempt to beguile you from the grief of a loss so overwhelming; but I cannot refrain from tendering to you the consolation that may be found in the thanks of the Republic they died to save.

I pray that our heavenly Father may assuage the anguish of your bereavement and leave you only the cherished memory of the loved and lost, and the solemn pride that must be yours to have laid so costly a sacrifice on the altar of Freedom.

ABRAHAM LINCOLN, *(1809–1865)*.
16th President of the U.S.A. Born in a Kentucky log cabin. In his famous Gettysburg speech referred to America as a 'nation conceived in liberty, and dedicated to the proposition that all men are created equal', and that government of the people, by the people, and for the people, shall not perish from the earth.

May 17th

ALL WHO JOY WOULD WIN; MUST SHARE IT. HAPPINESS WAS BORN A TWIN.

HAPPINESS is like a crystal, fair and exquisite and clear ... Broken in a million pieces, shattered, scattered far and near ... Now and then along life's pathway, Lo! Some shining fragments fall; But there are so many pieces, no one ever finds them all.

You may find a bit of beauty, or an honest share of wealth ... While another just beside you, gathers honour, love and health ... Vain to choose or grasp unduly, broken is the perfect ball ... And there are so many pieces, no one ever finds them all.

Yet the wise, as on they journey, treasure every fragment clear ... Fit them as they may together, Imagining the shattered sphere ... Learning ever to be thankful, though their share of it is small ... For it has so many pieces, no one ever finds them all.

PRISCILLA LEONARD.

May 18th

GOD NEVER STRIKES BUT IN LOVE, NOR TAKES AWAY SAVE TO GIVE AGAIN.

Fenelon.

OURS was a grubby little back yard in the centre of a town where soot fell like black snow. My wife wanted so much to have a little garden, but try as she did, nothing ever seemed to thrive. Someone gave her a rose bush and it grew, but not well. Even mint, which seemed to spread like a weed everywhere else, had a hard time. Last spring, we planted a forsythia and it took root but that was about all. But the rose was my wife's pet. How she worked and worried over it.

I shouldn't have allowed any of this. She was a very sick girl. She had had a heart condition since childhood and I knew her time with me would not be long. However, her attempts at gardening seemed to give her joy and a purpose that I thought outweighed its harm. As time passed she grew more frail and finally in a desperate attempt I took her to a hospital in Boston for surgery. The day before the operation she stood beside her bed and looked out the window.

"What a beautiful day," she said, "what lovely colours."

I felt a throb in my heart as I somehow knew then that we were too late. We were. She slipped away several days later.

With a heavy heart I turned to face life again. But I avoided the yard where she had worked so hard. Then one morning, unaware of what I was doing, I walked into the little yard and looked about. The forsythia was a mass of vivid green, the mint a carpet of fragrant new leaves. And the rose, the rose was large and alive with bursting buds.

Welcome home, my darling.

EMMET P. LECOMPTE.

Sincere thanks to the author we have been unable to contact.

May 19th

ART IS LONG, AND TIME IS FLEETING. WHATSOEVER MY HAND FINDS TO DO, I'LL DO IT WITH ALL MY MIGHT.

"O YE gifted ones, follow your calling, for, however various your talents may be, you can have but one calling capable of leading you to eminence and renown. Follow resolutely the one straight path before you; it is that of your good angel. Let neither obstacles nor temptations induce you to leave it. Bound along if you can; if not, on hands and knees follow it; perish in it, if needful. But you need not fear that; no one ever yet died in the true path of his calling before he had obtained the pinnacle. Turn into other paths, and for a momentary advantage or gratification you have sold your inheritance, your immortality."

GEORGE BORROW.
British author and traveller. Born 1803 at East Dereham, Norfolk. Travelled on foot through England, Germany, France, Spain and Russia. A man of the open road. Died 1881. From: Lavengro.

May 20th

WHERE THERE IS HATRED, LET ME SOW LOVE—WHERE DESPAIR, HOPE

(St. Francis).

"I'VE gossiped about my neighbour," the woman confessed to her minister. "One day I saw her stagger about the yard, so I told a few friends that she had been drunk. Now I find that her staggering was caused by a leg injury. How can I undo this gossip I started?"

The minister excused himself for a moment, returned with a pillow and asked the woman to follow him to the side porch. He took out a knife, cut a hole in the pillow and emptied the feathers over the porch railing.

A small breeze soon scattered tiny feathers all about the yard, among shrubs, flowers, even up in the trees. A few feathers floated across the street, heading for unknown destinations.

The minister turned to the woman. "Will you go out now and gather up every one of the feathers?"

The woman looked stunned. "Why that would be impossible!"

"Exactly," replied the minister sorrowfully. "So it is with your gossip."

AUTHOR UNKNOWN.

May 21st

I ATTRACT TO MYSELF ONLY WHAT CORRESPONDS TO MY DOMINANT QUALITY OF THOUGHT. HOPE AND TRANQUILLITY OPEN-UP FOR ME CHANNELS OF NEW VITALITY.

SAYS one of deep insight into the nature of things: "The law of correspondences between spiritual and material things is wonderfully exact in its workings. People ruled by the mood of gloom attract to them gloomy things. People always discouraged and despondent do not succeed in anything, and live only by burdening someone else. The hopeful, confident, and cheerful attract the elements of success. A man's front or back yard will advertise that man's ruling mood in the way it is kept. A woman at home shows her state of mind in her dress. A slattern advertises the ruling mood of hopelessness, carelessness and lack of system. Rags, tatters, and dirt are always in the mind before being in the body. The thought that is most put out brings its correspondingly visible element to crystallize about you as surely and literally as the visible bit of copper in solution attracts to it the invisible copper in that solution. A mind always hopeful, confident, courageous, and determined on its set purpose, and keeping itself to that purpose, attracts to itself out of the elements things and powers favourable to that purpose.

"Every thought of yours has a literal value to you in every possible way. The strength of your body, the strength of your mind, your success in business, and the pleasure your company brings others, depends on the nature of your thoughts.

" . . . So to do good, is to bring to yourself all the elements in nature of power and good."

RALPH WALDO TRINE.
"In Tune with the Infinite"

May 22nd

"IN WHATSOEVER SET OF CIRCUMSTANCES I FIND MYSELF, I AM CONTENT."

KATHLEEN Ferrier was perhaps the greatest contralto who ever lived. Her character was as big and as rich as her voice. In the face of adversity she had all the courage and moral fibre of other Lancashire lassies who have made their mark on the artistic and industrial life of our country. Enquiries into her health by her devoted friends before she was so untimely taken from us were met with a reply: "Don't let's go into that, luv, it's too boring. I'm feeling fine." Let us hear what Bernadine Hammond said about her.

"One of the amazing things about her was her complete acceptance of whatever came her way. If it was something good, then it was added to her mental list of blessings to be ever thankful for. This was an enormous help to her. At times when it seemed that she had more than any normal human could be expected to cope with, there would suddenly be that quick smile and there she was counting over what yet remained to her, and feeling very sorry for people she considered worse off than herself. She hardly ever complained; on such rare occasions as she did, a saint would have done the same. She was her own greatest, most valiant helper, and never once did she let herself down. Any difficulty she looked upon in the light of a challenge and anything trying she said would pass the time.

"Kath enjoyed life from the moment she woke and purred over her morning cup of tea till I had removed Rosie the cat from under her bed at night. During the day she would say so often, 'Lucky, lucky, Kath!' "

"KATHLEEN FERRIER."
Edited by Neville Cardus. (Pub. Hamish Hamilton.).

May 23rd

I PAUSE TO RE-FIT. I STICK TO THE HELM WHEN I'M HARDEST HIT. IT'S WHEN THE STORM WINDS BREAK THAT I JUST WON'T QUIT.

WHEN the lean and weatherbeaten figure of Francis Chichester sailed into Plymouth Harbour, England, on 28th May 1967, the world had something to cheer about.

The 65-year-old adventurer had just completed an epic voyage around the globe in 226 days—farther and faster alone than any other man in nautical history.

Many weeks before, Chichester had nearly given up in despair. Heavy seas in the South Indian Ocean battering his 53-foot sailboat, "Gipsy Moth IV", had broken his most precious piece of equipment—the automatic steering gear.

With 17,000 miles still ahead of him, he knew that without the automatic pilot he could scarcely sleep, eat, navigate, change sails or perform other essential tasks.

But, making that added effort for which he is justly famous, he patched together a makeshift self-steering rig. With it he managed to complete the remaining 2,750 miles to Sydney, Australia, his only stop.

In Sydney he rested for some weeks to regain the 25 pounds he had lost and to re-fit his severely damaged vessel. Then Chichester set off across the Pacific for the most dangerous part of his journey—the rounding of Cape Horn at the tip of South America.

"There is something nightmarish about deep, breaking seas and screaming winds," he said later. "I had a feeling of helplessness before the power of the waves rolling down on top of me. It all has ten times the impact when alone."

Despite driving rain, mountainous seas and freezing winds of up to 100 m.p.h., the dauntless mariner rounded the Cape and sailed on to the eventual goal of Plymouth Harbour.

At any point, Francis Chichester could have "called it quits". But he heaped effort upon effort—and in the victory of his human spirit we all became a little richer.

Why did his lonely adventure capture the imagination of the world? Perhaps it was because his battle with the high seas dramatized the uphill struggle of millions of people. All his "can-do" spirit inspired them to renew their own dedication.

THE CHRISTOPHERS.

May 24th

I AM ALERT, ALIVE, AWAKE, JOYOUS AND ENTHUSIASTIC ABOUT LIFE ... MY GREATEST PLEASURE IS SOMETHING NEW TO LEARN TO DO.

THE fear of growing old can strike you at almost any age. As a consulting psychologist, specializing in problems of the aged, I find that a good percentage of my clients are still in their thirties—men and women who are already worried by the spectre of approaching age. What I tell them can be read with profit by anyone from seventeen to seventy who's interested in remaining young ...

My formula for staying young is simple: Concentrate on the part of you that's still young and growing—your brain. Keep your mind awake and you'll stay young all over. These are exciting times. Take an interest in the world around you. And make a point of learning at least one new thing every day. Above all, don't "settle down" ...

... Regardless of your age it's not too late to make your life more interesting. I know a housewife who, at fifty, with no previous experience made herself into an outstanding industrial engineer. I know a retired electrical engineer who has become a highly-paid ceramic artist. One of my clients—a woman of seventy whose children thought she should retire to the shelf—conducts a successful cookery school for brides.

Get over the idea that you're ever too old to go back to school. I know a man who entered medical college at seventy. He got his degree with honours and became an eminent physician. Another man went to law school at seventy-one and is now an active lawyer. And a ninety-one-year-old woman has just gone back to college for a refresher course in history. I know a woman who learned to paint at seventy-seven, held a "one-man" show at eighty, and today, at eighty-six is still going strong. It's never too late to add another skill to those you now possess.

Irrespective of years, staying young is easy for those who live in the future. You can do it, if you care enough to try. Keep your mind awake and active. That's the only youth elixir guaranteed to work.

DR GEORGE LAWTON.
Sincere thanks to the author whose address we are unable to trace.

May 25th

THOUGH I DON'T LIKE THE CREW, I WON'T SINK THE SHIP. IN FACT, IN TIME OF STORM, I'LL DO MY BEST TO SAVE IT. YOU SEE WE ARE ALL IN THIS CRAFT AND MUST SINK OR SWIM TOGETHER.

Daniel Defoe.

STRANGE is our situation here upon earth. Each of us comes for a short visit, not knowing why, yet sometimes seeming to divine a purpose. From the standpoint of daily life, however, there is one thing we do know: That Man Is Here for the Sake of Other Men ... for the countless unknown souls with whose fate we are connected by a bond of sympathy. Many times a day I realize how much my own outer and inner life is built upon the labours of my fellow men, both living and dead, and how earnestly I must exert myself in order to give in return as much as I have received and am still receiving.

ALBERT EINSTEIN.

German-Swiss physicist famous for his theory of relativity. Born at Ulm, of Jewish parents. Fled from Germany during the Hitler regime and settled in America

May 26th

THIS IS MY OPPORTUNITY TO BEGIN AGAIN ... I TRUST IN GOD WHO GUIDES AND STRENGTHENS ME ... I KNOW I CAN DO IT.

PLEASE, God, when I ride home on the train, help me to keep myself as straight and strong as those tracks of steel.

Help me remember, God, when I walk in my front door how many times I walked through a different kind of door ... a door with bars of steel. When I walk through the park and breathe the fresh air and hear the laughter of children, help me, God, to appreciate how sweet freedom is. When I cash my first pay cheque and stop on my way home to buy a shirt or maybe shoes, help me, God, to appreciate my independence.

That's about it, God, and if you don't mind my asking, please don't judge me for what I was, but for what I can be.

BY H. S.
—*House of Correction, Chicago, USA.*

May 27th

MY FIRST THOUGHT SHALL BE THE SAFETY OF OTHERS ...
MY SECOND, TO DO ALL TO PROMOTE THEIR HAPPINESS.

BECAUSE of a little piece of paper today is a very special day. This world suddenly belongs to me in a way it never did before. I also belong to it in a new way.

That child pedalling his bicycle along the road—I see the years of love and sacrifice that brought him to this place. I realize the incalculable heartbreak if some accident should befall this child.

The man approaching me in a pick-up truck is a very ordinary looking man. But doubtless he is the heart and mainstay of some nearby home.

The old lady glancing about hesitantly before crossing the street is elderly and slightly stooped, walking with studied care. How precious these late September days must be to her.

God, make me alert that no action of mine may darken or shorten the life of one of Your people.

Today is a very special day for me. I hold in my hand a little piece of paper that is a passport to a broader world of freedom and discovery. God, grant that I use it only for good.

Today I received my driver's licence.

Julia C. Mahon.

May 28th

TODAY I WILL KEEP A FRIENDSHIP ALIVE
BY PHONING OR WRITING TO A FRIEND.

> Life is sweet just because of our Friends,
> And the things in which we all share:
> We want to live on, not because of ourselves,
> But because of the people who care;
> It's giving and doing for somebody else,
> On that all Life's splendour depends,
> And all the joys of this wonderful world
> Are found in the keeping of Friends.

Anonymous.

May 29th

THE MORE WE LIVE BY OUR INTELLECT, THE LESS WE UNDERSTAND THE MEANING OF LIFE.
William James.

I DO not pray that you may be delivered from your troubles, but I pray God earnestly that He would give you strength and patience to bear them as long as He pleases ... Happy are those who suffer with Him. The men of the world do not comprehend these truths, nor is it to be wondered at, since they suffer as lovers of the world, and not as lovers of Christ.

Men of the world consider sickness as a pain of nature, and not as from God. They see it only in that light. They find nothing in it but grief and distress. But those who consider sickness as coming from the hand of God, as an effect of His mercy, and the means which He employs for their salvation—such find in it great consolation.

BROTHER LAWRENCE, (1611–1691).

May 30th

TO WORK ... TO HELP ... TO LEARN SYMPATHY THROUGH SUFFERING ... TO LEARN FAITH THROUGH PERPLEXITY ... TO REACH TRUTH THROUGH WONDER ... THIS IS WHAT IT MEANS TO PROSPER ... THIS IS WHAT IT IS TO LIVE.

Phillip Brooks.

ETERNAL providence has appointed me to watch over the life and health of Your creatures. May the love of my art motivate me at all times. May neither avarice, greed, the thirst for public acclaim or reputation engage my mind. The enemies of truth and social service can easily deceive me, making me forgetful of my dedication to do good to Your children.

May I never see in the patient anything but a fellow being in pain.

Lord, grant me strength, time and opportunity to develop what I have acquired, always to extend its domain; for knowledge is without limit. The spirit of a man can extend infinitely to enrich him daily with new demands upon his talents. Today he can discover his errors of yesterday. Tomorrow, he may obtain a new light on what he holds in confidence today.

O God, Who has appointed me to watch over the life and death of Your creatures, I am ready for my vocation.

MAIMONIDES.
Jewish Physician, 12th Century.

May 31st

I WILL BE STRONG AND OF A GOOD COURAGE. I ACT FOR THE BEST, AND TAKE WHAT COMES.

I HAVE, myself, full confidence that if all do their duty, if nothing is neglected, and if the best arrangements are made, as they are being made we shall once again prove ourselves able to defend our island home, to ride out the storm, and to outlive the menace of tyranny. At any rate, that is what we are trying to do. That is the resolve of His Majesty's Government—every man of them . . .

. . . We shall not flag or fail. We shall go on to the end. We shall fight in France, we shall fight on the seas and oceans. We shall fight with growing confidence and growing strength in the air, we shall defend our island, whatever the cost may be. We shall fight on the beaches, we shall fight on the landing grounds, we shall fight in the fields and in the streets, we shall fight in the hills. We shall never surrender.

SIR WINSTON CHURCHILL.
3rd June, 1940.

A WOMAN knows the face of the man she loves as a sailor knows the open sea.
Honor De Balzac.

FAREWELL.
By Ralph Todd (1852-1932).
Whitford & Hughes, London, UK,
Bridgeman Art Library, London & New York.

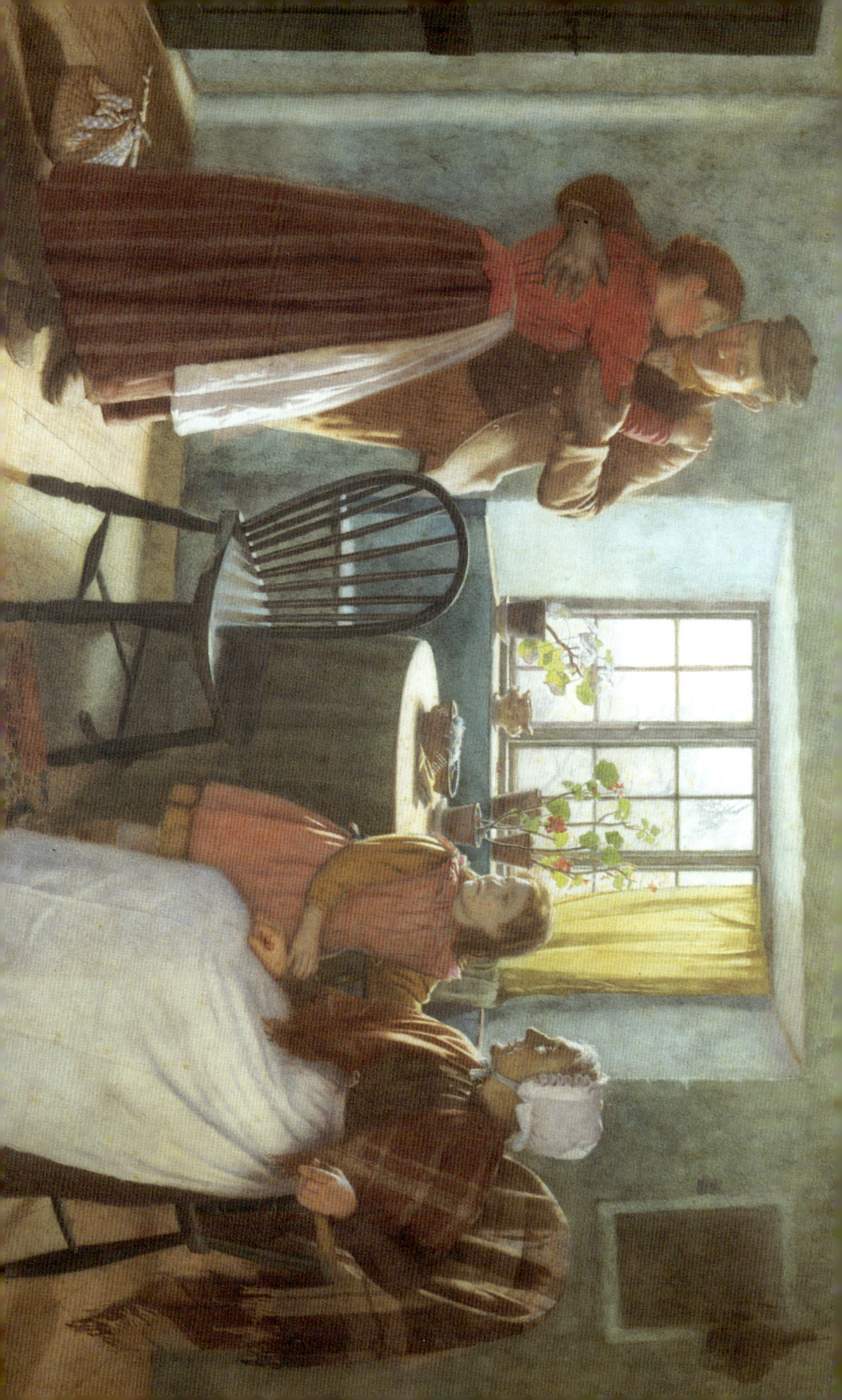

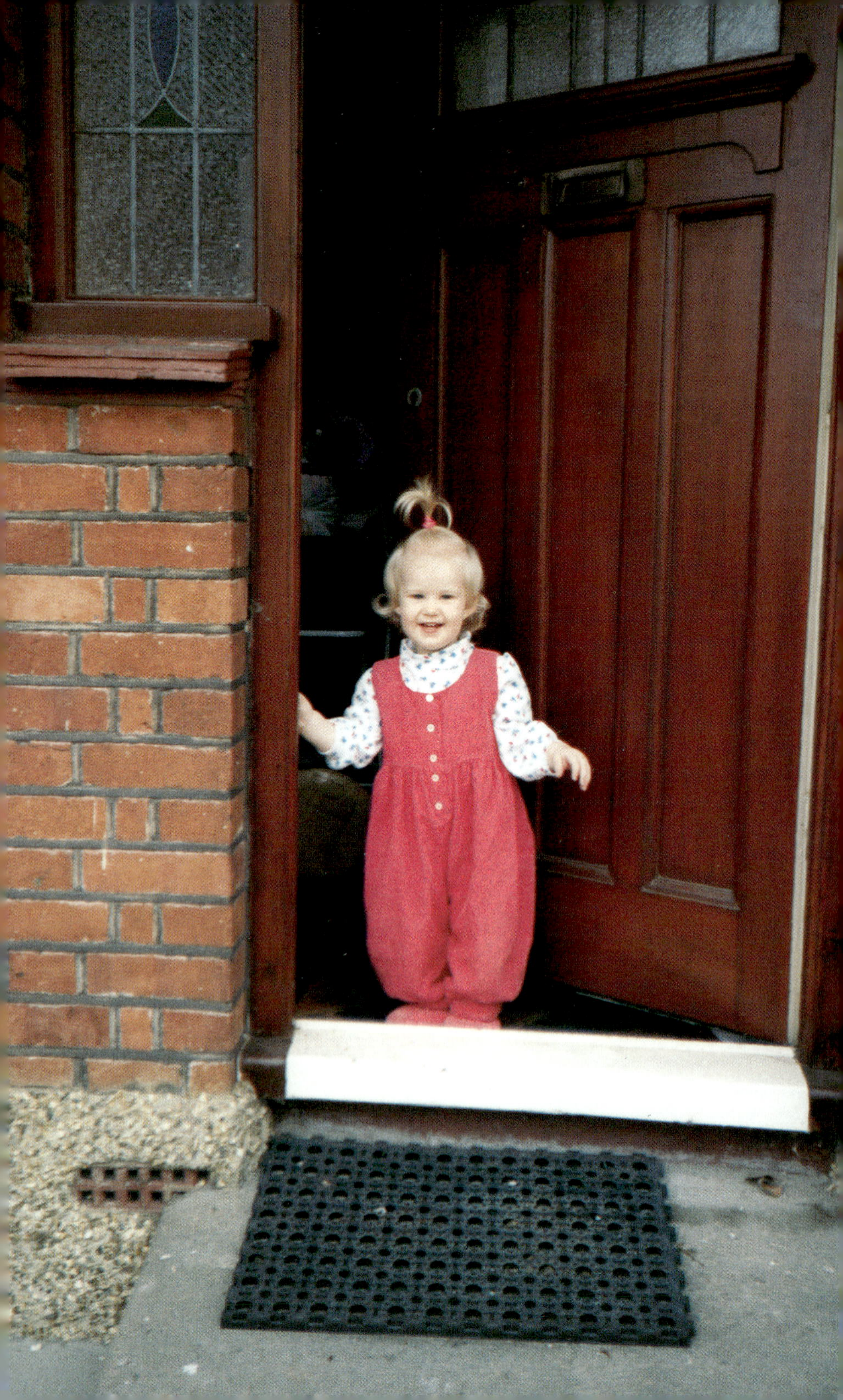

June 1st

I LOVE LIFE ... I WANT TO LIVE ... ALL OF LIFE'S
GOODNESS ... ALL THAT IT HAS TO GIVE ...
Song.

I LOOK upon Life as the greatest adventure.

Often ... too often ... I meet someone who says, "What's the bargain in living? What's the sense in striving and straining? What's the use of this rat race? Why go through all this? Life isn't that good! Life isn't that important!"

Through the years I have had literally hundreds of people say something along those lines.

Well, to me, life is beautiful. It's a great and glorious and wonderful adventure and experience. I would not have missed it for the world. I take time regularly to raise my head and eyes towards the sky or heavens and I mutter a few kind expressions to my maker that indicate my feelings and my gratitude for the privilege of being a part of this wonderful universe.

Let it not be denied that at times I have found life a wee bit difficult, when things didn't go my way, but mainly it was due to the fact, as I see it now, that I was not well and a person who is sick or ailing cannot appreciate the beauties of life. It is only when one is in good health and I should say, deservedly good health, by following a proper way of living, that he can truly appreciate the beauties, the glories and the wonders of our universe.

Fortunately I find no pleasure in drinking or in smoking, but in spite of this I enjoy every moment of my life. I am not depressed when it rains or snows or thunders or the skies are dark. I don't even feel better when the sun is shining, because I feel the same, rain or shine. And I maintain this is so because I am well and for this blessing I am grateful with all my heart.

JOHN TOBE.

One of Canada's most popular writers. Studied health from the ground upwards, having started his career as a nurseryman. At 39 was a physical wreck, but achieved health after adopting natural methods of healing.

WELCOME HOME. (Sarah).
By courtesy of Mr & Mrs Douglas Higgs, Ruislip, Middlesex.

June 2nd

THE WORLD IS A LOOKING-GLASS ... IT GIVES BACK TO EVERY MAN A REFLECTION OF HIS OWN FACE ... FROWN INTO IT, AND IT WILL LOOK SOURLY AT YOU ... LAUGH AT IT, AND WITH IT, AND IT IS A JOLLY COMPANION, KINDNESS ITSELF.

Thackeray.

TEN recommendations for human relations:
1. Speak to people. There is nothing as nice as a cheerful word of greeting.
2. Smile at people. It takes seventy-two muscles to frown—only fourteen to smile.
3. Call people by name. The sweetest music to anyone's ears is the sound of his own name.
4. Be friendly. If you would have friends, be friendly.
5. Be cordial. Speak and act as if everything you do is a genuine pleasure.
6. Be genuinely interested in people. You can like everybody if you try.
7. Be generous with praise—cautious with criticism.
8. Be considerate of the feelings of others. It will be appreciated.
9. Be thoughtful of the opinions of others. There are three sides to a controversy—yours, the other fellow's, and the right one.
10. Be alert to help and give service. What counts most in life is what we do for others.

"Sunshine Magazine".

THE true way to live is to enjoy every moment as it passes, and surely it is in the everyday things around us that the beauty of life lies.

Laura I. Wilder.

June 3rd

I WELCOME CHANGE, AND REGARD IT AS A FRIEND. THIS PRESENT UNCERTAIN SITUATION HAS MORE POWER FOR GOOD THAN FOR EVIL. NO MATTER HOW COMPLICATED THE PLOT, IT CAN BE THE OPENING SENTENCE TO A NEW RICH CHAPTER IN MY LIFE.

ONE reason that people get old and bored is that change baffles them: they feel they can't cope with it. So they retire from the confusion and sit back with their horse-and-buggy memories, losing momentum, gathering years and little else. But welcome change as a friend; try to visualise new possibilities and the blessings change is bound to bring you.

Let it excite you, arouse your curiosity and transfuse you with its own vitality and you'll never grow old, even if you live to be 100. If you stay interested in everything around you, in new ways of life, in new people, in new places and ideas, you'll stay young, no matter what your age. Never stop learning and never stop growing: that's the key to a rich and fascinating life.

ALEXANDER P. DE SEVERSKY,
in Quote.

June 4th

I NO LONGER CONVERSE TO CONTRADICT MY FRIENDS' CHERISHED BELIEFS FOR THE SAKE OF ARGUMENT. I TRY TO LOVE MUCH; TO UNDERSTAND MORE; NOT ASPIRING TO EMINENCE BUT WILLINGLY ADJUSTING TO HUMBLER STATIONS.

I WONDER if you ever change human beings with arguments alone: either by peppering them with little sharp facts or by blowing them up with great guns of truth. You scare them, but do you change them?

I wonder if you ever make any real difference in human beings without understanding them and loving them. For when you argue with a man, you are somehow trying to pull him down and make him less; but when you try to understand him, when you like him, how eager is he then to know the truth you have; and you add to him in some strange way, you make him more than he was before; and at the same time, you yourself become more.

DAVID GRAYSON.

June 5th

FROM MY RELAXED BODY AND TRANQUIL MIND SECRET MAGNETISMS FLOW, INCESSANTLY LEADING TO WIDER CREATIVITY, NEW DISCOVERY AND INCREASED ABILITY.

JUST as a farmer knows his fields must lie fallow from time to time, so has every great thinker known that he must give his mind a rest periodically if he is to produce good work.

But this apparent inactivity of the mind is really only the inactivity of one layer of it. The conscious mind may be at rest, but the unconscious is always busy. And the secret of great men is that they know how to use their unconscious mind. When they desire to produce original work on some topic, they supply all the material they can to their mind, knowing it will sink into the unconscious, and then they proceed to "forget" the subject for a week or more.

And all the while they are playing or sleeping or talking, this unconscious activity of the mind is going on, collating, associating. Then one day they will feel an uncontrollable desire to express themselves either on paper or in the workshop or the laboratory, and that which they produce will be the result of their unconscious thinking.

Constance Williams.

June 6th

NOTHING HAS THE POWER TO WORRY ME ANY MORE. I KNOW THAT FOR THE FUTURE 'ALL IS WELL'.

MILLIONAIRE dictators are being assassinated, kings and queens deposed and roaming about the world, people are being robbed of thousands of pounds' worth of valuables, banks are being daily robbed, big monied firms are merging to make more money, the rich and not-so-rich are flying from place to place to get away from it all—and can't.

Yet, no one tries to rob me of my old age pension book. I cannot be deposed; no one wants to assassinate me; no one can stop me from access to fresh air (it cannot be controlled or they would sell it or tax it); no one can stop me from a walk by the sea, a look at beautiful flowers and beautiful women. I can admire the stars and freely go to church to thank God for all these free lovely things.

The moral seems obvious—keep out of high places and big money if you want to live safely, in peace and happiness.

David Moss,
Bure Lane, Christchurch.

June 7th

I AM ABLE TO FACE LIFE AT ANY POINT. I CAN MEET ANY SITUATION. NOTHING CAN DESTROY THE JOY AND PEACE WHICH ARE RIGHTFULLY MINE.

HOW do we become true and good, happy and genuine, joyful and free? Never by magic, never by chance, never by sitting and waiting, but only by getting in touch with good, true, happy, genuine human beings, only by seeking the company of the strong and the free, only by catching spontaneity and freedom from those who are themselves spontaneous and free.

You will then develop a sharpness of perception to differentiate unerringly between the true and the phoney, the beautiful and the hideous, the noble and the mean. You will develop the ability to blush, the ability to cry and shed tears, the ability to repent, the ability to fall on your knees and pray, the ability to become a real, moral human person.

Should you read the Bible—both Old and New Testaments, especially the Psalms and the Gospels—reverently and prayerfully every day; should you read the deepest and purest saints and men of God, should you faithfully serve the Church and participate in the fullness of its life despite its endless frailties and imperfections and tribulations; should you practise the great art of mental and moral discipline; should you seek, with love and expectation and self-giving, the company of those who do these things, I guarantee you two things: first, that you will experience in your own life and being a taste of what is beautiful and strong and certain and free; and second, you will develop such a sharpness of vision as to distinguish the true from the false whenever you come across them. And both your being and your vision will grant you some knowledge of God.

CHARLES MALIK.
President of the United Nations General Assembly.

TIME TO TALK.
After a sightseeing-tour of Warwick Castle, England, friends pause to relax beside the River Avon.
Photograph by Dennis Mansell

June 8th

TODAY IS MADE FOR BRIGHT GREEN FIELDS ... FOR THE JOY OF SUMMER ... I FEEL THE TOUCH OF LIFE, AND THE QUIET POWER OF EARTH FLOWING INTO ME.

ALL that is sweet, delightful, and amiable in this world, in the serenity of the air, the fineness of seasons, the joy of light, the melody of sounds, the beauty of colours, the fragrancy of smells, the splendour of precious stones, is nothing else but Heaven breaking through the veil of this world, manifesting itself in such a degree and darting forth in such variety so much of its own nature.

WILLIAM LAW.
British mystic, 1686–1761.

June 9th

THE WORLD IS INCOMPLETE WITHOUT ME. I AM HERE FOR A PURPOSE. OTHERS RELY UPON MY HONESTY, KINDNESS AND STEADFASTNESS. I SHALL NOT FAIL THEM.

Dear Andrew,

IF I should not see you again I wish you to remember and treasure up some things I have already said to you: in this world you will have to make your own way. To do that you must have friends. You can make friends by being honest, and you can keep them by being steadfast. You must keep in mind that friends worth having will in the long run expect as much from you as they will give to you.

To forget an obligation or be ungrateful for a kindness is a base crime—not merely a fault or a sin but an actual crime. Men guilty of it sooner or later must suffer the penalty.

In personal conduct always be polite, but never obsequious. No one will respect you more than you esteem yourself. Avoid quarrels as long as you can without yielding to imposition. But sustain your manhood always ...

Never wound the feelings of others. If ever you have to vindicate your feelings or defend your honour, do it calmly. If angry at first, wait till your wrath cools before you proceed.

Love, Mother.

The Andrew of this letter was none other than Andrew Jackson, 7th President of the United States.

June 10th

> WHEN THE SUN RISES, I GO TO WORK,
> WHEN THE SUN GOES DOWN, I TAKE MY REST,
> I DIG THE WELL FROM WHICH I DRINK,
> I FARM THE SOIL THAT YIELDS MY FOOD,
> I SHARE CREATION ... KINGS CAN DO NO MORE.
>
> *Ancient Chinese, 2500 B.C.*

"NOTHING is too high for me to reach. My step-ladder will be positive thinking and each rung of the way, courage and confidence." Broaden your interests, learn something new every day, because the measure of your interests is the amount of information you possess. Don't let your life go by without discovering the thrill of appreciating good music, wonderful paintings and the treasures in great books.

Rely on your own taste and judgment, and try not to feel before praising a book or picture, you have to look round to see if anyone else thinks it's good. Determine to use your own mind and project your own personality. You are the boss, not your circumstances.

The climate of your life is within you and not outside you. You must believe that wholly, for faith that sets limits to itself is not faith at all. Believe wholeheartedly and circumstances will yield to you; your life will be moulded into the pattern you want. But remember if we want great lives, adventurous lives, successful lives, happy lives, we must not ask for easy lives.

AUTHOR UNKNOWN.

June 11th

> 'TIS TIME FOR ME TO DRAW ASIDE FROM LIFE AND ALL ITS PROBLEMS—MAYBE, ONLY FOR A MINUTE. I TUNE INTO PEACE AND POWER.

THERE comes a day when the worrisome chequebook, the jangling telephone, the brainstorming conference, the pressures of being a man in the jet age have to be set aside. It is a time for him to be alone, to think things through, to put the 'out-to-lunch' sign on his heart and nervous system. Time to go roaming through Nature's woods. Time to sit in the sun and dream. He will then assume his role as a better man, a better friend, a better worker, if he is let to be alone in the while, out of the tenseness of glare of a demanding man-made turmoil, and into the tranquil world of Nature.

AUTHOR UNKNOWN.

June 12th

A KIND WORD IS NEVER LOST. IT KEEPS GOING ON AND ON FROM ONE PERSON TO ANOTHER, UNTIL AT LAST IT COMES BACK TO ME AGAIN.

SHOULD I feel inclined to censure . . . Faults I may in others view . . . I'll ask my own heart, ere I venture . . . If that has not failings, too . . . Let not friendly vows be broken . . . Rather strive a friend to gain . . . Many a word in anger spoken . . . Finds its passage home again . . . I'll not, then, in idle pleasure . . . Trifle with a brother's fame . . . But guard it as a valued treasure . . . Sacred as my own good name . . . I'll not form opinions blindly . . . Hastiness to trouble tends . . . Those of whom I thought unkindly . . . Oft become my warmest friends.

Author unknown.

June 13th

HAVING LEARNT TO WALK ALONE I WILL NEVER BE LONELY ANY MORE. I WILL SERVE OTHERS AS BEST AS I CAN AND LEAVE THE REST TO THE ANGELS.

WHEN man's hand has been turned against me, and I have felt unloved and spurned, my own love unreturned, I have found solace in the song of little friendly birds, in shafts of sunlight falling upon bright flowers, and in the long shadows of junipers at eventide. I have sought the company and strength of mighty trees which breathed tranquillity into my soul by their stability, their endurance against wind and rain and tempest. They have given me patience. I have found the balm of compassion in the understanding purr of cats, in the fidelity of dogs, and in the affection of many small animals.

I have found sanctuary by stepping into opal sunset clouds, into rosy lagoons amid the purple hills and rugged mountains suspended against a turquoise infinity. I have learned the lesson I had to learn—to be able to walk alone. No reassuring and beloved hand holding my elbow. But I have come to know the light touch of unseen hands upon my head and the tingle of loving presences in my room when I have closed the door. "When you can walk alone", they seem to say, "You will never be lonely any more. Serve others as best you can, and leave the rest to us—the Silent Watchers . . ."

Peggy Mason.

June 14th

WISDOM IS OFTTIMES NEARER WHEN WE LOOK BACK INTO THE PAST, THAN WHEN OUR THOUGHTS SOAR INTO THE FUTURE.

WHEN we talk of our development I fancy we mean little more than that we have changed with the changing world; and if we are writers or intellectuals, that our ideas have changed with the changing fashions of thought, and therefore not always for the better.

I think that if any of us examines his life, he will find that most good has come to him from a few loyalties, and a few discoveries made many generations before he was born, which must always be made anew. These, too, may sometimes appear to come by chance, but in the infinite web of things and events, chance must be something different from what we think it to be. To comprehend this is not given to us, and to think of it is to recognize a mystery, and to acknowledge the necessity of faith.

As I look back on the part of the mystery which is my own life, my own fable, what I am most aware of is that we receive more than we can ever give: we receive it from the past, on which we draw with every breath, but also—and this is a point of faith—from the Source of the mystery itself, by the means which some people call Grace.

The last paragraph of Edwin Muir's autobiography.
British writer and distinguished poet. Born in the Orkneys. Famous for the
novel: The Three Brothers.

June 15th

"I LOOK UPWARD, I THINK UPWARD, I LIVE UPWARD."

"I AM going to let go of the past. 'All things are possible'—that means health, perfect order, and plenty. I feel that strength, joy and harmony are making their home in me. Health is contagious. I am made vigorous and strong. I am constantly being called to greater things and higher achievements. 'I can do all things through Christ Who is strengthening me'.

The windows of Heaven are open, and I am filled with the energies of God. I am thankful for the breath which is vitalizing and renewing every cell in my body. I am conscious of the good flowing through me, and pour it out into the lives of all with whom I come into contact. I am radiantly, vitally and fully alive."

THOMAS.

June 16th

I DARE TO DARE. I HAVE WHAT IT TAKES. I CAN DO ANYTHING IF I SET MY MIND TO IT.

PSYCHOLOGIST William James described our condition very accurately: "Most people live, whether physically, intellectually or morally, in a very restricted circle of their potential being. They make use of a very small portion of their possible consciousness . . . "

Not Rebecca Johnson. Mrs. Johnson, 23, decided to test her endurance by paddling a canoe down the Mississippi from Minnesota to the Gulf of Mexico—alone.

Along the way, she met plenty of people who predicted she'd never make it. "When I got within 200 miles of New Orleans, people asked me where I was going and then they'd say: 'Lady, that's a long way'. I'd say; 'not when you've already paddled 2,200 miles!'"

Was it worth the effort? Rebecca Johnson feels it was. "I've learned so much on this river," she says. "You learn about handling yourself. I think I could handle anything anybody wanted to throw at me now."

We don't have to paddle the length of the Mississippi to find out who we are. Sometimes, it takes a personal crisis or a severe physical, mental or emotional handicap. But not always. Each day holds the chance to challenge ourselves a little more, to ask a slightly tougher question, to go a little further out of our way to serve someone, or explore something. No one expects us to be foolhardy. But "playing it safe" is a sure way to cut down our chances of truly becoming all that we are. Dare to dare. You have what it takes.

THE CHRISTOPHERS.

A quitter never wins.
A winner never quits.

June 17th

LET ME FORGET THE HURT AND PAIN … FOUND ALONG
LIFE'S WAY … LET ME REMEMBER A KINDLY WORD …
TO PASS ON EVERY DAY.

EARLY one Saturday morning, I stood with a girl friend in a long queue, waiting to be conducted on a sightseeing tour. Never at my best at 8.30 am, I observed with admiration my friend's immaculate grooming and her well-pressed, becoming outfit.

After we had been standing about half an hour, a distinguished-looking woman with her hands full of documents walked down the corridor, wearing an expression of deep concentration. As she came level with us, her face suddenly lightened. Pausing for an infinitesimal second, she smiled at my friend and said, "You *do* look nice!" and then went briskly on towards her destination.

My friend blushed with pleasure. Buoyed by a stranger's recognition of her efforts to look attractive, she lifted her chin, straightened her shoulders and forgot that her feet were tired. Seeing her reaction, I wondered why I hadn't made the remark myself. I had always valued my friend's taste and standards, but had simply never put that appreciation into words.

Perhaps that is what recognition really is—appreciation *expressed*. Often we fail to bestow it out of diffidence, tacit acceptance of familiar virtues or the expectation that people can read our minds. The rare occasions when it is tendered usually come at the end of a career—or even at the end of a life. But the spontaneous acknowledgement of excellence, exhibited by average people involved in routine work—the unsolicited salute to skill or talent or intelligence or character traits that is so nourishing to the spirit, and so rare—is the sort of recognition that can make a day, halo a year, change a life. We all possess this extraordinary power that requires almost nothing but the will to communicate.

MARGARET COUSINS.
Our sincere thanks to the author who we have been unable to trace.

June 18th

IN ALL MY WAYS I ACKNOWLEDGE HIM, AND HE SHALL DIRECT MY PATH.

OH GREAT SPIRIT
Whose voice I heard in the wind
Whose breath gives life to the world
Hear me
I come to you as one of your many children
I am small and weak
I need your strength and your wisdom
May I walk in beauty
Make my eyes ever behold the red and purple sunset
Make my hands respect the things that you have made
And my ears sharp to hear your voice
Make me wise so that I may know the things you have taught your children
The lessons you have hidden in every leaf and rock
Make me strong, not to be superior to my brothers
But to be able to fight my greatest enemy—myself
Make me ever ready to come to you with straight eyes
So that when life fades as the fading sun sets
My spirit will come to you without shame.

CHIEF DAN GEORGE.
Submitted by Gilberte C. Lamontagne, Quebec, Canada.

BY LOVE may He be grasped and understood . . . by intellect never.
The Cloud of Unknowing.

June 19th

IT IS IN THE HEARTS OF MEN THAT WE MUST LAY THE FOUNDATIONS OF WORLD PEACE.

THE battle for Tobruk was a see-saw affair in the African campaign, the British and the Germans alternately holding the city. A captain in charge of a British hospital unit related his experience.

When Rommel's troops took Tobruk in a sudden thrust, this hospital unit carried on calmly, even handling whatever wounded the enemy stretcher-bearers brought in, German and British alike. Later there was a hush as a figure darkened the door. It was General Rommel himself. The General stood for a moment, gazing at the rows of hospital cots. He strode to a wounded German soldier, asked a crisp question, and listened attentively to the soldier's reply. Then he walked between the rows, pausing to question other German wounded.

At last Rommel beckoned to the British captain. "My men tell me they are getting exactly the same treatment as your British wounded. Also, that you are short of medical supplies, but they are receiving their fair share of what you have. I will have supplies sent to you. Carry on as you are doing. No one will molest you." He strode out.

Promised supplies and drugs arrived promptly, and the hospital unit was able to employ them to good effect, saving both British and German lives. As the General had promised, there was no interference with the hospital's routine.

A few days later came another abrupt change in the fortunes of war. Rommel's forces were in flight, but in retreating they left the hospital unharmed. Neither defeat nor victory had interrupted its work of mercy.

Major P. W. Rainer,
in Pipeline to Victory.
<small>Sincere thanks to the author whose address we are unable to trace.</small>

June 20th

I AM ON MY OWN. HOWEVER MENACING THE OUTLOOK I AM DETERMINED NOT TO YIELD WITHOUT A FIGHT. I INTEND TO LOSE MYSELF IN ACTION. I WILL NEVER BE BEATEN.

WHAT General Weygand called "The Battle of France" is over. I expect that the battle of Britain is about to begin. Upon this battle depends the survival of Christian civilization. Upon it depends our own British life and the long continuity of our institutions and our Empire. The whole fury and might of the enemy must very soon be turned upon us. Hitler knows that he will have to break us in this island or lose the war. If we can stand up to him all Europe may be free, and the life of the world may move forward into broad, sunlit uplands, but if we fail then the whole world, including the United States and all that we have known and cared for, will sink into the abyss of a new dark age, made more sinister, and perhaps more prolonged, by the lights of a perverted science. Let us therefore brace ourselves to our duty and so bear ourselves that if the British Commonwealth and Empire lasts for a thousand years men will still say: "This was their finest hour".

Sir Winston Churchill.
In a war speech, 18th June, 1940.
Leader of Britain in her 'finest hour'. British statesman. Descendant of the great Duke of Marlborough, born at Blenheim Palace, 30th November, 1874.

June 21st

I BELIEVE IN THE HOLINESS OF LIGHT, WHICH LIKE A WINTER'S DAY MUST HAVE SOME DARKNESS TO REVEAL ITS HIDDEN MEANING.

EVERYTHING that he saw from the carriage window, in the pale light of the dying day, appeared to him just as fresh, happy, and strong as he himself. The roofs of the houses shining in the setting sun, the sharp outlines of fences and corner buildings, the forms of occasional pedestrians, the motionless leaves, the green grass, the fields with their straight rows of potatoes, the slanting shadows from the houses, trees, and bushes—everything was beautiful, like an exquisite landscape fresh from the artist's hand.

Tolstoy.
From 'Anna Karenina'.

June 22nd

ALL GOOD GIFTS AROUND US
ARE SENT FROM HEAVEN ABOVE;
THEN THANK THE LORD, O THANK THE LORD,
FOR ALL HIS LOVE.

I OFFER thanks ... For the dawn as it comes slowly over the hill, with the birds waking and starting to sing ... For giving me the noontide when the sun stands high, and whistles blow so that people rush to dine ... For the quiet afternoon when the sun moves lazily westward to set in majestic glory ... For the evening, when the night begins to tuck us in, and a moon beckons us out to watch it settle ... For the stars giving a brilliant welcome to lovers in the crisp, cool air ... For the land on which I thrive and the goodness we get from it ... And when I grow weary of treading through fallen leaves, or plunging into the snowdrift, or imbibing the spring's sweetness ... I offer thanks for the home I may go to, and for the care and comfort I receive from the guardians placed in my home ... For the country I live in and the freedoms I enjoy ... For the people who are my friends, neighbours, and fellow countrymen ... For all these, and much more, I offer my sincere thanks.

Esther M. Mishler.

Our sincere thanks to owners of copyright we have been unable to contact.

GRATITUDE is the rosemary of the heart.
Minna Antrim.

June 23rd

BY GRACE I AM SAVED, THROUGH FAITH, AND THIS IS NOT OF MY OWN WILL ... IT IS A GIFT OF GOD, NOT FROM ANYTHING I DO ... LEST I SHOULD HAVE A CAUSE TO BOAST.
Ephesians 2: 8–9.

GRACE is more than mercy. It is more than a multitude of tender mercies. Grace is more than love. It is more than innocent love. Grace is holy love, but it is holy love in spontaneous movement going out in eager quest toward the unholy and the unlovely, that by the ministry of its own sacrifice it might redeem the unholy and unlovely into its own strength and beauty.

The Grace of God is holy love on the move to thee and me, and the like of thee and me. It is God unmerited, undeserved, going out towards the children of men, that He might win them into the glory and brightness of His own likeness ... At the Cross the grim monarchies of sin and death die in the unutterable death of the Son of God. And it is all of Grace. "The gift of God is eternal life through Jesus Christ our Lord."

ARTHUR PORITT.

June 24th

THE OIL OF GLADNESS IS MINE IN ABUNDANCE. I CHEERFULLY POUR IT INTO THE LIVES OF ALL.

THERE is a story of an old man who carried a little can of oil with him everywhere he went, and if he passed through a door that squeaked, he poured a little oil on the hinges. If the gate was hard to open, he oiled the latch. And thus he passed through life lubricating the hard places and making it easier for those who came after him.

People called him eccentric, queer, and cranky, but the old man went steadily on, refilling his oil can when it became empty and oiling the hard places he found.

There are many lives that creak and grate harshly as they are lived day by day. Nothing goes right with them. They need lubricating with the oil of gladness, gentleness, and thoughtfulness. Have you your own oil can with you? Be ready with your oil of helpfulness in the early morning to the one nearest you. It may lubricate the whole day for him. The oil of good cheer to the downhearted one—Oh, how much it may mean! The word of courage to the despairing, let's speak it.

KATHLEEN V. MUSGRAVE,
Bournemouth.

June 25th

SOME OF YOUR GRIEFS YOU HAVE CURED ... AND THE SHARPEST YOU STILL HAVE SURVIVED ... BUT WHAT TORMENTS OF PAIN YOU ENDURED ... FROM EVILS THAT NEVER ARRIVED.

Credit: Old French proverb.

FEAR and lack of faith go hand in hand. The one is born of the other. Tell me how much one is given to fear, and I will tell you how much he lacks in faith. Fear is a most expensive guest to entertain, as also is worry: so expensive are they that no one can afford to entertain them.

We invite what we fear, just as, by a different attitude of mind, we invite and attract the influences and conditions we desire. The mind dominated by fear opens the door for the entrance of the very things, for the actualization of the conditions it fears.

"Where are you going?" asked an Eastern pilgrim on meeting the plague one day. "I am going to Baghdad to kill five thousand people," was the reply. A few days later the same pilgrim met the plague returning. "You told me you were going to Baghdad to kill five thousand people," said he, "but instead, you killed fifty thousand." "No," said the plague. "I killed only five thousand, as I told you I would; the others died of fright."

Fear can paralyze every muscle in the body. Fear affects the flow of blood, likewise the normal and healthy action of all the life forces. Fear can make the body rigid, motionless, and powerless to move.

Not only do we attract to ourselves the things we fear, but we also aid in attracting to others the conditions we, in our own minds, hold them in fear of. This we do in proportion to the strength of our own thought, and in the degree in which they are sensitively organised and so influenced by our thought, and this, although it is unconscious both on their part and on ours.

RALPH WALDO TRINE.
"In Tune with the Infinite"

WHO IS MY NEIGHBOUR?
From the drawing by Edmund J. Sullivan. Bibby's Annual.

June 26th

I ENJOY MUCH LOVE, MUCH LIFE—HEALTHY, VIBRANT AND ABOUNDING LIFE.

O GIVE me the joy of living ... And some glorious work to do ... A spirit of thanksgiving ... With loyal heart and true ... Some pathway to make brighter ... Where tired feet now stray ... Some burden to make lighter ... While 'tis day.

In the fields of the Master gleaning ... May my hands and heart be strong ... May I know life's deepest meaning ... May I sing life's sweetest song ... With some faithful friends to love me ... May I always do my best ... And at last with heaven above me ... Let me rest.

From an old Reward of Merit card.

June 27th

I HAVE WITHIN ME SOME KNOWN OR UNKNOWN TALENT THAT I HAVE NEVER BEEN AWARE OF ... I HOLD IN MY MIND THE IMAGE OF MYSELF SUCCEEDING ... AND MAKE THAT IMAGE BECOME FACT.

WHEN Alec Templeton came to our town, it seemed the whole town turned out to hear him play the piano. He was blind. Yet the magic of his fingers brought beautiful music from the piano such as we had never heard. He was witty and kept us laughing at his jokes. But, when he played, the audience grew strangely silent. We were listening to a master.

It is some years now since that night I heard Alec Templeton play. Yet, one scene stands out in my memory. It happened when he asked people in the audience to name three notes. The notes could be any three notes picked at random. Then, from these three notes, this blind pianist wove a melody.

From those notes he played a stirring march. Then the mood changed to a gay, capricious air, and eventually the notes became a lilting waltz. He played them as Beethoven might have used them. Or Wagner. When he finished, the audience went into ecstasies of applause.

Life gives to each person certain notes to play. At times, these notes may seem to be discordant. Life handed to Alec Templeton himself the tragic note of blindness. Yet, he was able to rise above that handicap and become a fine musician. It takes an artist to use the notes that are given, and to play a melody of beauty with them. But it can be done. Not alone, though, but by the grace and power of Almighty God—plus a great determination on your part.

HARLEIGH M. ROSENBERGER,
in "Sunshine" Magazine.

USE the talent you possess, for the woods would be very silent if no birds sang except the best.

From the Vagabond.

June 28th

I ACQUIRE A PURPOSE IN LIFE. I NOW LIVE CREATIVELY ... AND AM CONSTANTLY ON THE ALERT FOR NEW IDEAS.

CREATIVITY is a way of life. In 1928, Sir Alexander Fleming, British bacteriologist, was engaged in research on influenza. He noticed that mould had developed accidentally on a culture plate. It had created a bacteria-free circle around itself. This observation led to his Nobel prize-winning discovery of penicillin.

Important insights are rarely accidents. Creativity thrives in the presence of:

Awareness. We are most deeply aware, say psychologists, in the areas in which we are most intensely committed.

Curiosity. Searching for the "how" and "why" of things broadens our perspective. It nurtures our ability to judge.

Openness to new ideas. Thomas Edison, inventor, once said: "I'll try anything. I'll even try cheese!" The more we can keep the door open for a flow of ideas, the better the chance for usable solutions.

Patience with being unsettled. In the process of letting go of old answers and comfortable patterns there is anxiety. It is akin to the chemical process of fermentation which brings into being a new substance.

Sense of humour. Humour contains the same opposing elements found in most definitions of creative behaviour: playfulness and seriousness, originality and reality, non-sense and purpose, the irrational and the rational.

Living creatively is being ready for almost anything!

THE CHRISTOPHERS.

June 29th

TO ME, EVERY HOUR OF THE DAY AND NIGHT IS AN UNSPEAKABLE MIRACLE
Walt Whitman.

THE little Arizona town lay parched and lifeless in the heat of the day. The narrow, dusty streets were empty and quiet. At the foot of a sprawling hill of tailing deposited by the copper mill stood the house that was to be our home. In years gone by, it had been painted a dark green, but now it was peeling and dull.

Though I was only nine years old, I was thinking some pretty mournful thoughts as I looked at the drab surroundings, the misshapen tree next door, and I remembered the pleasant home we had left.

In a moment of silence I said in a plaintive voice, "Now we are really poor, aren't we?"

My mother looked at me. Then she said, with an edge in her voice, "Don't ever say we are poor, because we aren't, and we never will be as long as we look for the good things around us. There will be blessings here just as there are everywhere—if we have the eyes to see them. Now please go out and sweep the porch."

I picked up the stubby old broom and went outside. Soon the porch was clean and the sun had dropped suddenly out of sight. And then it happened. A few thin clouds turned to pink and lavender in the afterglow, and the hill of waste was bathed in a magical light. The neighbour's huge peach tree seemed to lean across our fence to drop a shower of lovely petals.

The whisper in my soul seemed to repeat the words of my mother: If we search with expectation and faith, we will always find a blooming tree to shower us with petals of hope.

JOSEPHINE MILLARD.
Sincere thanks to the author whose address we are unable to trace.

June 30th

IT IS MY GOOD FORTUNE TO OWN A FRIEND, I WILL DO ALL RATHER THAN LOSE HIM. I WILL LIVE AND LET LIVE, GIVE AND FORGIVE, RATHER THAN LOSE THE MOST PRECIOUS OF ALL EARTHLY POSSESSIONS.
Charles Kingsley.

NEW friends I cherish and treasure their worth,
But old friends to me are the salt of the earth.
Friends are like garments that everyone wears,
New ones are needed for dress-up affairs,
But when we're at leisure, we're more apt to choose
The clothes that we purchased with last season's shoes.

Things we grow used to are things we love best,
The ones we are certain have weathered the test.
And isn't it true, since we're talking of friends,
That new ones bring pleasure when everything blends?
But when we want someone who thinks as we do,
And who fits, as I said, like last summer's shoe,
We turn to the friends who have stuck through the years,
Who echo our laughter and dry up our tears.
They know every weakness and fault we possess,
But somehow forget them in friendship's caress.

The story is old, yet fragrant and sweet,
I've said it before, but just let me repeat,
New friends I cherish and treasure their worth,
But old friends to me are the salt of the earth
Author Unknown.

THE most I can do for my friend is simply to be his friend. I have no wealth to bestow on him. If he knows that I am happy in loving him, he will want no other reward. Is not friendship divine in this?
Henry David Thoreau.

July 1st

TO ME, EVERY MOMENT OF THE YEAR HAS ITS OWN BEAUTY ... I SEE, IN EVERY HOUR, A PICTURE WHICH HAS NEVER BEEN SEEN BEFORE ... AND WHICH WILL NEVER BE SEEN AGAIN.

Ralph Waldo Emerson.

BESIDES the singing and calling, there is a peculiar sound which is only heard in summer. Waiting quietly to discover what birds are about, I become aware of a sound in the very air. It is not the mid-summer hum which will soon be heard over the heated hay in the valley and over the cooler hills alike.

It is not enough to be called a hum, and does but just tremble at the extreme edge of hearing. If the branches wave and rustle they overbear it; the buzz of a passing bee is so much louder it overcomes all of it that is in the whole field. I cannot define it, except by calling the hours of winter to mind—they are silent; you hear a branch crack or creak as it rubs another in the wood, you hear the hoar frost crunch on the grass beneath your feet, but the air is without sound in itself.

The sound of summer is everywhere—in the passing breeze, in the hedge, in the broad-branching trees, in the grass as it swings; all the myriad particles that together make the summer are in motion. The sap moves in the trees, the pollen is pushed out from grass and flower, and yet again these acres and acres of leaves and square miles of grass blades—for they would cover acres and square miles if reckoned edge to edge—are drawing their strength from the atmosphere.

Exceedingly minute as these vibrations must be, their numbers perhaps may give them a volume almost reaching in the aggregate to the power of the ear. Besides the quivering leaf, the swinging grass, the fluttering bird's wing, and the thousand oval membranes which innumerable insects whirl about, a faint resonance seems to come from the very earth itself.

The fervour of the sunbeams descending in a tidal flood rings on the strung harp of earth. It is this exquisite undertone, heard and yet unheard, which brings the mind into sweet accordance with the wonderful instrument of nature.

RICHARD JEFFERIES.

19th century naturalist and writer. Son of a Wiltshire Farmer. Successful novel: The Gamekeeper at Home. Gifted with acute powers of description of Nature and the English countryside. From: The Story of My Heart, written when struggling with ill-health.

July 2nd

I STRIKE A TRUE BALANCE OF GIVE AND TAKE ... I KEEP MY HOME LIFE HAPPY

LET your marriage, if any, be a sharing of mutual interests, mutual accomplishments, as well as mutual affection. Let it strike a true balance of give and take. Now is the time for a husband to turn domestic, if he wants to. In one highly delightful household of my acquaintance, the husband (retired vice-president of a textile company) does all the marketing and cooking. He has become famous for his modernly prepared meals and all their friends are eager to be invited to dinner. His wife never liked cooking, and nowadays she is too busy. She has learned handloom weaving, has air-conditioned the attic, and is doing a thriving textile businesss of her own.

A marriage that refuses to grow old is an adventurous one, not bothered by tradition, not concerned about "what will people say?" Such a marriage can exemplify, in itself, all the special charms and advantages of the second half of life.

The first "must" for a well-balanced marriage is, of course, good health. Sound nutrition, regular checkups, plenty of sleep, exercise and rest.

The second "must" is good grooming. Carelessness in personal habits can wreck marriage, at any age; in later years it is inexcusable.

The third "must" is forget your children. They are grown up now. Forget that they are your children. Think of them as adults and friends. Give them love, a helping hand, advice when they ask for it. But live your own separate individual lives.

The fifth "must" is a very important one: keep your sense of humour. If you do not have a good one, develop it. A marriage seasoned with laughter, enriched by mature humour, can never grow stale.

GAYELORD HAUSER.
"Look Younger—Live Longer".
Reproduced by permission of Faber & Faber Ltd.

THE SPIRIT of a household reaches farther than from the front door to the back. It shines forth from a child's eyes and shows in the way a man hurries back to his home.

Author Unknown.

July 3rd

ENCOURAGEMENT, LIKE SUNLIGHT, MAKES ALL THINGS GROW ...

THE Bible tells us to train the child in the way he should go. But it also says, "Do not provoke your children, lest they become discouraged." Discipline is necessary, but understanding, love and encouragement help too.

The importance of encouragement was demonstrated one day when a boy discovered some bottles of coloured ink in his home. His mother had gone out, leaving him in charge of his little sister, Sally. The bottles were a temptation, and the boy began to paint Sally's portrait. In doing so, he made a terrible mess of things with ink blots all over.

When his mother returned she saw the mess but also saw the drawing. She said nothing about the blots but said, "Why, it's Sally!" Then she stooped and kissed her son.

The boy, Benjamin West, went on to become a world famous artist, who used to say proudly, "My mother's kiss made me a painter."

Her encouragement did more than any rebuke could ever do. We, too, need to look beyond the mess and see the beauty in every situation.

KEN MORTONSON.

July 4th

I WILL BE STILL. THERE IS STRENGTH IN SILENCE.

... IT HAS often occurred to me that a seeker after truth has to be silent. I know the wonderful efficacy of silence. I visited a monastery of Trappists in South Africa. A beautiful place it was. Most of the inmates of the place were under a vow of silence. I enquired of the father the motive of it and he said that "the motive is apparent. We are frail human beings. We do not know very often what we say. If we want to listen to the still small voice that is always speaking within us, it will not be heard if we continually speak." I understood that precious lesson. I know the secret of silence.

MAHATMA GANDHI.
One of the most magnetic personalities of India's history. Born October 2, 1869, at Potbandar, India. Son of merchant-class parents. Studied law in London, returning to India as a qualified barrister. Friend of Leo Tolstoy, Russian novelist, and of Thoreau, American naturalist. He developed his philosophy of non-violence for political ends.

July 5th

1 AM A FREEBORN CITIZEN IN THIS BOUNDLESS UNIVERSE. NOTHING CAN BIND ME, HOLD ME OR LIMIT ME BUT MY OWN OPINIONS AND MY OWN ACTIONS.

TODAY is here. I will start with a smile, and resolve to be agreeable. I will not criticize. I refuse to waste my valuable time.

Today has one thing in which I know I am equal with others—time. All of us draw the same salary in seconds, minutes, hours . . .

Today I will not waste my time, because the minutes I wasted yesterday are as lost as a vanished thought.

Today I refuse to spend time worrying about what might happen. I am going to spend my time making things happen . . .

Today I am determined to do things I should do. I firmly determine to stop doing the things I should not do.

Today I begin by doing, and not wasting my time. In one week I will be miles beyond the person I am today.

Today I will not imagine what I would do if things were different. They are not different. I will make success with what material I have.

Today I will stop saying, "If I had time", for I never will "find time" for anything—if I want it I must take it.

Today I will act toward other people as though this might be my last day on earth. I will not wait for tomorrow. Tomorrow never comes.

Author Unknown.

ARE you in earnest?   Seize this very minute;
What can you do, or dream you can, begin it;
Boldness has genius, power and magic in it.
Only engage, and then the mind grows heated,
Begin, and then the work will be completed.
—*Goethe.*

July 6th

IN LOVELY HARMONY THE WOOD HAS PUT ON ITS GREEN MANTLE, AND SUMMER IS ON THE THRONE, PLAYING ITS STRING MUSIC. THE WILLOW … NOW GIVES FORTH ITS MELODY—HUSH! LISTEN! THE WORLD IS ALIVE.

Thomas T. Evans.

HE SAID the pleasantest manner of spending a hot July day was lying from morning till evening on a bank of heath in the middle of the moors, with the bees humming dreamily about among the bloom, and the larks singing high up overhead, and the blue sky and bright sun shining steadily and cloudlessly.

That was his most perfect idea of heaven's happiness. Mine was rocking in a rustling green tree, with a west wind blowing, and bright white clouds flitting rapidly above; and not only larks, but throstles, and blackbirds, and linnets, and cuckoos pouring out music on every side, and the moors seen at a distance, broken into cool, dusky dells. I loved the great swells of long grass undulating in waves to the breeze; and woods and sounding water, and the whole world awake and wild with joy.

EMILY BRONTE,
British poet and novelist, 1818–48.

July 7th

MY HEART LIFTS TO A SILENT SKY BEFORE DAWN, THE CLEAN TOUCH OF FROST ON QUEEN'S LACE, AND A PALE WINTER SUN RISING BETWEEN NAKED TREES.

IT IS the great mystery of human life that old grief passes gradually into quiet, tender joy. The mild serenity of age takes the place of the riotous blood of youth. I bless the rising sun each day, and, as before, my heart sings to meet it, but now I love even more its setting, its long slanting rays and the soft, tender, gentle memories that come with them, the dear images from the whole of my long, happy life—and over all the Divine Truth, softening, reconciling, forgiving!

My life is ending, I know that well, but every day that is left me I feel how my earthly life is in touch with a new infinite, unknown, but approaching life, the nearness of which sets my soul quivering with rapture, my mind glowing and my heart weeping with joy.

DOSTOEVSKY.
The Brothers Karamazov.

July 8th

> TO HAVE FAITH IS TO CREATE ... TO HAVE HOPE IS TO CALL DOWN BLESSING ... TO HAVE COMPASSION IS TO WORK MIRACLES.
>
> *Michael Fairless.*

DURING World War II, 10,000 soldiers—many the remnants of the Bataan Death March—were eking out survival in a Japanese prisoner of war camp.

Intolerable living conditions—overcrowding, vermin, no beds, no baths, no toilet facilities, barely enough water for drinking, and grossly inadequate food supplies had pushed the death rate to more than 100 prisoners monthly.

One day a pigeon broke its wing flying into an overhead power line. A man rushed to pick it up. Though starving, he didn't kill it. Instead, he took it to a doctor, who was also a prisoner. The doctor improvised a miniature splint from a stick and some twine.

After that the man made the bird a constant companion, sharing with it his few grains of rice. Soon other men began to offer part of their meagre rations also. They watched as the bird's wing began to heal, offering advice and help. Then compassion worked a strange and wonderful miracle. In this one compound during the next few months, the death rate dropped 60 per cent.

HARRY F. BEARSE.

July 9th

> A GENTLE WORD IS NEVER LOST;
> OH, NEVER THEN REFUSE ONE.
> IT CHEERS THE HEART WHEN ABOUT I'M BOSSED,
> AND LULLS THE CARES THAT BRUISE ONE.
>
> *Author Unknown.*

HE HAS achieved success who has lived well, laughed often, and loved much; who has gained the respect of intelligent men, and the love of little children; who has filled his niche and accomplished his task; who has left the world better than he found it, whether by an improved poppy, a perfect poem, or a rescued soul; who has never lacked appreciation of earth's beauty, or failed to express it; who has always looked for the best in others and given the best he had; whose life was an inspiration; whose memory a benediction.

B. A. STANLEY.

July 10th

I LEARN TO ACCEPT GRACE FROM WHATEVER SOURCE IT SPRINGS. MY MIND IS AS OPEN AS A UNIVERSE OF STARS IN WHICH IS FOUND A PLACE FOR THE LOVE OF SIMPLE THINGS.

FOR a few days recently I was snowed in at home—alone. I was alone but not lonely.

Some of my most cherished books were re-read. What faithful companions, what proven friends they are!

The best of music stirred and enriched my soul. How fortunate are we who can hear and appreciate great music.

Treasured paintings that have hung on the walls for years suddenly revealed new facets of beauty and inspiration as I took time to study and see them anew.

Gradually I became grateful for each log which I somewhat reluctantly and almost reverently placed on the hearth. The fireplace became more than the focus of my attention—it had taken on spiritual qualities. It had become an altar.

Gratitude became an unceasing prayer. Stark, barren trees were transformed into majestic, living statues.

What joy, what blessings await us in hours of solitude, where we can be alone but not lonely.

WILLIAM ARTHUR WARD,
In "Sunshine" Magazine.

SUCH is the mystery of Grace . . . it never comes too late.

Francois Mauriac.

July 11th

WITH SUMMER GRIEF GIVES PLACE TO JOY … SKIES ARE BLUE, FLOWERS IN COLOURFUL ARRAY … EVERYTHING IS RADIANT NOW.

THE love which speaks and sings and sighs in one part of creation is revealed in the other half in the form of flowers. All this efflorescence, with its wealth of forms and colours and perfumes, which gives splendour to the fields, is the expression of love, is love itself, which celebrates its sweet mysteries in the bosom of every flower. The blossoming branch, the bird that perches thereon to sing or build his nest, the man who gazes at the branch and at the bird, are all moved by the same principle at different degrees of perfection.

Maurice De Guérin.

July 12th

THE SWEETEST OF SOUNDS IS PRAISE … I THINK OF THOSE AROUND ME … I ENCOURAGE OTHERS … GOOD WORK!

ENCOURAGEMENT. Derived from the Latin "cor" or "heart", this word is plainly defined as "to give heart". Webster's Dictionary tells us that to encourage is to "give courage, hope or confidence, to; to give support or help".

How often have you yourself felt discouraged, and all it took to get your motivation in gear was the enthusiastic encouragement of a friend? When you encourage others, you build.

Sometimes, people become discouraged simply because they lack the support of family and friends. By telling them, "you can do it" or "I give you credit for trying so hard, don't give up," you fuel their perseverance and help them fulfil their potential. Encouragement is a welcome display of support and love that says, "I believe in you!"

Children have a special need for encouragement. Parents can express support by assisting them in homework or offering a ride to some after-school activity. In every task a child undertakes, there lies an opportunity for parents to offer encouragement.

In a study to determine how best to motivate employees, a large business company found that "our people just wanted to be recognised for the job they do. The good old-fashioned 'pat on the back' did more to satisfy needs than anything."

The Christophers.

July 13th

I ACCEPT THE LAWS OF NATURE. I WILL BREATHE MORE PURE AIR, CONSUME FEWER 'CONVENIENCE' FOODS, AND REDUCE STRESS THROUGH EXERCISE. MY SENSE OF CONFIDENCE AND WELL-BEING RISES DAILY.

HEALTH comes from obedience to natural laws; disease is the result of their violation.

Man must know himself to comprehend Nature; he must study Nature to understand himself; his highest comprehension of God comes from his knowledge of himself and Nature, and their relation to each other.

The study of man and Nature is the study of health, the highest revelation of God in Nature, the foundation of strength, beauty, intellect, and happiness. Health is the greatest of blessings because it includes all the other blessings; it is also the simplest and most easily attained.

Health comes from the simple life of Nature, disease from the artificial life of civilization. A state of disease is but a partial life. A sick man is more or less dead. Health is the fullness of life.

Heat and cold up to a certain point stimulate the vital powers; carried too far they are alike debilitating. In breathing the air of a crowded and unventilated room you inhale the breath of other people and not only get less oxygen than you require and more carbonic acid than is good for you, but you also take in noxious effluvia, diseased emanations, and impurities. There is no disease which may not be aggravated by breathing impure air.

The natural diet of adult man consists of seeds, fruits, and roots. The vegetable world offers us a vast variety of healthful foods.

T. L. NICHOLS, M.D.
Secrets of Health.

MORNING IN THE STUDIO, AEDILEA
By Patrick William Adam, 1854 - 1930.
By courtesy of Sotheby's, London.

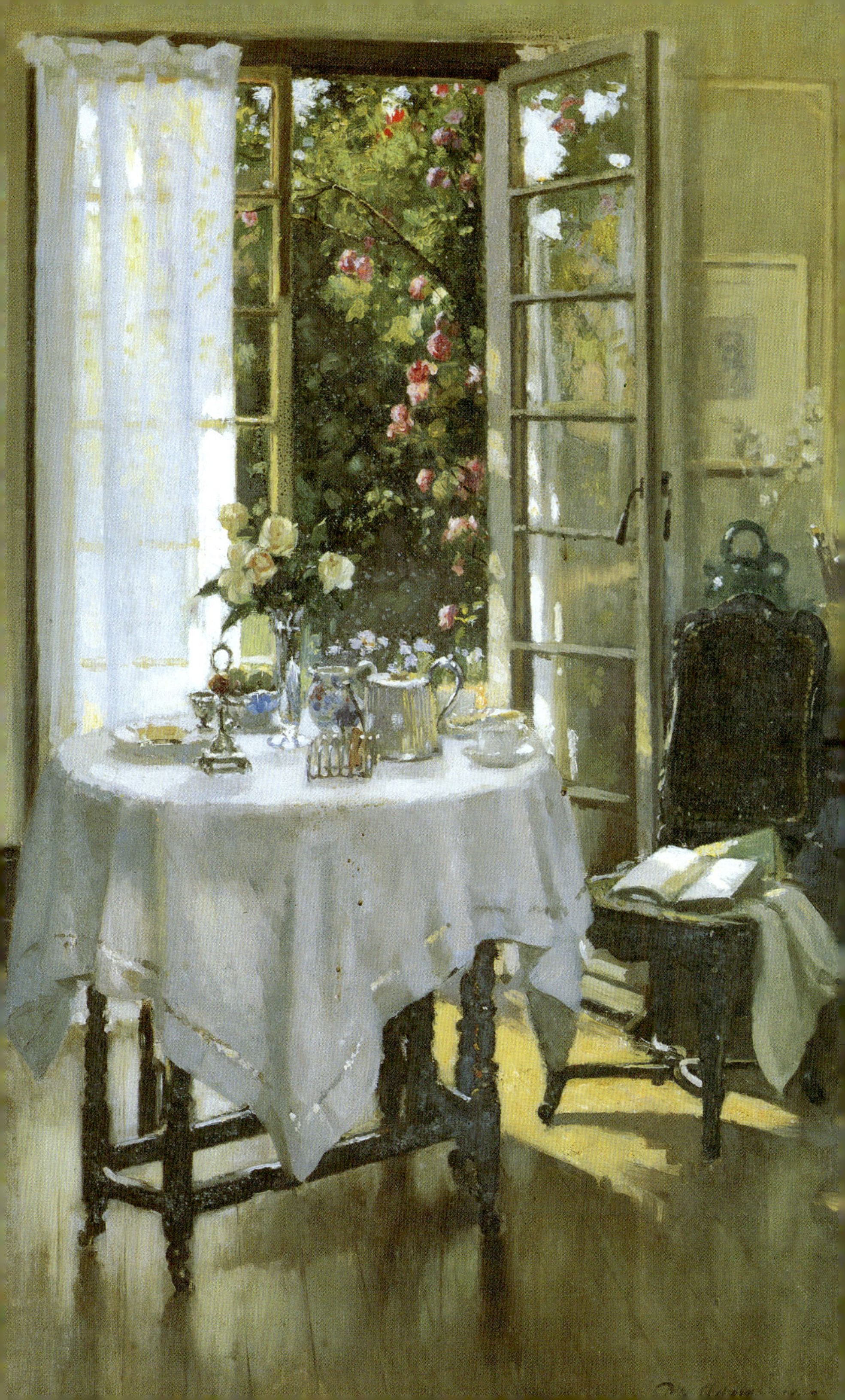

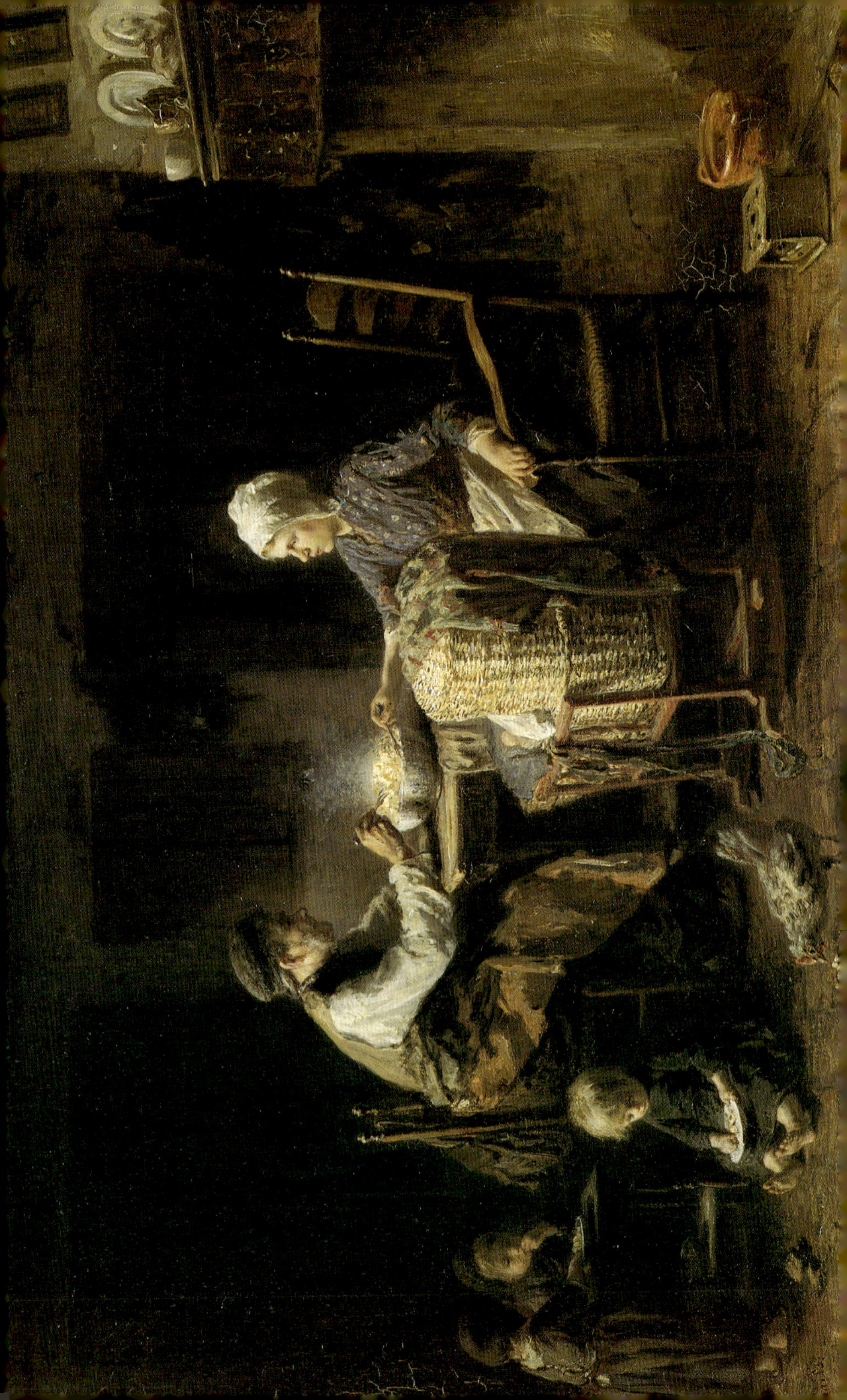

July 14th

I TAKE TIME OFF TO WALK. I WALK MYSELF INTO FITNESS.

'WALKING not only activates circulation of the blood, it also speeds up and intensifies respiration and enables greater absorption of oxygen ... The body of the walker is absolutely free, the feet only are put periodically on the earth and rolled off. In no other position ... will blood circulation be nearly as free ... Walking in addition, brings a whole orchestra of large and small muscles into action and to an accord ... Their "eurythmic" ... sends the blood towards the heart as the valves of the heart only allow this direction ... Walking has a healing influence and balances large and small psychical troubles and conflicts ... With the distance from home one also gains distance more easily from the miseries of the world. Perspectives, the "blue horizons" enable personal grievances to be put in a better proportion to the sorrow rucksack of the world ... a walk taken in harmony with nature very often replaces the psychiatrist.'

Dr Felix Oesch.
Medical Commissioner, City of Berne.

The All-Provider

Providence never fails the heart that trusts her. It is truly amazing how provision can be made in a very tangible way for physical sustenance in time of need. It may be small in time of extremity. But however humble the circumstances a simple trust will not go unrewarded.

Joseph Israels excelled in painting the beauty of contemporary life. Here, he mirrors with tender and unfailing sympathy a touching human situation. Grace has been said. The family settles down to a meal won by an honest day's work. They are poor by today's standards. We live like princes on twenty times their wealth. A soft ethereal light hallows the humble bowl of porridge. Standards of living have increased fantastically. But some things remain the same. One thing is Gratitude, which begets its own special blessing and assurance. True, man does not live by bread alone. But it goes a long way towards his survival. No matter how uncertain the world's future food supplies, a rich inner contentment rises like a spring in a thirsty land to sustain the family which has learnt to rely on the El Shaddai—the All-Provider.

Thomas.

THE FRUGAL MEAL,
from the painting by Israels.
By kind permission of the Glasgow Art Gallery and Museum.

July 15th

> HE WHO BLESSES MOST IS BLEST ...
> AND GOD AND MAN SHALL OWN HIS WORTH
> WHO TOILS TO LEAVE AT HIS BEQUEST
> AN ADDED BEAUTY ON THE EARTH.
>
> *Whittier.*

WHEN I go from here, I want to leave behind me a world that will be richer for the experience of me.

I want the creatures—the animals and birds—to be a little less afraid of human beings because they have known me, because I have blessed them and love them and, far from doing them any harm, have done them good.

I want to leave trees that are rustling with my thoughts, trees that have heard me speaking to them when we were alone together; trees that, one day, long after my form has disappeared, shall still in some mysterious way, cherish in their very beings their secret knowledge of me, so that others who shelter from the rain or who seek shade under their branches, shall catch the peace that went out from me.

I want to leave the whole of Nature nearer to the whole of man. I want to store up riches in the wind, and to leave blessings travelling upward to the stars. I want to leave my peace in the grass. I want the tears that I have shed for the sake of high love to come again in the dew. I want to leave Nature richer for having known me.

I want to leave my fellow man more sure that there is a Divinity that shapes his ends. I want to leave him with a wider vision and a greater sense of purpose. I want to leave him with the knowledge that death is nothing and that life is everything.

When I go from here, I want to leave behind me a deeper sense of God.

Derek Neville.

SYMPATHY with nature is evidence of perfect health. You cannot perceive beauty but with a serene mind.

Henry David Thoreau, 1817 - 1862.

July 16th

BUILD A STURDY FENCE OF TRUST AROUND TODAY,
FILL THE SPACE WITH LOVING WORK, AND THEREIN STAY.
LOOK NOT THROUGH SHELTERING BARS UPON TOMORROW
GOD WILL HELP YOU BEAR WHAT COMES, OF JOY OR
SORROW.

Author unknown.

MY FRIENDS: No one, not in my situation, can appreciate my feeling of sadness at this parting. To this place, and the kindness of these people, I owe everything. Here I have lived a quarter of a century, and have passed from a youth to an old man. Here my children have been born and one is buried. I now leave, not knowing when or whether I may return, with a task before me greater than that which rested upon Washington. Without the assistance of that Divine Being who ever attended him, I cannot succeed. With that assistance, I cannot fail. Trusting in Him who can go with me, and remain with you, and be everywhere for good, let us confidently hope that all will yet be well. To His care commending you, as I hope in your prayers you will commend me, I bid you an affectionately farewell.

ABRAHAM LINCOLN,
on leaving Springfield, Illinois, for Washington, D.C.

July 17th

THIS DAY IS A NEW BEGINNING FOR ME. I GO FORWARD
EAGER, HAPPY AND UNAFRAID. NOTHING IS IMPOSSIBLE.

"A FASCINATING medical theory is being propounded by one of Britain's most eminent surgeons. He is convinced that a cheerful state of mind can by itself cure certain diseases. The idea that an easy mind can help with the healing of ulcers and tuberculosis is striking enough. But Sir Heneage Oglivie, surgeon to Guy's Hospital, London, goes much further. He suggests the revolutionary idea that happiness keeps the growth of the body cells under proper control. That means happiness can prevent cancer. Often, as he says in 'The Lancet', he caught himself thinking about a professional colleague: 'So-and-so has started to look unhappy. He's either unhappy because he's got cancer or he is going to get cancer because he's unhappy.' In a few months that doctor died. Sir Heneage has noticed that cancer frequently starts immediately after some disaster, such as a death in the patient's family, the break-up of a close relationship or a financial crisis."

New Zealand Truth.

The Night Has a Thousand Eyes

The night has a thousand eyes,
And the day but one;
Yet the light of the bright world dies
With the dying sun.

The mind has a thousand eyes,
And the heart but one;
Yet the light of a whole life dies
When love is done.
Francis William Bourdillon, 1852 - 1921.

July 18th

SCORNING ALL THE CARE THAT FATE AND FORTUNE BRINGS, I MAKE THE HEAVEN MY BOOK, MY WISDOM HEAVENLY THINGS.

Thomas Campion.

THERE is always a little fire of wood on the open hearth in the kitchen when I get home at night; the old lady says it is "company" for her, and sits in the lonely twilight, her knotted hands lying quiet on her lap, her listening eyes fixed on the burning sticks.

I wonder sometimes whether she hears music in the leap and lick of the fiery tongues, music such as he of Bayreuth draws from the violins till the hot energy of the fire spirit is on us, embodied in sound. She hears some voice, that lonely old woman on whom is set the seal of great silence. (She was deaf and dumb.)

It is a great truth tenderly said that God builds the nest for the blind bird; and may it not be that He opens closed eyes and unstops deaf ears to sights and sounds from which others by these very senses are debarred?

Here the best of us see through a mist of tears men as trees walking; it is only in the land which is very far off and yet very near that we shall have fullness of sight and see the King in His beauty; and I cannot think that any listening ears listen in vain.

MICHAEL FAIRLESS.
"The Roadmender" (Duckworth).

FAIR QUIET, have I found thee here?
Andrew Marvell.

July 19th

ACCEPTANCE IS AN ESSENTIAL PRINCIPLE OF NATURE. BEHIND ALL MOVEMENT THERE IS REST; BEHIND ALL SOUND THERE IS STILLNESS; BEHIND A BUSY LIFE THERE IS A POOL OF QUIET WITHIN.

NOTHING that happens in the world happens by chance. God is a God of order. Everything is arranged upon definite principles, and never at random. The world, even the religious world, is governed by law. The Christian experiences are governed by law. Men, forgetting this, expect Rest, Joy, Peace, Faith, to drop into their souls from the air like snow or rain. But in point of fact they do not do so; and if they did they would no less have their origin in previous activities and be controlled by natural laws. Rain and snow do drop from the air, but not without a long previous history. They are the mature effects of former causes. Equally so are Rest, and Peace, and Joy. They, too, have each a previous history. Storms and winds and calms are not accidents, but are brought about by antecedent circumstances. Rest and Peace are but calms in man's inward nature, and arise through causes as definite and as inevitable. Realize it thoroughly. It is a methodical not an accidental world.

HENRY DRUMMOND.
From "The Greatest Thing in the World".

July 20th

NOW IS THE TIME TO FORGET THE QUARREL AND MEND THE FRIENDSHIP. GOODWILL AND SOFT WORDS HAVE BROUGHT MANY A DIFFICULT THING TO PASS.

MEND a quarrel. Search out a forgotten friend. Dismiss suspicion and replace it with trust. Write a love letter. Share some treasure. Give a soft answer. Encourage youth. Manifest your loyalty in a word or deed.

Keep a promise. Find the time. Forgo a grudge. Forgive an enemy. Listen. Apologize if you were wrong. Try to understand. Flout envy. Examine your demands on others. Think first of someone else. Appreciate, be kind, be gentle. Laugh a little more.

Deserve confidence. Take up arms against malice. Decry complacency. Express your gratitude. Worship your God. Gladden the heart of a child. Take pleasure in the beauty and wonder of the earth. Speak your love. Speak it again. Speak it still once again.

AUTHOR UNKNOWN.

July 21st

A THING OF BEAUTY IS A JOY FOREVER—ESPECIALLY WHEN EVERYTHING GOES WRONG.

EVERYTHING seemed to go wrong that long-ago winter when I was in boarding school near a small Vermont village. Heavy snowstorms virtually imprisoned us. Then the water pipes froze, and water had to be rationed.

At first the other students enjoyed the extra ice-skating, skiing and sledging; but I, a city-bred 15, was not adept at winter sports. I guess I became the leader in the griping and irritability that followed. I wanted to return home to the city and the warm comforts of "civilized living".

One morning we students went to the frozen lake to watch some men from town cut ice. The men sang as they worked. They looked frozen but happy. Their mood was contagious, and soon all the students were singing with them.

I looked about me at the lake's smooth mirrored ice, the snow-covered hills and the trees lining the lake. Bent with the weight of snow, they looked like ballet dancers taking a bow. In a special moment of truth, I saw that the country had a loveliness all its own. I had been so occupied with what I did not like, with the discomforts, that I had missed the real beauty about me.

That moment of awareness not only made me appreciate that time and place but, in years since. has helped me to adapt to other inconveniences and seek out the good in bad situations.

LILIAN GARDNER.

July 22nd

MY FRIENDS RESPOND TO A POSITIVE SUGGESTION. I WILL NOT HESITATE TO EMBOLDEN AND INCREASE CONFIDENCE OF SUCCESS IN TIMES OF DESPAIR AND DOUBT. ENCOURAGEMENT IS A GREAT INVIGORATOR.

EDWARD Steichen, who eventually became one of the world's most renowned photographers, almost gave up the day he shot his first pictures.

At 16, young Steichen bought a camera and took 50 photos. Only one turned out—a portrait of his sister at the piano.

Edward's father thought that was a poor showing. But his mother insisted that the photograph of his sister was so beautiful that it more than compensated for 49 failures.

Her encouragement convinced the youngster to stick with his new hobby. He stayed with it for the rest of his life. But it had been a close call.

What tipped the scales? A person who had enough vision to spot a little excellence in the midst of a lot of failure; who cared enough to point out a small achievement instead of dwelling on obvious shortcomings; who gave a gentle word of encouragement instead of a thoughtless putdown.

Each of us faces choices every day. Our decisions may not drastically affect anyone's life. But they might. We won't know in advance. One thing is certain—if we don't choose to "build up", we'll never know. Why build up? The strain in our communities, our nation and our world show too clearly the results of the "me first" attitude. It is better to light one candle than to curse the darkness.

THE CHRISTOPHERS.

ALL the darkness of the world cannot put out the light of one small candle.

Author Unknown.

July 23rd

I BELIEVE THE POWER BEHIND ME IS GREATER THAN THE ODDS AGAINST ME ... DAFFODILS CAN DO IT ... WHY CAN'T I?

IT WAS earlier this year that we first noticed the curious little humps which appeared at intervals in the smooth pathway of our garden. All the more curious considering the fact that just prior to our removal here, the pathway had been re-surfaced with a thick layer of tar macadam.

Had the time of year been summer instead of winter, we might have supposed that the strong rays of the sun had melted the tar and drawn these parts of the pathway upward—but even that would have seemed improbable—the surface of the pathway seemed so firm and solid. Ant hills: we considered the idea.

"It is probably the roots of a tree," said my husband, "They are very strong and it is surprising how far they can reach out."

Each week we watched the little humps continue to grow, until at last one day, like miniature mountains in eruption, the tops of the humps burst open to reveal delicate green shoots of bulbs. We looked at them in amazement. Tender green shoots pushing through the tarmac!

Just down the road, on the main thoroughfare, some men were boring through the tarmac to dig a hole for an electric cable. To get through the pavement they were using a noisy pneumatic drill. In one sense, what was happening on the road was happening in our garden—tarmac was being removed for a purpose. The noisy hurried power of the drill; the silent, patient power of nature.

LILIAN GREAVES.
Grange-over-Sands, Lancashire.

July 24th

> HERE IN MY HEART IS ALL THE GOLD
> THAT I SHALL EVER OWN;
> HERE ARE THE MEMORIES OF OLD;
> THE FRIENDS THAT I HAVE KNOWN.
>
> *Robert Hill.*

I HAVE been living in England for just over three years. In the dark days of 1940 I was one with you in the decision to resist the Germans. I shared your joy in success and I shared your confidence in final victory. I made many real friends to whom I must now say or write my farewell.

During these three years, in the towns and villages of Great Britain, in trains and on roads, in parks and streets, in shops and shelters, pubs and clubs, in drawing-rooms and in factories, so many faces smiled at me, so many eyes greeted me, so many friendly hands shook mine, and so many lips spoke a kindly welcome to me.

They all belong to friends whose names and addresses are unknown to me. This letter to you, Sir, is the only way I can say goodbye to your people, whom I have found to be the kindest people in the world. To say through your columns "I thank you" is the only way in which I can make a small repayment for so much that they have given me.

I am leaving here soon. To me it seems to be the way home. Home—where I was with all my feeling, with all my memories, with every wish and thought. I dreamt how wonderful it would be and how happy I should be when the time came to return. But it was not so. My heart is heavy with the sadness of leaving something one loves.

I say thank you to all my friends whose names and addresses I do not know, but whom I know as the English people. Behind this short phrase "I thank you" is so much affection for you that I am unable to say goodbye; I say to you au revoir. Yours affectionately,

CZECHOSLOVAK OFFICER.
"The Times", *October 19th, 1943.*

July 25th

> I HAVE BEEN DRIVEN MANY TIMES TO MY KNEES BY THE OVERWHELMING CONVICTION THAT I HAD NOWHERE ELSE TO GO. MY OWN WISDOM, AND THAT OF ALL ABOUT ME, SEEMED INSUFFICIENT FOR THE DAY.
>
> *Lincoln.*

THE boy, Abe Lincoln, was only nine when his mother, Nancy Hanks Lincoln, died. Nine years seems a brief allotment for a mother to impress a child for life; but so deep was the influence of Nancy on the impressionable Abe that in later life Lincoln declared, "All that I am or hope to be, I owe to my angel mother."

Why was Nancy Lincoln so special to her son? She was just an ordinary woman given to the hard labours of a rugged frontier. Her life was brief and simple, but impressions she made upon the heart of her son truly lasted.

Adversity contended with Abraham Lincoln all the days of his life. During the trying years in the White House, grave problems burdened his mind and tested his spirit. When there seemed no other place to go for counsel and solace, Lincoln, by his own admission, went on his knees. He had learned early in life where to seek wisdom.

In his youth, Abe Lincoln's mother had taught him—by precept and example—the simple principle of prayer. Little Abe had knelt at his mother's knee. He had heard his mother talk with God. Years later he said, "I remember my mother's prayers and they have always followed me. They have clung to me all my life."

Lawrence R. Giles.
In "Sunshine" Magazine.

July 26th

JUST LOOK AHEAD TO TOMORROW ... AND TRUST YOU'LL FIND WAITING THERE ... THE SUNLIGHT THAT SEEMED TO BE HIDDEN ... BY YESTERDAY'S CLOUDS OF DESPAIR.
Helen Steiner Rice.

AN ENFORCED holiday in bed blamelessly releases us from a too-busy world, sharpens our mental and spiritual perceptions and permits a clearer perspective on our lives ... We enter a realm of introspection and self-analysis. We think soberly, perhaps for the first time, about our past and future. Former values are seen to be fallacious; habitual courses of action appear weak, foolish or stubborn. Illness, it seems, gives us that rarest thing in the world—a second chance, not only at health but at life itself!

Even pain confers spiritual insight, a beauty of outlook, a philosophy of life, an understanding and forgiveness of humanity—in short, a quality of peace and serenity—that can scarcely be acquired by the "owner of pure horse flesh". Suffering is a cleansing fire that chars away much of the meanness, triviality and restlessness of so-called "health". Milton declared, "Who best can suffer, best can do". The proof is his "Paradise Lost", written after he was stricken blind.

If you have never been sick, never lost so much as a day in bed—then you have missed something! When your turn comes, don't be dismayed. Remind yourself that pain and suffering may teach you something valuable, something that you could not have learned otherwise. Possibly it may change for the better the entire course of your life.

LOUIS E. BISCH, MD.
Sincere thanks to the author whose address we are unable to trace.

July 27th

I AM LEARNING TO DO ONE THING AT A TIME … ONLY THUS CAN I PRACTISE CONCENTRATION … THE GENTLE ART OF CONTROLLING THE ATTENTION.

Dr. Austen F. Rigg.

IN HANDLING troubles, I have taken as my motto the words of an old parrot that my father used to tell me about.

The parrot was kept in a cage hanging over the doorway in a hunting club in Pennsylvania. As the members of the club passed through the door, the parrot repeated over and over the only words he knew:

"One at a time, gentlemen, one at a time!"

Father taught me to handle my troubles that way: "One at a time, gentlemen, one at a time!"

I have found taking my troubles one at a time has helped me to maintain calm and composure amidst pressing duties and unending engagements.

SIR WILLIAM OSLER.

Sir William Osler, (1849–1919) British physician. Born in Canada. Regius professor of medicine at Oxford. Created a baronet in 1911. Distinguished for his work on diseases of the blood and spleen.

July 28th

I FILL MY MIND WITH THOUGHTS OF HAPPINESS, HEALTH, STRENGTH AND FRIENDS.

TEACH your child to understand the law of attraction. Let them know that if they form certain habits, and continue them until they become thoroughly fixed in their minds, they have through the power of thought become related to all people thinking and doing the things that have occupied their attention.

For instance, if it has been your habit to find fault with people, to criticize, through this habit of criticism all the fault-finding people of the world have become related to you.

If you are in the habit of thinking kindly and saying kind words, in a short time you will become mentally related to all kindly natured people in the world, and you will have the force of their kind loving thoughts pouring in upon you so that it will be easier for you to say a kind word than the reverse.

By indulging in healthy thoughts you attract to yourself everything necessary for your well-being—happiness, health, strength and friends.

HAMILTON WRIGHT MABIE.

July 29th

I NEVER FEAR BEING ALONE ... BECAUSE I AM NOT ALONE.

TEARS glistened in the eyes of Salvation Army Officer Shaw as he looked at the three men before him. Shaw was a medical missionary who had just arrived in India. It was the turn of the century, and the Salvation Army was taking over the care of the leper colony.

But these three lepers had manacles and fetters binding their hands and feet, cutting the diseased flesh. Captain Shaw turned to the guard and said, "Please unfasten the chains."

"It isn't safe," the guard replied. "These men are dangerous criminals as well as lepers."

"I'll be responsible. They're suffering enough," Captain Shaw said, as he put out his hand and took the keys. Then he knelt on the ground, tenderly removed the shackles and treated their bleeding ankles.

About two weeks later Captain Shaw had his first misgivings about freeing the criminals. He had to make an overnight trip and dreaded leaving his wife and child alone.

But his wife was also a Salvation Army officer whose life was dedicated to God. She insisted that she was not afraid.

The next morning when she went to her front door, she was startled to see the three criminals lying on her steps.

One explained, "We know doctor go. We stay here so no harm come to you." This was how 'dangerous men' responded to an act of love.

Evelyn Wick Smith.

July 30th

LORD, HELP ME TO REMEMBER THAT NOTHING IS GOING TO HAPPEN TO ME TODAY THAT YOU AND I TOGETHER CAN'T HANDLE.
Dr Norman Vincent Peale.

I'M A little old lady in my late 60s and I would like to tell you and all the ones that have no faith that with the power of faith one can achieve miracles. I'm sorry I have no education and can't even spell right, but I'm going to try to relate to you my first great problem of my life and how I did draw on the power of faith.

I was born with dislocation of both my hips and doctors said I would never walk, but as I grew up and looked at others walk I said to myself, "Please, God, help me. I know You love me." I was six years old and my heart was broke and so one day I tryed to stand up between two chairs and down I would go but I didn't give up. Every day I'd speak to God and tried again and again until I held myself up for a few seconds and I can't describe to you the joy in my heart being able to stand on my feet. I gave one scream to mama. "I'm up! I can walk!"

Then I went down again. I can't never forget the joy of my parents and when I tried again my mother handed me the end of a broomstick while she held the other end and said, "Give one step forward with one foot and then another," and that is how my faith helped me to walk the duck walk, that's what the doctors call it but I have been so grateful ever since then.

Three years ago I had an accident and I broke my left ankle and was in the hospital and they took X-rays of my legs. Then the doctors came to me and said lady how did you walk? And I said God was my doctor and they said it's a miracle you have no sockets and no joints on your hips how did you stand up? And memories came back to me and I have waited 60 years to find out that I have no sockets and no joints for I never knew why.

Then the doctors were afraid that with the accident and broken ankle and my age I would not walk again but God came to my rescue again and to the surprise of all I'm walking again, and still holding my job of taking care of four children of a widow mother while she works. I'm a widow too and had to work very hard to grow my children. My husband died with the Spanish flu. I had two little girls and a son was born two months later. I scrubbed floors on my knees for 17 years and never was sick in my life. I don't know what a headache is.

Letter received by DR NORMAN VINCENT PEALE,
from a woman who told of learning to walk when it was assumed she could never possibly do so. From: Treasury of Joy and Enthusiasm. (Foundation for Christian Living).

July 31st

WORK AND LIFE GO TOGETHER. EVERY DAY I ENJOY SO MUCH WORK—AN EXCITING, STRONG AND HEALTHY EXPRESSION OF ABOUNDING ENERGY AND VITALITY.

A NATURAL activity has saved me from many of the dangers of inactivity, but on certain occasions when I have been forced, or have given myself up to doing nothing. I have been able to estimate to the full the injurious and disintegrating effects of idleness. I really believe that it alone can cause illness, and that every invalid ought to work except when he is really unable to owing to extreme ill-health. I do not mean making a mere show of being occupied, or making efforts to fill up the empty hours with fruitless "pastimes", but real work, such as acquiring, or methodically bringing to perfection, some branch of knowledge or a language, or even embarking on some career compatible with confinement in bed.

But, you say, we all need distraction and relaxation. Granted, so let a certain amount of time be allotted to it. But the life of an invalid should not, any more than any other life, be spent in finding out ways of amusing oneself or drowning one's woes, but rather in discovering possibilities of setting one's forces to real work. For the "pastime", without other aim than that of "killing time", often calls for an expenditure of energy and application which amounts to no more than would be required for an occupation which might be useful to somebody else, or in some other way.

Killing time! But time is life. It must not be killed but utilized and made fruitful. Even were one paralyzed in all four limbs, as long as the mind can work clearly there exists not only the possibility but the duty of action.

Many people look upon work as slavery. Sickness should teach them that it is freedom.

Franco Pastorelli,
in *The Glorious Bondage of Illness.*

ONCE UPON A TIME . .
Manor County Primary School, Braintree, England.
Photograph by Dennis Mansell.

AMONG THE thousands of tiny things growing up all over the land, some of them under my very wing — watched and tended, unwatched and untended, loved, unloved, protected from danger, thrust into temptation — among them somewhere is the child who will write the novel that will stir men's hearts to nobler issues and incite them to better deeds.

There is the child who will paint the greatest picture or carve the greatest statue of the age . . . another who will deliver his country in an hour of peril . . . another who will give his life for a great principle . . . and another, born more of the spirit than of the flesh, who will live continually on the heights of moral being, and dying, draw men after him.

It may be that I shall preserve one of these children to the race . . . It is a peg big enough on which to hang a hope, for every child born into the world is a new incarnate thought of God, an ever-fresh and radiant possibility.

Kate Douglas Wiggin.

_{Our sincere thanks to the author who we have been unable to contact.}

August 1st

I DESIRE NO MORE THAN FALLS TO MY LOT ... WHAT GOD SENDS I ACCEPT WITH THANKFULNESS ... THIS TRUTH MAKES ME FREE ... I HAVE NO FEAR.

FLEE from the crowd and dwell in truthfulness ... Suffice you with your gifts, though they be small ... To hoard brings hate, to climb brings giddiness ... The crowd has envy, and success blinds all ... Desire no more than to your lot may fall ... Work well yourself, to counsel others clear ... And truth shall make you free, there is no fear!

Torment you not all crooked to redress ... Nor put your trust in fortune's turning ball ... Great peace is found in little busyness ... And war but kicks against the sharpened awl ... Strive not, you earthen pot, to break the wall ... Subdue yourself and others you shall hear ... and truth shall make you free, there is no fear!

What God shall send, receive in gladsomeness ... To wrestle for this world foretells a fall ... Here's not your home, here's but a wilderness ... Ever onward pilgrim; up, beast and leave your stall ... Know your country, look up, and thank God for all ... Hold the high way, your soul the pioneer ... And truth shall make you free, there is no fear!

GEOFFREY CHAUCER (1340–1400).
Father of English poetry. His most famous book: "The Canterbury Tales", a remarkable account of the life of his time, with a deep understanding of human nature.

Inspiration

I wonder if the human touch, which people have, is not one of the greatest assets that you can have. You meet some people, and immediately you feel their warmth of mind or heart. You read a book, sit before the performance of a fine actor, or read a poem – and there it is – something that streams into your consciousness ... Those who keep climbing higher, in their chosen work, all have this outstanding something. The nurse in the hospital, the man who delivers your mail, the clerk behind many a store counter, and the effective minister or public speaker. Without this human touch, hope has little on which to feed or thrive.

George M. Adams.

August 2nd

LET NOT YOUR HEART BE TROUBLED ... NEITHER LET IT BE AFRAID.
John 14:27.

CHAY BLYTH, B.E.M., was first to sail alone round the world from east to west, against the prevailing winds and currents. In the 59-foot ketch, *British Steel*, he also made the fastest time, departing October 1970 and arriving back August 1971, the 31-year-old Scot took only 292 days.

He describes how, on one occasion, the main sail was jammed halfway up the mast. "I prayed, and asked for strength and assistance. At my first try, down it came. I wrote in my log: "No one will ever say to me that there is no God without my remembering all these situations. To atheists I say 'Go sailing singlehanded for a few weeks'."

He also says, "Man is so pitifully small against such gigantic forces. You feel over and over again that it is only by God's will that you survive ... Ten months' solitude in some of the loneliest seas of the world strengthened every part of me, deepened every perception and gave me a new awareness of that power outside man which we call God. I am quite certain that without God's help many and many a time I could not have survived to complete my circum-navigation."

CHAY BLYTH.
The Impossible Voyage.
Reproduced by permission of Hodder & Stoughton Ltd.

August 3rd

LOVE IN MY HEART WASN'T PUT THERE TO STAY: LOVE ISN'T LOVE, TILL I GIVE IT AWAY.

IN MY practice at the Clinic people sometimes ask me what this psychiatric stuff is all about. It's increasingly clear to me that almost all emotional problems could be summed up in one word—love. "Love me," that's all. We go through a million different manipulations to get somebody to love us.

And that's the core of most emotional sickness.

The healthy people are walking around looking for someone to love. And, if you see changes in the people who are calling out "Love me, love me," it's when they realize that if they give up the call and take up the business of loving another human, they can get all the love they have been calling out for all their lives. It's hard to learn. But it's good when you learn it.

THOMAS MALONE, M.D.

August 4th

I AM THE MASTER OF MY EMOTIONS. I LEARN TO DELAY THE EMOTIONAL IMPACT OF NEGATIVE MEMORIES OR ACCIDENTAL HAPPENINGS. THE RHYTHM OF MY LIFE IS UNDISTURBED.

IF ONE is emotionally wrought up, it is easy to break a dish or spill what one is handling. Muscles miss by only a fraction of an inch in their co-ordination, but that fraction may mean a fatal slip. Some people never seem to drop nor break things they handle, nor to incur minor injuries by mis-steps. What do they do to avoid accidents? A very simple thing, really. They defer the emotional impact. They employ the technique of delayed reaction.

A surgeon whom I assisted years ago gave me the clue, and it has meant a great deal to me. One morning just before scrubbing-up for a major operation he was called to the telephone. We knew by his facial expression as he returned from the telephone that something disagreeable had happened.

He sat down for a few minutes, then went on with his preparations, performing the operation without any uncertain movements. Later he told us the news, and we marvelled that he could go through his task so unperturbed. He explained that he had felt shaken with the news at first, but realizing his duty and the need for steadiness, he simply put aside the entire matter as though he had not heard it, in something of the same fashion as Scarlet O'Hara in *Gone With the Wind*, when she said, "I can't think about that now. I haven't time. I'll think about that tomorrow when I am not so busy."

DR. REBECCA BEARD.
From "Everyman's Goal".

Publisher: Arthur James Ltd., 70, Cross Oak Road, Berkhamsted, Herts HP4 3HZ.

August 5th

AS SOME RARE PERFUME IN A VASE OF CLAY
PERVADES IT WITH A PRESENCE NOT ITS OWN;
SO WHEN THOU DWELLEST IN A MORTAL SOUL
ALL HEAVEN'S OWN SWEETNESS IS AROUND IT THROWN.
Harriet Beecher Stowe.

HE CAME from the bosom of the Father to the bosom of a woman. He put on humanity that we might put on divinity. He became man that we might become sons of God ...

In infancy He startled a king; in boyhood He puzzled the doctors; in manhood He ruled the course of nature. He walked upon the billows and hushed the sea to sleep. He healed the multitudes without medicine and made no charge for His services. He never wrote a book, yet not all the libraries of the world could hold the books that could be written about Him ...

Great men have come and gone, yet He lives on. Herod could not kill Him, Satan could not seduce Him, Death could not destroy Him, the grave could not hold Him ...

He laid aside His purple robe for a peasant's gown. He was rich, yet for our sake He became poor ... He slept in another's manger. He cruised the lake in another's boat. He rode on another man's ass. He was buried in another man's tomb. All failed, but He never. The ever-perfect One—He is the Chief among ten thousand. He is altogether lovely.

AUTHOR UNKNOWN.

August 6th

"IN COMMON THINGS THAT ROUND US LIE ...
SOME RANDOM TRUTHS WE CAN IMPART,
THE HARVEST OF A QUIET EYE
THAT BROODS AND SLEEPS ON OUR OWN HEART."

Author Unknown.

I HAVE never felt lonesome, or in the least depressed by a sense of solitude. But once, and that for a few weeks after I came to the woods, when, for an hour, I doubted if the near neighbourhood of men was not essential to a serene and healthy life.

In the midst of a gentle rain, while these thoughts prevailed, I was suddenly sensible of such sweet and beneficent society in Nature, in the very pattering of the drops, and in every sound and sight around my house, an infinite and unaccountable friendliness all at once like an atmosphere sustaining me. It made the fancied advantages of human neighbourhood insignificant, and I have never thought of them since.

Every little pine-needle expanded and swelled in sympathy, and befriended me. I was so distinctly made aware of the presence of something kindred to me, even in scenes which we were accustomed to call wild and dreary. The nearest of blood to me and most human was not a person nor a villager, and I thought no place could ever be strange to me again.

From Thoreau's "Walden".

THE easeful days, the dreamless nights ... The homely round of plain delights ... The calm, the unambitioned mind ... Which all men seek, and few men find.

Austin Dobson.

August 7th

OUR DOUBTS ARE TRAITORS, AND MAKE US LOSE THE GOOD WE OFT MIGHT WIN BY FEARING TO ATTEMPT.
Shakespeare.

THE things that haven't been done before ... Those are the things to try ... Columbus dreamed of an unknown shore ... At the rim of the far-flung sky ... And his heart was bold and his faith was strong ... As he ventured in dangers new ... And he paid no heed to the jeering throngs ... Or the fears of the doubting crew ... The things that haven't been done before ... Are the tasks worth while today.

Are you one of the flock that follows? ... Or are you one of the timid souls that quail? ... At the jeers of the doubting crew? ... Or dare you, whether you win or fail ... Strike out for the goal that's new?

AUTHOR UNKNOWN.

August 8th

I MAY NOT HAVE THE BEST OF EVERYTHING ... BUT I MAKE THE BEST OF EVERYTHING I HAVE.

SOME are widowed, separated or divorced. For some the road is far from smooth as this office worker observes: "I went through a period of incredible despair. I got sick to my stomach and was too tired even to take care of the children. But I learned to cope with those feelings by taking power over my life in small ways."

Here is expressed the pain of life experienced by so many single adults in similar circumstances. Fortunately, time does heal and the strength to carry on does come.

The single life is not incompatible with happiness; in fact, it has many advantages. Being a single adult who has never married, for most, means being free from the responsibilities of raising a family. There is a greater opportunity for travel, more free time, more privacy, greater financial independence.

The temptation is always there to use these advantages for selfish reasons. But most single adults are basically altruistic. They may only need a passing word of encouragement to put the creative power of mind, heart and soul into action. They care about others, and they care what becomes of the world.

THE CHRISTOPHERS.

August 9th

"IN HIM I LIVE, MOVE, AND HAVE MY BEING. THEREFORE, ALL IS WELL."

"MY HEART is filled with joy because I have a place in this world. I am meant to be here.

"If we wish to gain contentment, we might try such rules as these: (1) Allow ourselves to complain of nothing—not even the weather. (2) Never to picture ourselves under any circumstances in which we are not in reality. (3) Never to compare our own lot with that of another. (4) Never to allow ourselves to dwell on the wish that this or that should have been otherwise. God loves us better and more wisely than we do ourselves. (5) Never dwell upon tomorrow. Remember, it is His—not ours. The heaviest part of sorrow often is to look forward to it."

E. B. Pusey.

August 10th

LIFE IS FOR LIVING SO LIVE IT AND SEE HOW GREAT AND HOW BEAUTIFUL LIVING CAN BE.

NATURAL merriment is something that is rare in these days of non-stop so-called entertainment on television or radio. Many of the programmes inflicted on the public are supposed to be funny but a real comedian is a rare phenomenon now. Wit seems to have been crushed under the dull weight of vulgarity, though the instinct for laughter is still there. Occasionally one hears an outburst of it from children, a natural bubbling up of spontaneous laughter. This comes very near to pure joy. Laughter is good for the muscles of the stomach. It is also good for one's mental outlook on life. There is nothing like a good laugh for changing the perspective and making you see things from a different angle.

Laughter is one of God's loveliest gifts to man. The ability to smile is a safety valve. If you can smile at misfortune you have got the better of it. Without a word being uttered you can establish good relations with another person by the mere lifting of the corners of the lips into a smile and when this happens the eyes have a way of brightening. The face becomes a mirror reflecting happiness and goodwill. When you look at creatures like frogs, peacocks, grasshoppers, zebras or ducks you cannot resist the conclusion that the Creator was not lacking in a sense of humour.

Patience Strong.
"Life is for Living"

August 11th

I WILL CONCENTRATE ON BEING LOVING … LOVE MUST BE LEARNED AGAIN AND AGAIN … THERE IS NO END TO IT.

A WIFE is someone who always loves you. She'll marry you when your future is still a great big question mark, and then, she'll tell everybody she's the luckiest girl in the whole wide world.

She'll praise your virtues, ignore your faults, choose your clothes, govern your diet, tolerate your friends, cater to your relatives, and never quite admit she's doing it for you.

She'll build you up when you've been "put down"; she'll make your dreams seem like real possibilities. She'll nag a little and she'll worry a lot about your weight, and then serve you three of your favourite things at one meal.

If it's on a map, she can't find it. If it's in the house, she's the only one who *can* find it, If there's something to be done, she'll do it. If someone needs something, she'll give it to them. She may have trouble keeping a secret, but who else would you tell it to? And isn't it nice to know that no matter who is on the other side, she's on YOUR side?

Her companionship is your delight. Her laughter is your joy. Her dreams are your goals. Her faith is your strength. Her loyalty keeps your whole world steady. And as year follows year, she proves over and over again the thing you've known all along—because a wife is someone who always loves you!

Rey Wheeler.
Sunshine Magazine.

"I Love you to the level of every day's most quiet need … by sun and candlelight."
Elizabeth Barret Browning.

August 12th

SET YOUR AFFECTION ON THINGS ABOVE, NOT ON THINGS ON EARTH.
Colossians 3:2.

LOVE underlies it all! All was created in the Son of God's love. The eons will not cease to unfold until all shall respond and satisfy the longing of His heart. To display His love and create a response in the breasts of His creatures is the purpose of the eons. Does not this explain the pain, the sorrow, the despair, and the death which seem to have blighted all His efforts? These are but the background, the contrast so essential for the revelation of their opposites. They are the bitter ingredients without which we cannot know the balm, the joy, the ecstasy, the ineffable delight which God has prepared for us. Adam would never have known good if he had not eaten of the tree of the knowledge of good *and* evil. We can never know grace unless we first experience sin.

In Ephesians (The Bible) we see man at his worst and God at His best. There is the deepest degradation and the greatest grace. It is an epistle of superlatives. The last becomes first, the lowest highest. The dregs of earth become the elect of heaven. We are His achievement, a special and permanent display to exhibit to an admiring universe the multifarious wisdom and the immense wealth of grace there is in Him.

A. E. Knoch.
Concordant Publishing Concern, 15570 Knochaven Road, Santa Clarita, CA 91350-2799, U.S.A.

August 13th

HE WHO THINKS HE CAN, DEVELOPS WITHIN HIMSELF THE POWER THAT CAN.

DEATH and sorrow will be companions of our journey; hardship our garment; constancy and valour our only shield. We must be united; we must be undaunted; we must be inflexible. Our qualities and deeds must burn and glow through the gloom of Europe until they become the veritable beacon of its salvation.

Hitler has said "In three weeks England will have her neck wrung like a chicken". Some chicken; some neck.

SIR WINSTON CHURCHILL.

August 14th

I WANT TO BE SO GENIAL, SO KIND, SO ALIVE, THAT OTHERS FEEL INSTINCTIVELY THAT MY PRESENCE HAS DONE THEM GOOD.

Adapted from Henry Ward Beecher.

I KNOW of no better practice than that of a friend who continually holds himself in an attitude of mind that he continually sends out his love in the form of the thought—"Dear everybody, I love you." And when we realize the fact that a thought invariably produces its effect before it returns, or before it ceases, we can see how he is continually breathing out a blessing not only upon all with whom he comes in contact, but upon all the world. These same thoughts of love, moreover, tokened in various ways, are continually coming to him from all quarters.

Even animals feel the effects of these forces. Some animals are much more sensitively organized than many people are, and consequently they get the effect of our thoughts, our mental states, and emotions much more readily than many people do.

Therefore whenever we meet an animal we can do it good by sending out to it these thoughts of love. It will feel the effects whether we simply entertain or whether we voice them. And it is often interesting to note how quickly it responds, and how readily it gives evidence of its appreciation of this love and consideration on our part.

RALPH WALDO TRINE.
"In Tune with the Infinite".

August 15th

**FRIENDSHIP—PURE, UNSELFISH FRIENDSHIP,
ALL THROUGH LIFE'S ALLOTTED SPAN,
NURTURES, STRENGTHENS, WIDENS, LENGTHENS,
MAN'S AFFINITY WITH MAN.**

Author Unknown.

FRIENDSHIPS do not come by chance. Upon the loom of circumstances Fate weaves an intricate design—and threads of other lives entwine to make a pattern with our own. We were not made to walk alone. Our pathways lead to where we meet a friend in need. It seems it was meant to be. And how important is that little touch of kindness at a time when it was needed most.

There are kindnesses that you don't forget . . . The gesture of true sympathy that's made in all sincerity and comes when you are weary and upset . . . The understanding word that reaches down into your heart—at the very moment of your need . . . A well timed act of friendliness that saves you from despair—even though it may be small . . . A good turn done for you that shows that someone has concern for you . . . HOW much it really means—that good and timely deed! . . . The love that we appreciate is that which does not come too late to help us when we need it most of all! Friends are your best insurance against loneliness, and if you are going to be 100, that's a long time to be lonely . . . A friend is a priceless possession. Like good wine, friendship improves with keeping. You'll find it's the treasure you value most when you reach your 100th birthday.

AUTHOR UNKNOWN.

LIFE

He spake of life which all can take
but none can give; Life which all
creatures love and strive to keep;
wonderful; dear and pleasant to the meanest.
Yes, a boon to all where pity is,
For pity makes the world soft for the weak,
and noble for the strong.

Anonymous.

August 16th

WHILE WITH AN EYE MADE QUIET BY THE POWER OF HARMONY, AND THE DEEP POWER OF JOY, WE SEE INTO THE LIFE OF THINGS.

Wordsworth.

THE corn was orient and immortal wheat, which never should be reaped, nor was ever sown. I thought it had stood from everlasting to everlasting. The dust and stones of the street were as precious as gold. The gates were at the first end of the world. The green trees when I saw them first through one of the gates transported and ravished me. Their sweetness and unusual beauty made my heart to leap, and almost mad with ecstasy. They were such strange and wonderful things.

The Men! O what venerable and reverend creatures did the aged seem! Immortal Cherubims! And young men glittering and sparkling Angels. And maids strange seraphic pieces of life and beauty! Boys and girls tumbling into the street, and playing, were moving jewels. I knew not that they were born or should die. But all things abided eternally *as they were in their proper places.*

Eternity was manifest in the Light of the Day, and something infinite behind everything appeared: which talked with my expectation and moved my desire. The city seemed to stand in Eden, or to be built in Heaven. The streets were mine, the temple was mine, the people were mine, their clothes and gold and silver were mine, as much as their sparkling eyes, fair skins and ruddy faces. The skies were mine, and so were the sun and moon and stars, and all the world was mine; and I the only spectator and enjoyer of it . . . So that with much ado I was corrupted, and made to learn the dirty devices of this world.

THOMAS TRAHERNE (1638–1715).
Son of a Hereford shoemaker, Traherne was a poet who saw a new meaning in life through the loveliness of the natural world.

August 17th

I DON'T GROW OLD MERELY LIVING A NUMBER OF YEARS ... I GROW OLD BY DESERTING MY IDEALS ... YEARS MAY WRINKLE MY SKIN ... BUT TO GIVE UP IDEALS WRINKLES MY SOUL.
Douglas MacArthur (1880–1964).

YOUTH is not a time of life—it is a state of mind. It is not a matter of ripe cheeks, red lips and supple knees; it is a temper of the will, a quality of the imagination, a vigour of the emotions; it is a freshness of the deep springs of life.

Youth means a temperamental predominance of courage over timidity, of the appetite of adventure over love of ease. This often exists in a man of fifty more than a boy of twenty.

Nobody grows old by merely living a number of years; people grow old only by deserting their ideals. Years wrinkle the skin, but to give up enthusiasm wrinkles the soul. Worry, doubt, self-distrust, fear and despair—these are the long, long years that bow the head and turn the growing spirit back to dust.

Whether seventy or sixteen, there is in every being's heart the love of wonder, the sweet amazement at the stars and the star-like things and thoughts, the undaunted challenge of events, the unfailing child-like appetite for what comes next, and the joy and the game of life.

You are as young as your faith, as old as your doubt; as young as your self-confidence; as old as your fear; as young as your hope, as old as your despair.

In the central place of your heart there is a receiving station; so long as it receives messages of beauty, hope, cheer, courage, grandeur and power from the earth, from men and from the Infinite, so long are you young.

AUTHOR UNKNOWN.

August 18th

I DO NOT FEAR THE FUTURE ... THE NATURAL WORLD SPEAKS TO ME OF A BLESSED ASSURANCE THAT ALL IS WELL.

THERE is religion in everything around us—a calm and holy religion in the unbreathing things of Nature, which man would do well to imitate. It is a meek and blessed influence stealing in, as it were, unawares upon the heart; it comes quietly, and without excitement; it has no terror, no gloom in its approaches; it does not rouse up the passions; it is untrammelled by the creeds, and unshadowed by the superstitions of man; it is fresh from the hands of its Author, glowing from the immediate presence of the Great Spirit which pervades and quickens it; it is written on the arched sky; it looks out from every star.

It is on the sailing cloud and in the invisible wind; it is among the hills and valleys of the earth, where the shrubless mountaintop pierces the thin atmosphere of eternal winter, or where the mighty forest fluctuates, before the strong wind, with its dark waves of green foliage; it is spread out like a legible language, upon the broad face of the unsleeping ocean. This is the poetry of Nature; it is this which uplifts the spirit within us, until it is strong enough to overlook the shadows of our place of probation; it is that which breaks, link after link, the chain that binds us to materiality, and which opens to us a world of spiritual beauty and holiness.

JOHN RUSKIN.

August 19th

NEVER MIND YESTERDAY—LIFE IS TODAY! NEVER MIND YESTERDAY—LET IT AWAY! NEVER MIND ANYTHING—OVER AND DONE, HERE IS A NEW MOMENT—LIT WITH NEW SUN.

Author Unknown.

TO AWAKEN each morning with a smile brightening our face, to greet the day with reverence, for the opportunities it contains; to approach my work with a clean mind; to hold ever before me, even in the doing of little things, the Ultimate Purpose toward which I am working; to meet men and women with laughter on their lips and love in my heart; to be gentle, kind and courteous through all the hours; to approach the night with weariness that ever woos sleep and the joy that comes from work well done—this is how I desire to waste wisely my days.

THOMAS DREIER.

August 20th

GOD GRANT ME THE SERENITY
TO ACCEPT THE THINGS I CANNOT CHANGE:
THE COURAGE TO CHANGE THE THINGS I CAN;
AND THE WISDOM TO KNOW THE DIFFERENCE.
Niebuhl.

GO PLACIDLY amid the noise and haste, and remember what peace there may be in silence. As far as possible without surrender be on good terms with all persons. Speak your truth quietly and clearly; and listen to others, even the dull and ignorant; they too have their story. Avoid loud and aggressive persons, for they are vexations to the spirit. If you compare yourself with others, you may become vain and bitter; for always there will be greater or lesser persons than yourself. Enjoy your achievements as well as your plans. Keep interested in your own career, however humble; it is a real possession in the changing fortunes of time. Exercise caution in your business affairs; for the world is full of trickery, but let not this blind you to what virtue there is: many persons strive for high ideals; and everywhere life is full of heroism.

Be yourself. Especially, do not feign affection. Neither be cynical about love: for in the face of all heredity and disenchantment it is perennial as the grass. Take kindly the counsel of the years, gracefully surrendering the things of youth. Nurture strength in spirit to shield you in sudden misfortune. But do not distress yourself with imagining. Many fears are born of fatigue and loneliness. Beyond a wholesome discipline, be gentle with yourself.

You are a child of the universe, no less than the trees and stars; you have a right to be here. And whether or not it is clear to you, no doubt the universe is unfolding as it should. Therefore be at peace with God, whatever you conceive Him to be, and whatever your labours and aspirations, in the noisy confusion of life, keep peace with your soul. With all its sham, drudgery, and broken dreams, it is still a beautiful world. Be careful. Strive to be happy.

From a Manuscript to be seen in Old St. Paul's Anglican Church, Baltimore, Maryland, U.S.A.

MORNING RIDE.
Lower Slaughter, Cotswolds, Gloucestershire.
Photograph by Andy Williams.

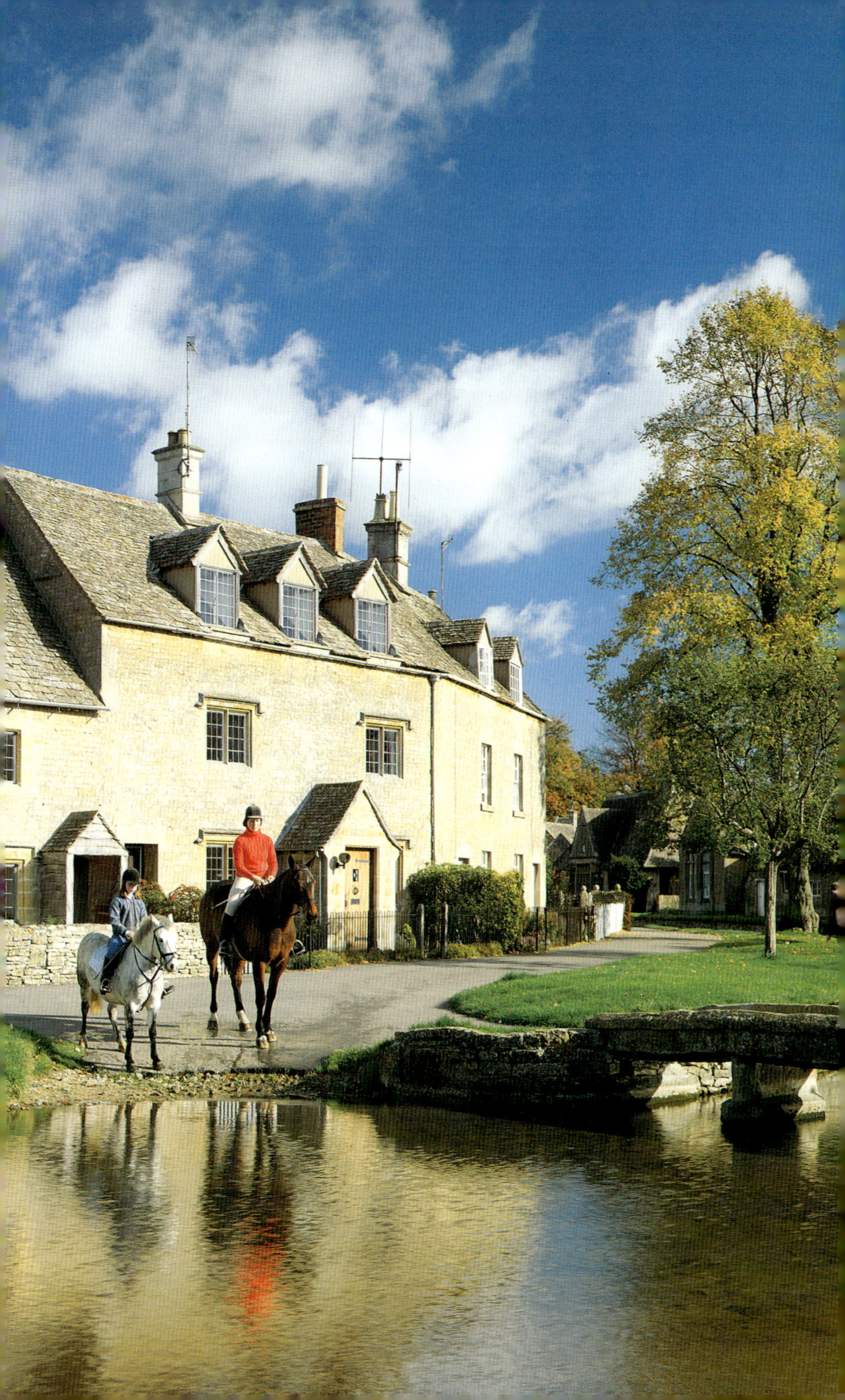

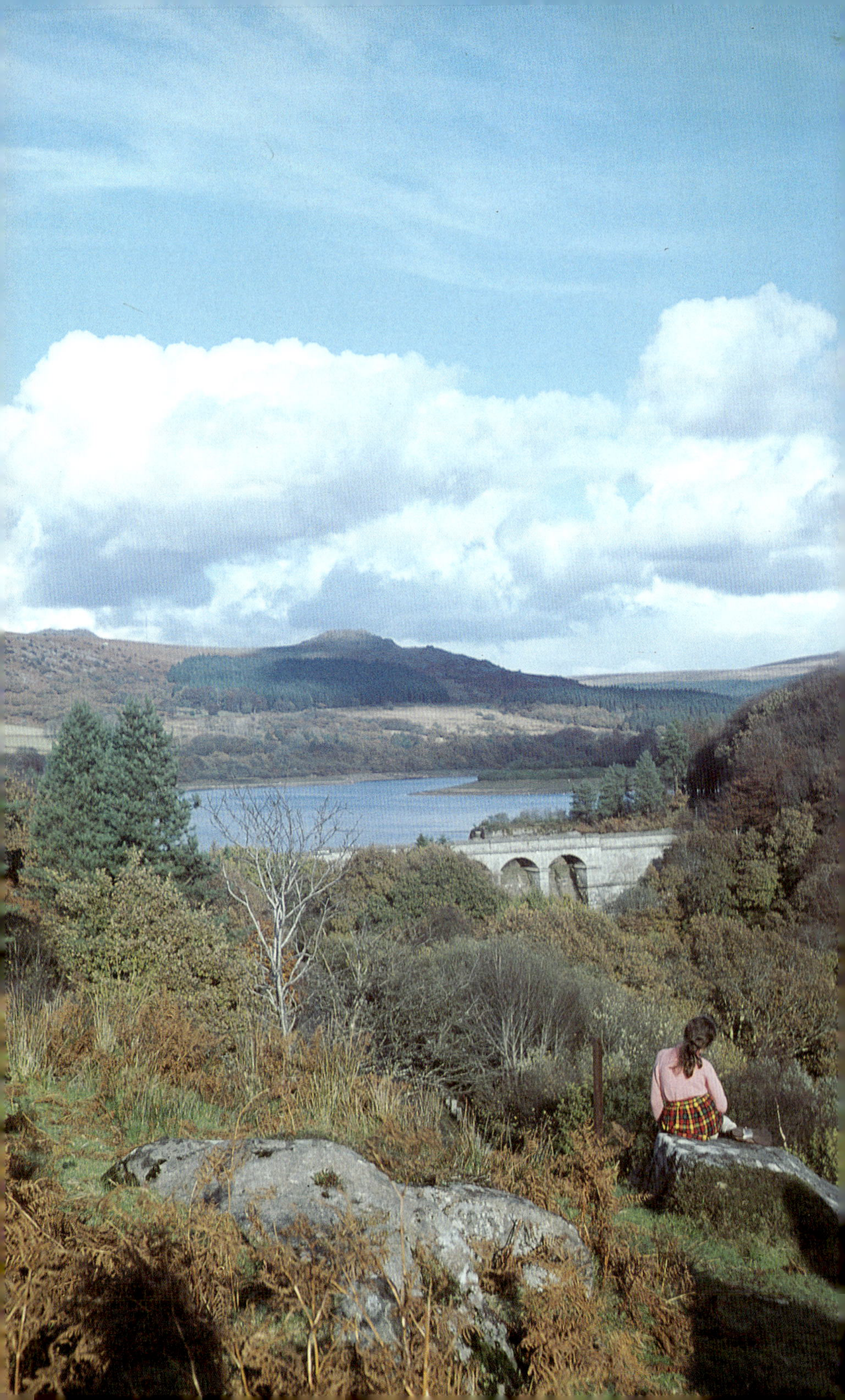

August 21st

I WISH YOU GOOD HEALTH
FOR YOU CANNOT DENY
THAT HEALTH IS A TREASURE
WHICH CASH CANNOT BUY.

DR. HANS SELYE, prominent medical research scientist, has a theory that all disease is caused by a disturbance in the chemistry of the body, due to stress. He bases this on the fact that the chemical balance within the body is governed by three tiny glands: the pituitary and the two adrenals.

Their job is to adapt the body to all kinds of stress. If you are chilled, the arteries constrict and raise the blood pressure to create greater warmth. When bacteria invade the body, the glands provide hormones to produce inflammation which walls off infection. In the case of severe injury, they hasten the clotting of blood, lower blood pressure, and control haemorrhage. They also increase blood sugar to provide quick energy, and decrease sensitivity to pain. It is the task of the adrenal hormones to combat stress and to fight off any threat to the body's welfare.

In this Hurry-Up World we are exposing ourselves to too many stresses. We hurry constantly and worry incessantly. The businessman drives himself at the office all day, then worries half the night. The housewife tries to run her home, maintain a social life, and at bedtime is so jangled that she takes a sleeping tablet. These glands pour out hormones to keep the body going. For a while they succeed and then the defence mechanism breaks down. The result? Arteries harden, blood pressure rises and heart trouble strikes.

Health is an orderly, harmonious functioning of all glands of the body, and this state of harmony continues as long as they are not hard-driven by excess chemical activity due to anxiety and stress.

AUTHOR UNKNOWN.

LOOKING INTO THE FUTURE.
Burrator Lake, Dartmoor, Devon.
Photograph by Roy Westlake.

August 22nd

> LOVE IS MY REASON FOR LIVING ...
> LOVE IS MY REASON FOR GIVING,
> LIFE WOULD BE ONLY EMPTY AND LONELY
> IF IT WERE NOT FOR LOVE.
>
> Ivor Novello.
Published by Chappell & Co Ltd.

WHEN I became acquainted with my husband's parents, my marriage was dewy new and life was a song. My husband exerted himself to please me, and I made up my mind *never* to nag such a perfect husband.

So when I heard my mother-in-law complain about little tasks her husband ignored, I was taken aback. It seemed she was always scolding.

When we went to see "the folks", I experienced a feeling of sadness. Grandma continually pecked at Grandpa, and he still neglected his tasks. She worried about him constantly—his health, his comfort. And Grandpa fussed at her—said she worked too hard. A funny way to live, I thought.

One spring evening, I stopped by to see them. The living room was dark, but a light shone through the dining room window. On impulse, I paused beside the open window.

There sat Grandpa with the big Swedish Bible on his knee. Grandma sat beside him, gnarled hands folded. A peaceful expression was on her lined face as she listened while he read aloud.

He read a few verses, smiled, and asked if she were tired. She patted his hand. "No, I like to hear your voice," she answered.

In this calm evening hour, petty annoyances were in the background, replaced by true companionship. I understood then that I shouldn't judge by superficialities. Regardless of minor differences, the years had welded Grandma and Grandpa together in enduring affection, understanding and love.

MRS. GRACE RINGBLOOM.
Sunshine Magazine.

> THE supreme happiness of life is the conviction that we are loved.
>
> Victor Hugo.

August 23rd

**THE TENDENCY TO BROOD AND FRET
NEVER SOLVED A PROBLEM YET.
WORRY IS A ROCKING CHAIR
THAT NEVER TAKES ME ANYWHERE.**

PELL-MELL, helter-skelter, we are dashing through life, eating time up alive and wearing our nerves to a frazzle. We are bombarded on every side by countless miscellaneous activities, clubs, social affairs, stupid meetings, flat concerts, pageants, parades, and a million and one interests that for ever nag at our resistance until they wear it down, and we lose our last drop of poise and serenity, while we promise the god of hurry to keep everlastingly on the jump in order to keep up with the hurrying, scurrying, worrying mob. We are becoming speed maniacs in all phases of our haste-driven journey through life ...

Nature did its best to make Britain a place to be calm and happy in. Are we blind to its beauty, failing to be blest and strengthened by it? Are we even marring the beauty about us by our ugly haste? It is something to think about.

Harriet Geithmann.

August 24th

**AS I GIVE THE BEST THAT IS WITHIN ME, SO I RECEIVE
THE BEST THAT IS WITHOUT ME ... AS I GIVE, SO I
RECEIVE.**

THE desire for a fuller, richer life runs as an unbroken threat throughout the history of mankind. This yearning and aspiration to attain perfection is given expression in nearly every object of art.

It is the dominant theme in literature and the inspiration of the world's great music. Religion, literature, music ... these are the inseparable trinity to which man intuitively turns with faith and confidence for strength to hold a forward course unswervingly through every trial.

It is in these, rather than in the material things, that the spirit finds complete contentment. These irresistible forces alone possess the power to exalt and unify and have inspired the noblest deeds of valour and sacrifice.

However difficult the path, everyone will find courage in the knowledge that the beautiful things in life endure for all time.

Author Unknown.

August 25th

THOUGH I WALK THROUGH THE VALLEY OF THE SHADOW OF DEATH I WILL FEAR NO EVIL.
Psalm 23.

PRAYER seems to be essentially a tension of the spirit towards the immaterial substratum of the world. In general, it consists of a complaint, a cry of anguish, a demand for succour. Sometimes it becomes a serene contemplation of the immanent and transcendent principle of all things. One can define it equally as an uplifting of the soul to God.

As an act of love and adoration towards Him from Whom comes the wonder which is life. In fact, prayer represents the effort of man to communicate with an invisible being, creator of all that exists, supreme wisdom, strength and beauty, father and saviour of each one of us.

Far from consisting of a simple recitation of formulas, true prayer represents a mystic state when the consciousness is absorbed in God. This state is not an intellectual state. Also it remains as inaccessible as incomprehensible to the philosophers and to the learned. Just as with the sense of beauty and of love, it demands no book knowledge.

The simple are conscious of God as naturally as of the warmth of the sun, or the perfume of a flower. But this God, so approachable by him who knows how to love, is hidden from him who knows only how to understand. Thought and word are at fault when it is a matter of describing this state. That is why prayer finds its highest expression in a soaring of love through the obscure night of the intelligence.

Dr. ALEXIS CARREL.
Sincere thanks to the author whose address we are unable to trace.

August 26th

ALWAYS REMEMBER ... THE HILLS AHEAD
ARE NEVER AS STEEP AS THEY SEEM:
AND WITH FAITH IN YOUR HEART—START UPWARD
AND CLIMB TILL YOU REACH YOUR DREAM.
Helen Steiner Rice.

DOES the road wind uphill all the way? ... Yes, to the very end. Will the day's journey take the whole long day? ... From morn to night, my friend.

But is there for the night a resting-place? ... A roof for when the slow dark hours begin? ... May not the darkness hide it from my face? ... You cannot miss that inn.

Shall I meet other wayfarers at night? ... Those who have gone before? ... Then must I knock or call when just in sight? ... They will not keep you standing at the door.

Shall I find comfort, travel-sore and weak? ... Of labour you shall find the sum ... Will there be beds for me and all who seek? ... Yea, beds for all who come.

CHRISTINA ROSSETTI, 1830–94.
British poet. Sister of Dante G. Rossetti.

August 27th

O HEAVENLY FATHER, PROTECT AND BLESS ALL THINGS
THAT HAVE BREATH: GUARD THEM FROM ALL EVIL AND
LET THEM SLEEP IN PEACE.
Albert Schweitzer when a child.

LORD, may I love all Thy creation, the whole and every grain of sand in it. May I love every leaf, every ray of Thy light. May I love the animals: Thou has given them the rudiments of thought and joy untroubled. Let me not trouble them, let me not harass them, let me not deprive them of their happiness, let me not work against Thine intent. For I acknowledge unto Thee that all is like an ocean, all is flowing and blending, and that to withhold any measure of love from anything in Thy universe is to withhold that same measure from Thee.

DOSTOEVSKY, 1821–1881.
Russian novelist.
From "The Conversations and Exhortations of Father Zossima"
from "The Brothers Karamazov".

August 28th

THE ANGELS KEEP THEIR ANCIENT PLACES –
TURN BUT A STONE, AND START A WING!
'TIS YOU, 'TIS YOUR ESTRANGED FACES,
THAT MISS THE MANY-SPLENDOURED THING.

Francis Thompson.

I HAVE never felt lonesome, or in the least oppressed by a sense of solitude, except once, and that was a few weeks after I came to the woods. Then, for an hour, I doubted if the nearness of man was not essential to a serene and healthy life.

To be alone was something unpleasant. But I was at the same time conscious of a slight melancholy in my mood, and seemed to foresee my recovery.

In the midst of a gentle rain, while these thoughts prevailed, I was suddenly sensible of such sweet and beneficent society in Nature, in the very pattering of the drops, and in every sight and sound around my house, an infinite and unaccountable friendliness came all at once, like an atmosphere sustaining me. It made the fancied advantages of human neighbourliness insignificant.

Every little pine-needle expanded and swelled with sympathy, and befriended me. I was so distinctly made aware of the presence of something kindred to me, even in scenes which we are accustomed to call wild and dreary. The nearest blood-relation to me was not a person. I thought no place could ever be strange to me again.

HENRY DAVID THOREAU, 1817–1872.
American naturalist and writer.
From: "Walden".

HOW sweet . . . How passing sweet . . . Is solitude.

Anonymous.

August 29th

EARTH HAS NOT ANYTHING TO SHOW MORE FAIR ...
William Wordsworth.

THE little cares that fretted me
I lost them yesterday
Among the fields, above the sea,
Among the winds that play.

Among the lowing of the herds,
The rustling of the trees,
Among the singing of the birds,
The humming of the bees.

The foolish fears of what might happen,
I cast them all away,
Among the clover-scented grass,
Among the new-mown hay,

Among the husking of the corn,
Where drowsy poppies nod,
Where ill thoughts die and good are born
Out in the fields with God.

AUTHOR UNKNOWN.

August 30th

THEY THAT SOW IN TEARS SHALL REAP IN JOY.

I SAY to the House, as I said to the Ministers who have joined this Government, I have nothing to offer but blood and toil and tears and sweat.

We have before all of us an ordeal of the most grievous kind. We have before us many, many long months of struggle and of suffering.

If you ask what is our policy I will say it is to wage war—war by air, land and sea, war with all our might and with all the strength that God can give us, and to wage war against a monstrous tyranny never surpassed in the dark and lamentable catalogue of human crime. That is our policy.

If you ask us what is our aim? I can answer in one word—victory. Victory at all costs, victory in spite of all terrors, victory however long and hard the road may be, for without victory there is no survival—and let that be realised—no survival for the British Empire, no survival for the urge and impulse of the ages that mankind shall move forward towards its goal.

I take up my task in buoyancy and hope. I feel sure that our cause will not be suffered to fail among men. I feel entitled, at this juncture and at this time, to claim the aid of all, and I say, "Come, then, let us go forward together in our united strength".

THE RT. HON. WINSTON CHURCHILL.
Prime Minister,
May 14th, 1940.

August 31st

CRISIS BRINGS POWER ... MAY EVEN CHANGE MY LIFE ... I LEARN TO TURN A CRISIS INTO A CREATIVE OPPORTUNITY.

IT WAS an autumn dusk in Tangier. A group of children were playing in the dusty street in front of a general stores. The shop assistant, Moulay, was getting a last breath of fresh air before serving the evening customers when to his horror he saw one of the urchins pick up a grenade from a pile of rubble and pull out the pin.

He dived at the child, grabbed the grenade and attempted to throw it to safety. There was not enough time. The grenade exploded, taking with it both his hands.

He didn't feel the pain—the shock was too great. There were two bleeding stumps where his hands had been a few seconds before. A police car came quickly and took him to hospital. The bleeding was stopped, and his life saved. For what? No one had seen an artificial hand in Tangier. No one without hands had ever had a job there.

Months went by, and no one thought about Moulay except some US naval officers and consular officials who couldn't forget the tragedy. They pooled their savings to provide transport to the United States, where a rehabilitation centre had promised to fit him with new hands and train him to use them.

It took only ten days to provide Moulay with modern mechanical hands—hands that functioned and had plastic skin that matched his own. A week later he painted a little picture, a bright oriental scene of his native city. In three weeks, he could meet all the demands of daily life and even manipulate fine tools.

The story of his thrilling victory over disability spread like wildfire in his country. When he arrived home, he was met by high government officials. The prime minister, after praising his fortitude, gave him a job and a purse of money to help him start a new life.

Moulay gave the children he saved the greatest gift of all—life itself. In turn, people who truly cared gave him new hands. But they were much more than new hands. The gift was actually a new life—a new life of value and dignity.

D<small>R</small> H<small>OWARD</small> R<small>USK</small>.

Sincere thanks to the author whose address we are unable to trace.

September 1st

GOD IS LOVE.

WHO shall separate us from the love of God? Shall tribulation, distress, persecution, famine, nakedness, peril, or sword? . . . No, in all these things we are the overcomers through Him Who loves us. For I am persuaded that neither death, nor life, nor angels, nor principalities, nor powers, nor things present, nor things to come, nor height, nor depth, nor any other creation (here, or elsewhere in the universe) shall be able to separate us from the love of God, which is in Christ Jesus.

ROMANS 8:25.

September 2nd

PRAISE IS A GRACE THAT FINDS ITS WAY INTO EVERY HEART.

TO PRAISE a person is not to flatter the face. Praise magnifies the tendency into a virtue—and calls forth response and reciprocation.

Praise is that warmth which unfolds hidden aptitudes and talents and inspires them to expression. Genius has often been ignited through simple appreciation. All things blossom and come to fruition through respect and esteem.

Approval is the way to every man's heart. Man is that sensitive being who lives for approval and responds to praise. What is more, he will involuntarily live up to and fulfil any virtue which receives commendation.

Claim the best that is in one—and it will grow to your expectations. Recognize the best that is in yourself, and the best will magnify itself. That which you look to—will look to you, and that which you acknowledge is quickened. Praise calls forth response and reciprocation.

Those who are constantly censured are stifled, and whatever attributes they may possess are soon withered and seared with the breath of condemnation. Magnified fallacies become great faults. Magnified virtues become great assets.

To find a virtue to praise in each soul is to enrich that person with a priceless possibility. Praise magnifies the minutest tendency into a virtue. It has the power to expand the smallest inclination into a great blessing.

SARAH ROBBINS.
in "Today".

September 3rd

I AM RESOLVED TO TALK HEALTH, HAPPINESS AND PROSPERITY; AND TO BE TOO LARGE FOR WORRY, TOO STRONG FOR FEAR, AND TOO HAPPY TO PERMIT THE PRESENCE OF TROUBLE.

Christian D. Larson.

THERE is a close tie-up between health and happiness. I realized this some 12 years ago when I arrived and started in general practice in New Zealand, expecting to find it a very healthy country. One of my first impressions was shock and surprise to find such large numbers of people flocking not only to doctors but to chiropractors, colour therapists, and faith healers of various kinds.

It seemed all wrong that in a country like New Zealand, with all its advantages, its high standard of living, its climate, open spaces, and opportunities for healthy living, so many people should be unwell.

One of my next impressions was the amount of misery and unhappiness, which also seemed so wrong in a country like this. The more I thought about these two facts, the more convinced I became that they were closely linked. Unhappiness tends to lead to ill-health; or, put the other way, happy people are much more likely to be healthy. I then discovered that Lord Horder, the great English physician of the last generation, had stated the same fact in similar words:

"Happiness, whatever its ingredients, is a large factor in preventing disease . . . a healthy nation tends to be happy, and a happy nation tends to be healthy. There is a considerable overlap between these two things."

DR. J. S. ROXBURGH,
Medical Officer of Health, Nelson, New Zealand.

CONTENTMENT is natural wealth.
Socrates.

September 4th

> WE MUST GO ON THINKING LESS ABOUT OURSELVES AND MORE FOR ONE ANOTHER; FOR SO, AND SO ONLY, CAN WE HOPE TO MAKE THE WORLD A BETTER PLACE, AND LIFE A WORTHIER THING.
>
> *King George VI.*

AUNT Frances lived in a village where the mountains crowded the cornfields and white plumes crowned the sky. On her widow's pension she supported her four children. She took in sewing, washing, and ironing. Sometimes she boarded children for social agencies until permanent homes could be found.

One cold February day Aunt Frances found an infant, warmly wrapped, upon her doorstep. Her heart was moved with pity. Tenderly, she took the baby inside, and sat in the rocker near the stove, crooning softly.

Years passed. Aunt Frances' own children were now grown up and married, living great distances away. Only Leah, the lovely "gift package", remained at home. Now a young and beautiful woman, she was eager to strike out on her own. "I know how much a nursing career means to you, Leah, dear," Aunt Frances told her. "You must go to the city. I can get along." With both joy and sadness, she watched her youngest fledgling leave the nest.

Aunt Frances grew old and feeble. The children she had borne in her youth were now selfish, and heedless of their mother's plight. While they lived miles away in luxury, Aunt Frances stuffed the seams and cracks in her old house with strips of newspaper. While they sent glowing letters recounting their own successes, Aunt Frances ate sparingly, closed off the rooms of the draughty house, and sat in the kitchen near the fire. While they counted their securities, Aunt Frances counted her change.

One wintry evening, Aunt Frances answered a knock on her door. "I've come home!" the girl on the porch said. Snow glistened on the dark hair under the nurse's cap. The blue woollen cape sparkled with snow. Aunt Frances stretched forth her arms, her eyes filled with tears, and Leah placed her own arms around the frail shoulders.

"It's my turn now," she said, patting the thin cheek. "You cared for me all those years. I've come to care for you!"

JUNE L. RICE,
in "Catholic Digest".

September 5th

MORE POWER IS WROUGHT BY PRAYER THAN THIS WORLD DREAMS OF.

Shakespeare.

OUR village loved Professor Graga. We all knew the story of the old man's collapse when the German invaders destroyed his beloved organ. His niece brought him to our war-torn countryside for proper nursing. Each day, at the home of little speechless Anna, the plaintive notes of his violin brought new life to her garden.

On this Sunday I joined them. Three Germans, two officers and an orderly, rode into the yard. The old man's lips moved in prayer as the trio dismounted and fastened their horses to the base of the tumbledown chimney. A young officer, bowing in mock respect, held up his crippled right hand.

I knew a little German, but could see that the arm of this glowering man was pierced by spikes from the Professor's pet porcupine. He had made a target of the great organ. Now, legs apart, with his revolver in his hand he taunted the feeble old man. Death hovered near. But, seemingly unaware of the danger this aged musician bent low over his moving bow, smiling calmly as a spine-tingling sound rose from his violin. The roots of my hair began to throb. Then, with a dull rumbling roar the massive chimney split in two, hiding the horses under a cloud of dust and debris.

Instantly the animals broke for the open road, with the shouting Germans at their heels. They did not return. The old man tucked his precious violin beneath his arm and led the way through the brambles to my grandmother's house.

When I tried to explain how a miracle had saved us, my grandmother nodded. "In ancient times," she said, "blasts of horns brought down the walls of Jericho. It was prayer that caused that chimney to crumble into dust."

ANN WIGMORE, D.D.
From "Why Suffer?"

Lunch break, Kinder Downfall, Derbyshire.
Photograph by Dennis Mansell.

AS WE GET OLDER we cling to our friends, those who have known us for many years, by whose side we have developed and changed and suffered. Those friendships are the real prizes we gain in this world-school in which we seek experience. So many work for the "glittering prizes" — titles, wealth, power and social advancement; but these things are only a transitory pleasure and by no means an undiluted one.

They bring added responsibilities, difficulties, problems, and both head and heartaches in their train. They can also bring a vast and empty loneliness unless they have been achieved in a spirit of love and unselfishness.

At the end of one's life, and indeed all through it, it is the friendship of one's fellow men which matters most. The handclasp when one is afraid, the encouraging word when in doubt, the comfort and kindness in sorrow and the warm companionshhip at all times.

Dame Barbara Cartland, MBE.
From:"The Light of Love", A Thought for Every Day. (Sheldon Press, London).

September 6th

I JOIN THE WHOLE OF CREATION OF INANIMATE THINGS IN HEART-FELT JOY THAT I AM ALIVE. I SEE THE SUN. I AM ON THIS GLORIOUS EARTH WHICH NATURE HAS MADE SO BEAUTIFUL AND WHICH IS MINE TO ENJOY.

BORN in the mountains of Lebanon, I have always loved the solitude of high peaks and deep gorges, and found peace in the company of fantastic rock formations. I do not recall the day, the month and the year in which the experience took place. But I do recall the spot and the hour of the day.

It was late summer afternoon, cool, clear and peaceful. I sat on a solitary rock, in the shade of a high wall of cliffs. Before me sloped to a deep gorge a stretch of land spattered with rocks and trees. Immediately to the left of me rose, almost perpendicularly, the rugged Mount Saneen—one of the highest and loveliest peaks of the Lebanon range. Now and then I could hear the twittering of a bird, the bleating of a ewe, the bellowing of a cow.

Drifting from one thing to another, my thoughts were finally caught in the net of such questions as to How? And When? And Why? And by Whom? All this came to be. Such questions had long been besieging me, although I was yet between 20 and 21 years of age. Oblivious to everything about me, I began to feel like one labouring in an endless labyrinth and seeking a way out. The search, however, did not seem to oppress me. On the contrary, I felt as if goaded on and on, and as if I were on the verge of breaking through.

Now subsiding, now flaring up, that feeling did not leave me until I suddenly emerged out of the labyrinth into a world flooded with dazzling light. How long I laboured in that labyrinth I do not recall. How long the sensation of light stayed with me—that also is hard to confine in seconds. It seemed like a fleeting twinkle of an eye; and it also seemed like an eternity.

So poignant, so deep, was that experience, that for the rest of the day, and for many days after, I lived and moved as one lifted on wings and given a glimpse of paradise. Nothing about me seemed alien to me, or unworthy of my love. I was at peace with all things.

Since then I have had no such experiences. Yet not infrequently, while writing, meditating, or simply drifting aimlessly, I have had a feeling of a Presence about me guiding my hand and mind, and helping me to turn smoothly and safely what appeared to me to be dangerous curves in my spiritual, literary and even social life.

Dr. Raynor C. Johnson,
"Watcher of the Hills".
Reproduced by permission of Hodder & Stoughton Ltd.

September 7th

WHO PLANTS A FLOWERING VINE OR A FRIENDLY TREE LOVES HIS NEIGHBOUR AS HIMSELF. A WORLDLY EMPIRE IS A BRIEF THING BUT BEAUTY IS ETERNAL.

Author Unknown.

A YOUNG woman, a lover of flowers, had planted a rare vine at the base of a stone wall. Though it grew vigorously, the woman noticed that it did not bloom, despite the good care lavished on it day after day. One morning, as the young lady stood disappointedly before it, her invalid neighbour, whose back yard adjoined her own, called her over and said, "You can't imagine how much I have been enjoying the blooms of that vine you planted."

The owner looked, and on the other side of the wall, she saw a mass of blossoms. The vine had crept through the crevices and had flowered where the neighbour could enjoy the beauty.

There is a lesson for everyone here. Often we cannot see the fruits of our labours and think they've been lost. But in God's service, somewhere, all our efforts bear their fruit—and some hearts receive their blessing and joy.

From "Forward".

September 8th

NOTHING IS TOO HIGH FOR ME TO REACH. MY STEP-LADDER WILL BE POSITIVE THINKING AND EACH RUNG OF THE WAY, COURAGE AND CONFIDENCE.

BROADEN your interests, learn something new every day, because the measure of your interests is the amount of information your possess. Don't let your life go by without discovering the thrill of appreciating good music, wonderful painting, the treasures in great books ... Rely on your own taste and judgement, and try not to feel that before praising a book or picture, you have to look round to see if anyone else thinks it's good. Determine to use your own mind, and project your own personality. You are the boss, not your circumstances. The climate of your life is within you and not outside you. You must believe that wholly, for faith that sets limits to itself, is no faith at all. Believe wholeheartedly and circumstance will yield to you; your life will be moulded into the pattern you want.

But remember if we want great lives, adventurous lives, successful lives, happy lives, we must not ask for easy lives.

AUTHOR UNKNOWN.

September 9th

THE BEAUTY OF MY HOUSE IS ORDER,
THE BLESSING OF MY HOUSE IS CONTENTMENT,
THE GLORY OF MY HOUSE IS HOSPITALITY,
THE CROWN OF MY HOUSE IS GODLINESS.
Author Unknown.

LORD, behold our family here assembled. We thank Thee for this place in which we dwell; for the love that unites us; for the peace accorded us this day; for the hope with which we expect the morrow; for the health, the work, the food and the bright skies that make our lives delightful; for our friends in all parts of the earth.

Let peace abound in our small company. Purge out of every heart the lurking grudge. Give us peace and strength to forbear and to persevere. Offenders, give us the grace to accept and to forgive offenders. Forgetful ourselves, help us to bear cheerfully the forgetfulness of others.

Give us courage and gaiety and the quiet mind. Spare to us our friends, soften to us our enemies. Bless us, if it may be, in all our innocent endeavours. If it may not, give us the strength to encounter that which is to come, that we be brave in peril, constant in tribulation, temperate in wrath and in all changes of fortune, and down to the gates of death loyal and loving one to another.

As the clay to the potter, as the windmill to the wind, as children of their sire, we beseech of Thee this help and mercy for Christ's sake. Amen.

ROBERT LOUIS STEVENSON.

September 10th

EVERY NIGHT I ASK GOD FOR STRENGTH TO HANG ON UNTIL THINGS GET BETTER ... I KEEP BUSY ... I KEEP MOVING ... I MAKE NEW FRIENDS ... I GO THROUGH IT.

MANY married women have left financial and business affairs entirely to their husbands. When they are widowed, they feel lost and unable to handle these responsibilities by themselves. After a life of shared decision-making, it is a shock to make them alone. Of course it is wisdom to consult competent friends or counsellors, but the final decision is one's own and must be taken, for once made one has to live with it.

It is generally agreed that it is not wise for a widow to make far-reaching decisions too soon after bereavement, when still in a state of deep shock. Acting precipitately may bring later regrets. When decisions have to be made, James counsel should be acted upon:

"If any of you lack wisdom—and who does not?—he (or she) should put their petition to God who gives generously to all without finding fault, and it will be given to him (or her)." (*James 1:5*)

Here is a definite undertaking by God that He will impart wisdom in decision-making to the one who asks for it. It is a promise to be believed and acted upon.

With this assurance, and the facts of the case before us, we can confidently trust Him to guide us in our mental processes as we weigh up the pros and cons.

J. OSWALD SANDERS,
in "Facing Loneliness"

Sincere thanks to the author whose address we are unable to trac

---

COME to me all you who labour and are heavy laden, and I will give you rest.

Jesus.

September 11th

EVERY PERSON I MEET TODAY IS A UNIQUE INDIVIDUAL DESERVING SOME DIGNITY AND RESPECT. MY MIND IS COOL IN THE FACE OF A THOUSAND AGGRAVATIONS. GENEROSITY TOWARDS THE OTHER PERSON IS THE HALLMARK OF A MATURE PERSONALITY.

HOW delightful is the company of generous people, who overlook trifles and keep their minds instinctively fixed on whatever is good and positive in the world about them. People of small calibre are always carping. They are bent on showing their own superiority, their knowledge or prowess or good breeding. But magnanimous people have no vanity, they have no jealousy, they have no reserves, and they feed on the true and the solid wherever they find it. And, what is more, they find it everywhere.

VAN WYCK BROOKS.

September 12th

A NEW LOVE OF PEOPLE QUICKENS WITHIN ME. ALL THE WORLD IS FRIENDLY.

ONE day when I was despondent because my efforts to solve some of my problems seemed to be of no avail, I felt the need to sit quietly for a while and hear the comfort of another voice.

At that very moment my cleaning lady arrived, ready to help with the weekly chores. Mary's sweet, ageing face greeted me in the usual way. Her smile was friendly, her greeting, timid and quiet.

"Let's not do any work today, Mary," I said to her impulsively. "Let's have a cup of tea and chat a while."

We did exactly that, and spoke of many things. Of Mary's grandchildren, and how green the grass was getting on the lawn outside my window. Of the weather, and of Mary's birthplace, a small town in Ireland where once I had visited. I did not speak of my inner turmoil, but soon I felt much better.

Months later, Mary mentioned that bright morning in my rooms. "I don't know what I would have done without those few quiet hours," she said. Then she told me that on that very morning before coming to work, she had learned that her youngest son had died—in Korea.

How marvellously God had used my own small troubles to help another bear a far more grievous burden!

Olive Bradshaw, Milwaukee, Wisconsin, USA.

September 13th

MY GRACE IS SUFFICIENT FOR YOU ... FOR IN WEAKNESS IS MY STRENGTH MADE PERFECT.
2 Corinthians 12:9.

GRACE ... never betrays the heart that loves her. She is as real, as living, and as active as Holy Spirit which is her mother. She is the filial sister of mercy; the heir and brother of truth. A gift from the Heights, she slumbers deep within the citadel of every heart where God dwells. We cannot earn her favours.

Enriched by her in-dwelling, we are indeed sons of God, irradiated by her bright shining. Treasure her dearly. She was bought at tremendous cost by the one Man. Kingdoms of the earth perish on the wheel of time, but her beauty is indestructible and eternal. She is the light in the eye of the searcher as he stumbles upon the pearl of great price. Possessing within herself power to produce her own energy she is indeed a day-spring from on high, transporting us into the kingdom of the Son of His love. Passing of years cannot diminish her splendour. Neither is the world able to quench that joy unspeakable upspringing in a pilgrim's heart as he strides unafraid through all the changing scenes of life.

THOMAS.

September 14th

I CAN DO EVERYTHING THROUGH CHRIST WHO IS STRENGTHENING ME.

IT HAS been my lot in life, living in the wilderness as I do, to be out in storms a great many times. I never knew one that did not do me good. For a storm, whether it be physical or spiritual, is always a challenge; and there is something in the heart that rises up to meet it. No other kind of occasion calls it forth. Storms rend and mar; but they strengthen, they build, and they may bring forth serene and changeless beauty.

We are prone to lament that the world is not better. Yet the fact that it is full of trouble affords us our only chance to spend our hearts. And it is not in times and places of peace that we find our heroes and heroines. A time of prosperity is a dangerous time; the soul loafs and grows fat. Times of storms and peril are the ones that show what we are made of. Loss and grief are always life's summonses to us to be great.

ARCHIBALD RUTLEDGE.
'Beauty in the Heart'

September 15th

> AND GOOD MAY EVER CONQUER ILL,
> HEALTH WALK WHERE PAIN HAS TROD;
> "AS A MAN THINKETH, SO IS HE,"
> RISE, THEN, AND THINK WITH GOD.
>
> *Author Unknown.*

THE diagnosis of intestinal carcinoma was confirmed in hospital by X-ray photographs and an exploratory operation. The cancer was growing rapidly, and it was held that the major operation should be performed within a week. But before admission to hospital I had committed myself afresh to Christ, for life or death without reservation, and in this *I found release from all fear.*

I entered hospital as a cancer patient on August 10th. I left it again on August 21st without undergoing a drastic major operation which, the surgeons had said, was my only hope of living for more than two or three months. An immediate improvement was steadily maintained, and long before the end of the year health was back to normal.

HUGH REDWOOD, O.B.E.
From: Is There Life After Death?

Publisher: Arthur James Ltd., 70 Cross Oak Road, Berkhamsted, Herts HP4 3HZ.

September 16th

> LED BY A KINDLIER HAND THAN OURS ...
> WE JOURNEY THROUGH THIS EARTHLY SCENE
> ... AND SHOULD NOT, IN OUR WEARY HOURS
> ... TURN TO REGRET WHAT MIGHT HAVE BEEN.

LOVE pervades all of God's operations. May we not imagine that God's judgements and dire disasters are due to a lack of affection? The very opposite is true. These are due to His desire for response to His goodness and grace. If we lived in a world of constant light, we would not appreciate it. But when the sun's bright rays shine through darkness and disaster we welcome them the most.

Our present trials may lead us to doubt His fond care. But our future bliss will be measured mostly by the blackness of its background. Even the sceptical will look back to their judgement in thankfulness, when they also will be justified and reconciled, when they realize how it has enabled them to appreciate His all-embracing love.

Unsearchable Riches.
Bimonthly magazine for God and His Word.
15570 Knochaven Road, Santa Clarita, CA 91350, USA

September 17th

> NEVER A TEAR BEDIMS THE EYE
> THAT TIME AND PATIENCE WILL NOT DRY:
> NEVER A LIP IS CURVED WITH PAIN
> THAT CAN'T BE KISSED INTO SMILES AGAIN.
>
> *Francis Brett Hart.*

AS A new mother my responsibilities weighed heavily upon me. After giving birth to two sons in as many years, I was a classic example of the "baby blues". I was exhausted from the physical demands of two close pregnancies. And added to that was the emotional drain of being a constant source of love and affection for my offspring.

A beautiful spring day found me sitting amidst the clutter of my living room floor mulling over my inadequacies. My two-week-old infant slept peacefully in the crib while his 18-month-old brother busied himself with rearranging the pots and pans.

Against my will the tears began to flow. When the clatter from the kitchen abruptly ceased, I was sure my son was about to present yet another demand. Instead he had seen my distress and was about to come to my rescue. He put his tiny arm around my neck and planted a soggy kiss on my already wet cheek. Without saying a word, he toddled off to resume his game.

Since that time my children have brought me a great deal of pleasure. They have given back to me in many ways the love I have shown to them. But the memory of that special day will always be dear to me. On that day I received the first fruits of a harvest I planted with loving care.

Suzanne Grosser.
Sunshine Magazine.

HOME is the place where character is built, where sacrifices to contribute to the happiness of others are made, and where love has taken up its abode.

Elijah Kellog.

September 18th

WHATEVER COMES, OR MAY NOT COME,
I WILL NOT BE AFRAID.
King George VI.
Christmas 1950.

PRIVATE Clifford Elwood, of High Street, Nantyfyllon, Bridgend, Glamorganshire, and Bugler Robert Hunt, of King Street, Mansfield Woodhouse, Nottinghamshire, both stretcher-bearers, were returning to their lines on the Arakan front with a casualty when they heard a rustling in the bushes and the click of a rifle-bolt.

Out into their path stepped a six-foot Japanese with his rifle at the ready. He looked at the two men and the third man they carried on the stretcher, and then without a word or gesture dropped the muzzle of his rifle and stepped back into the jungle.

Leicester Evening Mail, 19th May, 1944.

September 19th

THE GREAT OUT-OF-DOORS CALLS US WITH MANY VOICES. HER MOST GENTLE AND MOST SUBTLE CALL IS THAT OF THE GARDEN, OF THE TENDER CARE OF PLANTS, AND THE TOUCH OF THE DEAR BROWN EARTH.

HAPPINESS, I have discovered, is nearly always a rebound from hard work. It is one of the follies of men to imagine that they can enjoy mere thought, or emotion, or sentiment. As well try to eat beauty! For happiness must be tricked! She loves to see men at work. She loves sweat, weariness, self-sacrifice. She will be found not in palaces but lurking in cornfields and factories and hovering over littered desks; she crowns the unconscious head of the busy child. If you look up suddenly from hard work you will see her, but if you look too long she fades sorrowfully away.

There is something fine in hard physical labour. One actually stops thinking. I often work long without any thought whatsoever, so far as I know, save that connected with the monotonous repetition of the labour itself—down with the spade, out with it, up with it, over with it—and repeat. And yet sometimes, mostly in the forenoon when I am not at all tired, I will suddenly have a sense as of the world opening around me—a sense of its beauty and its meaning—giving me a peculiar deep happiness, that is near complete content.

DAVID GRAYSON.

September 20th

THIS DAY I EXERCISE ALL MY TALENTS: I AM CONSTANTLY ALERT FOR NEW IDEAS: I FIND IN MYSELF NEW AND UNEXPECTED GIFTS.

WE ARE each of us part of the total life and energy manifest in this world as it circles round the Sun. Our bodies bear the imprint of all forms of life in the immense past. Our minds carry within them, below the surface of consciousness, the experience of the human race in past ages. Both mentally and physically we need to be in rhythm with night and day and the changing seasons.

Our well-being as active and conscious persons depends on the degree to which we realise both our intimate relation to rock and river, plant and animal, light and air, and on the measure of good sense with which we seek to enrich our life through turning to account our material environment. All things are ours: hence our responsibility.

If we neglect to husband the fertility of cultivated soils, and if we persistently eat impoverished and refined food, the body reflects these errors in lowered vitality and manifold forms of disease. And if we exploit our inheritance or refuse to use the light of reason in all our affairs, we fall a prey to social and economic ills.

Centred in our individual make-up is creative energy, which seeks to find expression in diverse ways. Insofar as our bodies are lacking in the free flow of normal wellbeing, insofar as our minds are clouded or confused, this creative energy is frustrated.

EDGAR SAXON.
Nutritionist.

AS LONG as I live, I'll hear waterfalls and birds and winds sing. I'll interpret the rocks, learn the language of flood, storm and avalanche. I'll acquaint myself with the glaciers and wild gardens, and get as near the heart of the world as I can.

John Muir.

September 21st

I FILL MY MIND WITH THOUGHTS OF AN EVER-PRESENT PEACE AND POWER.

LOOK to this day, for it is Life . . . The very life of life . . . Within its brief span lie all the verities and realities of your existence . . . The bliss of growth . . . the glory of action . . . the splendour of beauty . . . yesterday is but a dream . . . tomorrow is but a vision . . . But today well lived makes every yesterday a dream of happiness and every tomorrow a vision of hope . . . Look well therefore to this day . . . Such is the salutation of the Dawn.

SANSKRIT.

Sanskrit is the language of ancient India, the oldest form of which is the Vedic, from 1500 BC.

September 22nd

I RESOLVE TO CONFRONT DIFFICULTIES AS THEY ARISE— TO DO SOMETHING HARD EVERY DAY—AND TO THINK-THINGS-THROUGH FOR MYSELF.

ALBERT Einstein, asked what he would say to science students, replied without hesitation, "I would advise them to spend an hour every day rejecting the ideas of others and thinking things out for themselves. This will be a hard thing to do, but rewarding."

The human brain can be an amazing instrument when it is *forced* to function. It can create a Beethoven sonata, a Hamlet, a rocket to the moon, television, the sculpture of Michelangelo, skyscrapers, pyramids—but never until it is driven to the hard job of thinking.

Countless areas offer challenges. "Doing something hard every day" could mean reading a profound book, forcing one's mind to stretch to its utmost capacity. As learned a scholar as Charles Darwin once said he regretted the lack of attention he had given to the stretching of his own mind with unfamiliar interests. "If I had my life to live over," he said, "I would have made a rule to read some poetry and listen to some music at least once a week; for perhaps the parts of my brain now atrophied would thus have been kept active through use."

OSCAR SCHISGALL,
in "Christian Herald".

September 23rd

I'LL TAKE TIME TO ENJOY THE FLOWERS, AND BASK IN AUTUMN'S GOLDEN HOURS.

HE NEVER saw again what he saw that morning. The children on their way to school, the silvery grey pigeons that flew from the roofs to the pavement, the little loaves of bread that some invisible hand had put out, all seemed to him divine. Two little boys ran towards a pigeon and looked smilingly at Levin; the pigeon fluttered its wings and flew off, glistening in the sun, through the quivering snow-dust in the air; from a window came the odour of freshly-baked bread, as a few little rolls were laid on the sill ...

TOLSTOY,
Russian novelist. From: Anna Karenina.

September 24th

THERE IS A MUSICAL SENSE; A SENSE OF BEAUTY; A SENSE OF COLOUR; AND ABOVE ALL A SENSE OF WISDOM. I WILL SEEK HER WITH MY WHOLE HEART.

WISDOM I loved and sought out from my youth, and I sought to take her for my bride, and I became enamoured of her beauty. She glorified her noble birth in that it is given her to live with God, and the Sovereign Lord of all loved her. For she is initiated into the knowledge of God, and she chooses out for him his works.

But if riches are a desired possession in life, what is richer than Wisdom, which works all things? And if understanding works, who more than wisdom is an artificer of the things that are? And if a man loves righteousness, the fruits of wisdom's labours are virtues, for she teaches soberness and understanding, righteousness and courage. There is nothing in life for men more profitable than these.

When I come into my house, I shall rest with her. Converse with her has no bitterness. To live with her has no pain, but gladness and joy.

When I considered these things in myself and took thought in my heart how that in kinship unto wisdom is immortality, and in her friendship is great delight, and in the labours of her hands is wealth that never fails, and in constant communion with her is understanding, and great renown in having fellowship with her words, I went about seeking how to take her to myself.

The Song of Solomon.

September 25th

> MY LIFE IS RICHER BECAUSE OF BENEFACTORS WHO HAVE GONE BEFORE ... IT IS SWEETER FOR THE NECTAR TAKEN FROM MY GARDEN TO SOME UNKNOWN HIVE.
> *Author Unknown*

MY GARDEN, that skirted the avenue of the Manse, was of precisely the right extent. An hour or two of morning labour was all that it required. But I used to visit and revisit it a dozen times a day, and stand in deep contemplation over my vegetable progeny, with a love that nobody could share or conceive of, who had never taken part in the process of creation.

It was one of the most bewitching sights in the world to observe a hill of beans thrusting aside the soil, or a row of early peas just peeping forth sufficiently to trace a line of delicate green.

Later in the season the song-birds were attracted to the blossoms of a peculiar variety of bean. They were a joy to me, those spiritual visitants, for deigning to sip airy food out of my nectar-cups. Multitudes of bees used to bury themselves in the yellow blossoms.

This, too, was a deep satisfaction. Although, when the bees had laden themselves with sweets, they flew away to some unknown hive, which would give back nothing in requital of what my garden had contributed. But I was so glad to fling a benefaction upon the passing breeze with the certainty that somebody must profit by it. There would be a little more honey in the world to allay the sourness and bitterness which mankind is always complaining of. Yes, indeed, my life was the sweeter for that honey.

NATHANIEL HAWTHORN.

September 26th

AN AMUSING FRIEND AND A CHEERFUL FACE BRING SUNSHINE IN THE DARKEST PLACE.

IT IS no earthly use telling people to be happy or to keep cheery. The utmost you can do is to set before them the good side by side with the ill, to show them the sunshine and also the shadow, to direct their attention to the kindness and gallantry in life as well as what is mean and deplorable; and if after that they cannot of themselves see how much more gold there is than dross, why, they must go on being miserable, and may heaven help them to enjoy it!

For seventeen days, ten of us were drifting about the Atlantic on a raft. Dick was the life and soul of the lot. The wind was as cold for him as for any of us, but he declared he'd never been one for muffling up. His ration was no bigger than anyone else had, but he used to say solemnly that doctors would go bankrupt if people didn't eat too much. When a ship passed us without seeing us, the disappointment was as bitter for him as for the rest, but Dick had an idea (or so he told us) that she was a German pocket-battleship. "And who wants to be taken to a Nazi prison-camp?" he demanded. "Tell you what," said Dick one day when we were all just about at the end of our tether, "I'll take badly to earning my living after leading the life of a gentleman all this time ... nothing to do and no one to tell you to do it!"

And when at last we were picked up, Dick was in better health than any of us.

From a letter written by the mate of a ship torpedoed early in 1943.

September 27th

I AM KEPT IN PERFECT PEACE, BECAUSE MY MIND IS STAYED ON THEE.

IT IS given to few men to experience the complete solitude that became the lot of the late Admiral Richard E. Byrd, the famed explorer, on one of his trips into the frozen wastes of the Antarctic, and about which he wrote so graphically in his book, "Alone". Trapped on a desolate barrier without the companionship of man or beast, and forced to remain there for a long time fighting courageously against cold, disease, and hunger, he had plenty of opportunities to reflect upon the meaning of life.

"My life became largely a life of the mind," he recounts. "Thinking things out alone on the barrier, I became better able to tell what in the world was wheat and what was chaff. I learned what philosophers have long insisted, that a man can live profoundly without masses of things. My definition of success itself changed. I came to believe that man's primary objective should be to seek a fair measure of harmony within himself and his family circle. Thus he achieves peace.

"I was conscious only of a mind utterly at peace, and yet I felt more alive than at any other time in my life. I saw my whole life pass in review. I realised how wrong my sense of values had been, and how I had failed to see that the simple, homely, unpretentious things of life are the most important. I thought of all I would do when I got home; and a thousand matters which had never been more than casual, now became attractive and important."

"Sunshine Magazine".

September 28th

FOR US THEY FIGHT, THEY WATCH AND DULY WARD,
AND THEIR BRIGHT SQUADRONS ROUND ABOUT US PLANT;
AND ALL FOR LOVE AND NOTHING FOR REWARD:
O, WHY SHOULD HEAVENLY GOD TO MEN HAVE SUCH REGARD?

Edmund Spenser, 1553–99.

PRAYER is the answer to every problem in life. It puts us in tune with divine wisdom, which knows how to adjust everything perfectly. So often we do not pray in certain situations, because from our standpoint the outlook is hopeless. But nothing is impossible with God.

Nothing is so entangled that it cannot be remedied; no human relationship is too strained for God to bring about human reconciliation and understanding; no habit so deep-rooted that it cannot be overcome; no one is so weak that he cannot be strong. No one is so ill that he cannot be healed. No mind is so dull that it cannot be made brilliant.

Whatever we need if we trust God, He will supply it. If anything is causing worry or anxiety, let us stop rehearsing the difficulty and trust God for healing, love, and power.

"Into the experience of all there come times of keen disappointment and utter discouragement—days when sorrow is the portion, and it is hard to believe that God is still the kind benefactor of His earthborn children; days when troubles harass the soul, till death seems preferable to life. It is then that many lose their hold on God and are brought into the slavery of doubt, the bondage of unbelief. Could we at such times discern with spiritual insight the meaning of God's providences we should see angels seeking to save us from ourselves, striving to plant our feet upon a foundation more firm than the everlasting hills, and new faith would spring into being."

ELLEN G. WHITE.
From: The Desire of Ages, a source of inspiration and enlightenment to readers all over the world.

September 29th

THE CYCLONE DERIVES ITS POWER FROM A CALM CENTRE. SO DOES A MAN. OUT OF RELAXATION COMES DRIVING ENERGY.

Dr Norman Vincent Peale.

RELAXATION while sitting. Sit upright in a comfortable chair without strain or tension, spine and head erect, the legs forming right-angles with the thighs (the chair should be neither too high nor too low). Rest the feet firmly on the floor, toes pointing slightly outwards, the forearms resting lightly upon the legs with the hands upon the knees. This should be accomplished without effort, for "effort" means "tension".

Dismiss all thoughts of hurry, care, worry, or fear and dwell upon the following thoughts:

"I am now completely relaxed in body and mind. I am receptive to Nature's harmonies and invigorating vibrations—they dispel the discordant and destructive vibrations of hurry, worry, fear and anger. New life, new health, new strength are entering into me with every breath, pervading my whole being."

Repeat these thoughts mentally, or, if it helps you, say them aloud several times, quietly and forcefully, impressing them deeply upon your inner consciousness.

After practising relaxation in this manner, lie down for a few minutes rest. If circumstances permit, practise "rhythmical breathing". Then return to your work and endeavour to maintain a calm, trustful, controlled attitude of mind.

If you are inclined to be irritable, suspicious, jealous, fault-finding, envious, etc. dwell on the following thought-pictures:

"I am now fully relaxed, at rest, at peace. The world is an echo. If I send out irritable, suspicious, hateful thought-vibrations, the like will return to me from other minds. I shall think such thoughts no longer.

"God is love, love is harmony, happiness, heaven. The more I send out love, the more I am like God; the more of love will God and men return to me; the more I shall realize true happiness, true health, true strength, and true success."

HENRY LINDLAHR, M.D.

From: "Nature Cure". "Philosophy and practise based on the unity of disease and cure."

September 30th

THIS IS A DAY THE LORD HAS MADE.
I WILL REJOICE AND BE GLAD IN IT.
The Psalms.

"JOY has a great therapeutic or healing value, whereas gloom and depression dry up creative life processes. Perhaps this is why Jesus so emphatically tells us to rejoice. One should learn to live the joy way. This does not mean, of course, to take a light or flippant view of the pain and realistic difficulties of contemporary life. But it does mean, certainly, to take a hopeful and optimistic attitude.

"One can think happy thoughts, say happy things, and seek in every way to put joy into people's lives. The more enthusiastically you do this, the more strength you will give to others, the better you will help to make the world, and the more surely you will keep your own spirit high.

"When low of spirit repeat this verse until its vitality lifts your depression."

Dr. Norman Vincent Peale.
"Inspiring Messages for Daily Living".

Rescued from the Plague

THE incident illustrated opposite is related to the diary of Samuel Pepys under the date of Sunday, 3rd September, 1665. The Great Plague was at its height. Over 10,000 victims had been carried off in London during the previous week. The authorities were at their wits' end, and tried to combat the pestilence by frantic and futile regulations. Sanitation and disinfection were unknown. It was ordered that the doors of infected houses should be fastened; that no one was to enter or leave them; and that the words "Lord have mercy upon us", with a cross, should be inscribed on the door in warning red – as can be seen in the picture – and the inhabitants left to their fate.

By ingenuity of love, a saddler of Gracechurch Street and his wife, themselves doomed, thought of a way to save their little girl, after burying all their other children of the Plague. They handed her, naked, from the window to a friend who had new fresh clothes ready; she was taken to Greenwich, and escaped.

Joseph Bibby, *Bibby's Annual.*

RESCUED FROM THE PLAGUE.
(Topham).
Guildhall Art Gallery/ Bridgman Art Library, London.

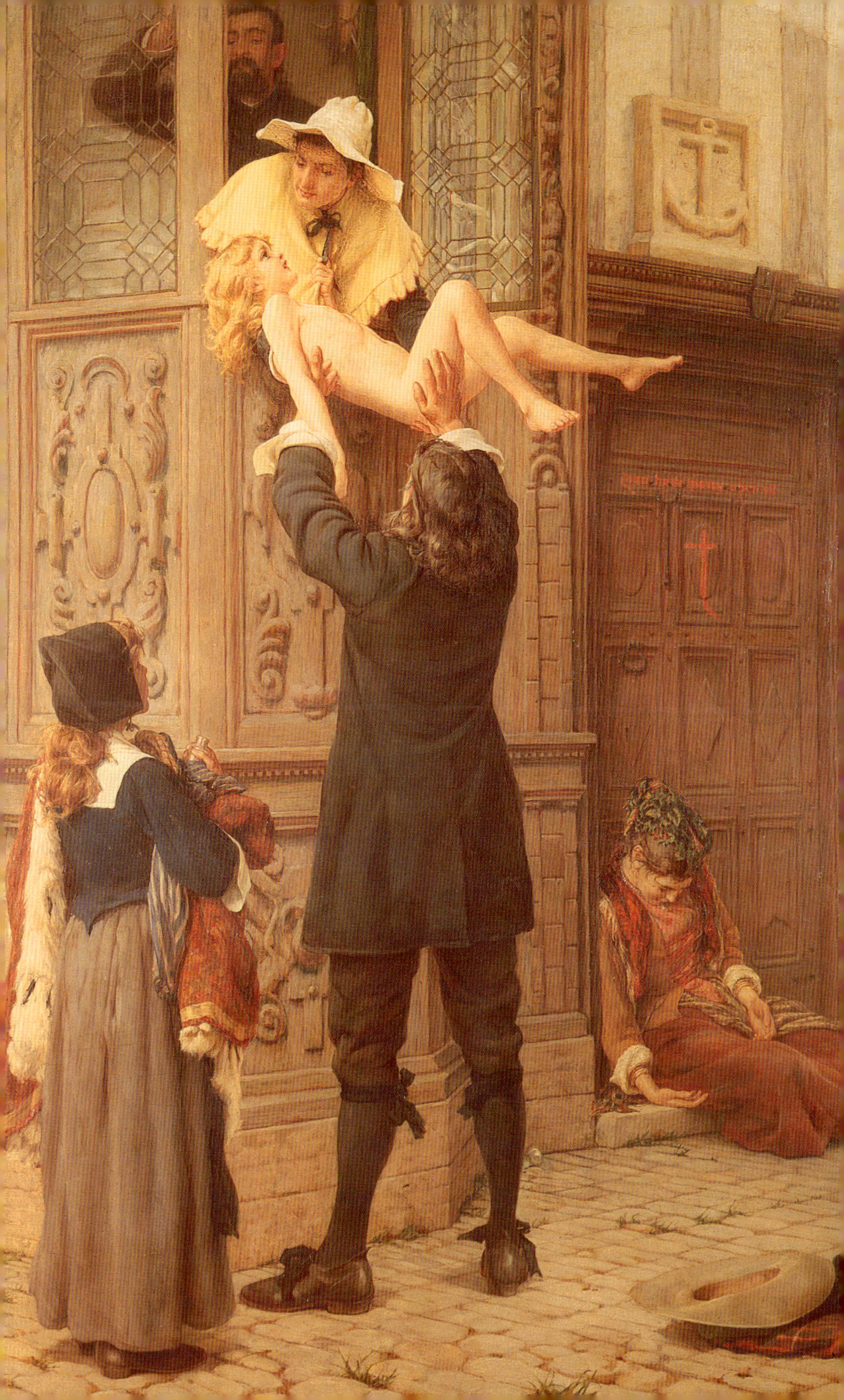

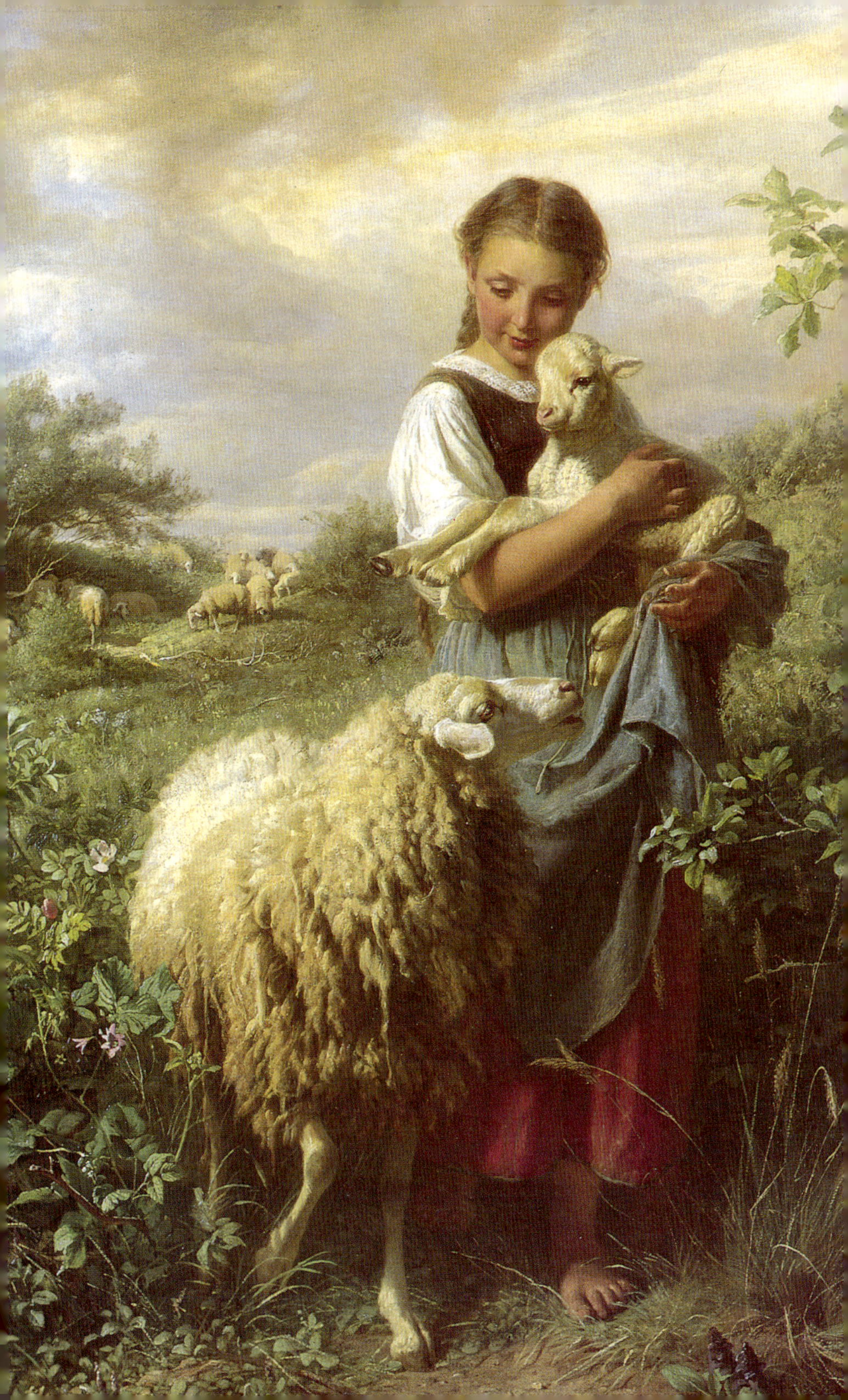

October 1st

> FROM QUIET HOMES AND FIRST BEGINNING,
> OUT TO THE UNDISCOVERED ENDS:
> THERE'S NOTHING WORTH THE WEAR OF WINNING
> BUT LAUGHTER AND THE LOVE OF FRIENDS.
>
> *Author Unknown.*

ALL that can be expected of any man is to make the best use of the things that are within his power. Only the contented man is rich, so we must look for the things that bring contentment.

And first of these is to find a friend. If you find two friends, you are indeed a lucky man. If you find three friends, real friends, then you are a rich and powerful man. In prosperity it is easy to find a friend, but in adversity it is most difficult of all things.

No matter how small a man's means may be, if he gives of what he has to his friend it is the same as if it were a great amount. A man's pleasures are ensured by sharing them with a friend. His griefs are reduced by securing the sympathy of a friend.

The counsel of a friend is the best counsel because it will be true advice; for when received from a mere acquaintance, it may be so filled with flattery that its value will be destroyed. Faithful and true counsel rarely comes except from a true friend.

It is said that in youth we have visions and in old age, dreams. The vision and the dream may give us an ideal of perfection; but experience and large contact with men compel us to accept the man who measures in his virtues only the substantial average.

If we view a man as a whole and find him good as a friend, we must not be diverted from the happy average ... the everyday, human average ... by using a magnifying glass upon his faults and frailties.

We must, in order to have and hold a friend, accept him as he is, demanding one thing in return for our affection ... his fidelity.

HARRY B. HAWES.

THE SHEPHERDESS.
By Johann-Baptist Hofner (1832-1913) – painter of animals and genre. Pupil of Piloty. He exhibited in Munich and Vienna from 1863; and died in Munich. Picture by courtesy of Christie's Images.

October 2nd

I AM RESOLVED TO MAKE NO SUBTLE ACCUSATIONS OR CUTTING REMARKS AS THOUGH OTHERS WERE RESPONSIBLE FOR MY LONELINESS. I INTEND TO EXCHANGE INSULARITY FOR POPULARITY.

IF ONLY we knew that the smiles we see
   Often hide the tears that would fain be free,
Would we not more tender and loving be
   If we only knew?

If we only knew that the words we say
   Oft drive the peace from some heart away,
Would we speak those words in the selfsame way
   If we only knew?

If we only knew that some weary heart
   Has been burdened more by our thoughtless art,
Would we cause the tears from those eyes to start
   If we only knew?

If we only knew, as we onward go,
   Many thanks that here we can never know,
For more patient love we would often show,
   If we only knew.

From an old scrapbook.

October 3rd

LIFE IS FULL OF SHADOWS
BUT THE SUNSHINE MAKES THEM ALL.

I DO not want to die without leaving a record of my belief that suffering can be overcome. For I do believe it. What must one do? There is no question of passing beyond it. This is false.

One must submit. Do not resist. Take it. Be overwhelmed. Accept it fully. Make it part of life. Everything in life that we really accept undergoes change. Bear it. And again bear it! Pain does not last for ever. It is only so terribly acute now. If you can cease reliving the shock and horror of it, *cease going over it*, you will get stronger.

Suffering is a kind of repairing process, so make it so. Try to learn the lesson it teaches. Life is a mystery. The fearful pain will fade. Turn to work. And put your agony into something and change it. "Sorrow shall be turned into joy." Try to lose yourself more utterly, to love more deeply, to feel oneself a part of life, not separate. Life Accept Me.

KATHERINE MANSFIELD.

Sincere thanks to the author whose address we are unable to trace.

October 4th

I AM GRATEFUL FOR PROBLEMS. AS EACH ONE
IS OVERCOME, I GROW STRONGER AND MORE
ABLE TO MEET THOSE YET TO COME. I THRIVE
ON MY DIFFICULTIES.

THERE is nothing which makes all evil worse than disquietude and worry. Birds are caught in nets and snares because when they are entrapped they struggle and move immoderately to escape and, in so doing, they entangle themselves much the more. When, then, you are pressed with the desire of being freed from some evil, or of attaining some good, place your spirit in a state of tranquillity, calm your judgement and your will. And then quite gently and softly, not negligently, pursue the end of your desire, taking in order the means which will be suitable . . . without worry and trouble and disquietude.

FRANCIS DE SALES, (1567–1622).

French saint. Born in Savoy. In 1610 founded the Order of Visitation, an assembly of nuns. Sales of his books in many languages run into millions.

October 5th

I WILL TAKE TIME TO LIVE;
THE WORLD HAS MUCH TO GIVE.

Thomas Clark.

IN SOME cloistered garden we may walk with peace, and in the joy of little things our vain efforts to comprehend the Universe may be forgotten. In tangible beauty is charm and solace. In visible Nature is comfort. Let us be eager to be pleased; grateful for every gleam of sunshine. Nature can comfort us and bring us joy. Are we not her children? Let us try, if it so pleases us, to understand her with the minds of sages, but let us enjoy her with the hearts of children.

So in the end let us seek a quiet home, and with earth radiant about us, face the setting sun. With thankful eyes and grateful hearts let us rejoice that it has been granted to us to live the length of our years in a world of beauty—to understand much, to divine much, and to come at last through pleasant paths to peace. Peace and understanding!

So with our last gaze let us face the serene sunset, content to have played our parts, and saying humbly:

Nature, from whose bosom I have come, take me back tenderly, lovingly. Forgive my faults, my failures, and now that my usefulness to you is ended, grant me to rest eternally. All is well!

ROBERT SERVICE.
Anglo-Canadian author. Born in Preston.
Famous for his ballads of the gold-rush days of the Yukon.

ADOPT the pace of nature . . . her secret is patience.

Emerson.

October 6th

"LOVE SO AMAZING, SO DIVINE,
DEMANDS MY SOUL,
MY LIFE, MY ALL."

WHEN I survey the wondrous cross
   On which the Prince of Glory died,
My richest gain I count but loss,
   And pour contempt on all my pride.

Forbid it, Lord, that I should boast,
   Save in the death of Christ my God;
All the vain things that charm me most,
   I sacrifice them to his blood.

See from his head, his hands, his feet,
   Sorry and love flow mingled down!
Did e'er such love and sorrow meet,
   Or thorns compose so rich a crown?

Were the whole realm of nature mine,
   That were an offering far too small;
Love so amazing, so divine,
   Demands my soul, my life, my all.

ISAAC WATTS (1674–1748).

October 7th

DAILY, WITH CONFIDENCE, I DO EVERYTHING WITHIN MY REACH. THE MOST DYNAMIC WORDS IN MY VOCABULARY ARE: "YES; NO; THANK YOU; NOT AT ALL; I'LL DO IT."

THE following are words I found in a composition which won first prize in a contest held by the *National Assembly for Youth Development* last year. "Every morning at our school, the Principal tells us to recite clearly the following five phrases and practise them. They are: 'Yes; No; Thank you; Not at all; I'll do it'."

Of the five, I myself have so far been trying to practise the first four. Of course, I am far from perfect in putting these four into practice, but I have now resolved to work on the last phrase, "I'll do it". This means doing things which must be done but which nobody else wants to do and this requires quite a lot of courage and determination. To start with, I have decided to do things I judge to be within my reach. I don't know how much I can accomplish in my lifetime, but I intend to work at it quietly.

When I see something that has to be done, I'll say, "I'll do it."

Seiji Kaya,
Professor Emeritius, Tokyo University.

October 8th

I RESOLVE TO FULFIL MY FIRST RESPONSIBILITY TO MYSELF—TO DO EVERYTHING IN MY POWER TO KEEP AS WELL AS POSSIBLE. I WILL FOLLOW THE EVERYDAY COMMONSENSE RULES OF HEALTHFUL, BALANCED LIVING.

Maurice Shefferman.

WISDOM and moderation in life up to middle-age will begin to pay off after fifty. Over-indulgence may be reflected in the waistline, the wind and the blood-pressure.

There is no need to be ashamed of the nap after lunch or before an evening engagement. Although older people require less sleep, they need it more often.

Breaking up the day in that way will help the older man keep up with the younger generation and the cultivation of young associates will lessen the chance of becoming a bore.

Institute of Directors Medical Unit.

October 9th

MY FAITH TURNS WEEPING INTO LAUGHTER, DESPAIR INTO JOY ... IN TOMORROW'S SUNRISE PROBLEMS RESOLVE THEMSELVES.

THERE are two days of the week upon which I never worry. Two carefree days. Yes, two, kept free from fear and apprehension.

One of these days is yesterday. Yesterday, with all its cares and frets, all its pains and aches, has passed forever beyond reach of my recall. I cannot undo an act that I have wrought, or unsay a word that I have said. All that it holds of my life's joys, regrets and sorrows is in the hands of mighty love that can bring honey out of rock, and sweet waters out of the barren desert. This is the love that can make all things right, that can turn weeping into laughter, that can give beauty for ashes, the garment of praise for the spirit of heaviness, the joy of the morning for the woe of the night. Save for the beautiful memories sweet and tender that linger like perfume of roses in the heart of the day that is gone. I have nothing to do with yesterday. It was mine. Now it is God's.

The other day about which I do not worry is tomorrow. Tomorrow, with all its possible adversities, burdens, perils and failures is as far beyond the reach of my mastery as its dead sister "yesterday". It is a day of God's.

Its sun will rise in roseate splendour behind a mask of weeping clouds. But it will rise. And the same love and patience will shine with tender promise as unfailingly as in the past. I have no possession in that unborn day of grace. Everything is in the safe keeping of that infinite love that holds forever treasures higher than the skies, deeper than the sea. Tomorrow is God's day.

I have left for myself but one day of the week, today. If there are cares and burdens to be carried they will be measured out to me "sufficient unto the day". Almighty love will surround me and a mighty strength sustain me moment by moment.

It is not the experience of today that drives men mad. It is remorse for something that has happened. Or fear of what may happen. Yesterday and tomorrow are God's days. I leave them to Him.

AUTHOR UNKNOWN.

October 10th

> HOME IS WHERE THE HEART IS,
> WHERE FRIENDSHIP IS A GUEST,
> WHERE LOVE AND FAITH AND GENTLENESS
> CAN SOOTHE A HEART AT REST.
>
> *Bessie Dunn.*

THIS is the true nature of home—it is the place of Peace; the shelter, not only from all injury, but from all terror, doubt and division. Insofar as it is not this, it is not home …

But so far as it is a sacred place, a vestal temple, a temple of the hearth watched over by household gods, before whose faces none may come but those whom they can receive with love—so far as it is this, and roof and fire are types only of a nobler shade and light—shade as of the rock in a weary land, and light as of the Pharos in the stormy sea—so far it vindicates the name, and fulfils the praise of home.

And wherever a true wife comes, this home is always round her. The stars may be only over her head; the glow-worm in the night—cold grass may be the only fire at her foot; but home is yet wherever she is. For a noble woman it stretches far around her, better than ceiled with cedar, or painted with vermilion, shedding its quiet light far, for those who else were homeless.

JOHN RUSKIN, 1819–1900.
British writer and art critic, born in London. His writings encouraged an appreciation of fine art and of the Pre-Raphaelites.

October 11th

> I BELIEVE THAT OUR DREAM OF A DIFFERENT MARRIAGE
> CAN STILL COME TRUE, IF WE BOTH TRY, AND KEEP ON
> TRYING. IT MAY TAKE TWO TO MAKE A QUARREL, BUT IT
> TAKES TWO TO GET ALONG.

OH, PROMISE me, that when the first intense excitement has died away, and the first bright lustre of our association has dulled, you will recall that this was your idea as well as mine … that you will always believe me to be the most desirable, and that the appearance of possession will not lull that desire into sleep … you will once more meditate on the theories we expounded in soft, hushed tones—that marriage merely gave us an option on each other, and both of us would try to keep that option desirable above all things …

Promise me, that you will forever believe those "magic words" were truly magic, and while they granted no rights, they blessed and sanctioned our privileges.

AUTHOR UNKNOWN.

Away over the Welsh hills.
Photograph by British Tourist Authority.

October 12th

FROM NOW ON ... I SHALL BE A DOER ... NOT A WORRIER.

WORRY never baked a cake, built a bridge, or solved a problem. Fretting does little more than make a bad situation worse. If you do your best, and try to find your fulfilment in making this a better world, there is little danger that you will overcome by fear of failure.

Thomas Edison tried two thousand experiments in search of a filament for the light bulb. When none worked to his satisfaction, his assistant complained, "All our work is in vain. We've gotten nowhere!"

"On the contrary," Edison replied, "we've come a long way and we've learned a lot. We now know that there are two thousand materials which will not make a good light bulb."

The assistant was a worrier, prone to discouragement, while Edison was a doer who was undaunted by set-backs. He kept his cool and ploughed ahead with confidence in all he did. In matters great and small it's always better to light one candle than curse the darkness.

THE CHRISTOPHERS.
12 E. 48th St., New York, NY 120017.

October 13th

LAUGHTER IS THE BEST MEDICINE, AS WELL AS THE MOST CIVILIZED MUSIC IN THE WORLD.

AT SOME time in our lives, we may ask ourselves, "What keeps us feeling young? What's the secret?"

The secret is laughter; something as simple as that. It is the language of mirth, humour, cheerfulness and joy. It is the greatest healer of all with no prescription required and it is available to anyone at any time. Laughter brings miracles. Its benefits are felt immediately.

It is heard in the sound of a child's gurgling laugh, of giggling children's voices echoing through a neighbour's fence. It is seen in the happy, smiling eyes of oldsters who know it can soothe a troubled spirit like no magic in the land. It takes so little to make us chuckle. It is contagious.

No matter how things may distress us, the gift of laughter is always free and it makes us stronger to run the race of life. Sharing laughter brings harmony and happiness to all our relationships. The ability to laugh and enjoy life is a life-saving medicine that wipes out despair and brings heartaches to an end.

There you have it! The secret turns out to be no secret at all. It is a natural thing that provides the invisible armour we need to protect us from the stresses of life.

LEA PALMER.
"Sunshine Magazine", *The House of Sunshine.*

Be the first to say, "Hello! Good to see you."

October 14th

IN QUIETNESS AND CONFIDENCE SHALL BE MY STRENGTH.

THERE is only one aristocracy that I believe in. It is the aristocracy of the spirit and is to be found among rich and poor alike.

I do not remember what people were wearing, when I met them. I remember their expressions.

I believe that people who love mountains unconsciously yearn to find themselves an inner height, from which to view themselves as well as the world around them.

I have sometimes reached the point of near despair. But there was always the quest to find the truth about the deeper meaning of life and to learn what to do about it. If some measure of understanding has been reached I wish to share it with my fellow men and women.

FREDERIKA, QUEEN MOTHER OF THE HELLENES.
From "A Measure of Understanding".

October 15th

HE PRAYETH WELL, WHO LOVETH WELL
BOTH MAN AND BIRD AND BEAST,
HE PRAYETH BEST, WHO LOVETH BEST
ALL THINGS BOTH GREAT AND SMALL;
FOR THE DEAR GOD WHO LOVETH US,
HE MADE AND LOVETH ALL.

Samuel Taylor Coleridge.

ALMIGHTY God, Father of all mercies, we thine unworthy servants do give thee most humble and hearty thanks for all thy goodness and loving-kindness to us, and to all men. We bless thee for our creation, preservation, and all the blessings of this life; but above all, for thine inestimable love in the redemption of the world by our Lord Jesus Christ; for the means of grace, and for the hope of glory. And, we beseech thee, give us that due sense of all thy mercies, that our hearts may be unfeignedly thankful, and that we shew forth thy praise, not only with our lips, but in our lives; by giving up ourselves to thy service, and by walking before thee in holiness and righteousness all our days; through Jesus Christ our Lord, to whom with thee and the Holy Ghost be all honour and glory, world without end.

Amen.
The Book of Common Prayer.

October 16th

I FIND DIFFICULTIES AND PROBLEMS ATTRACTIVE. IT IS ONLY BY COMING TO GRIPS WITH DIFFICULTY THAT I CAN REALIZE MY POTENTIAL.

Charles de Gaulle.

A MAN once said: "Every man takes the limits of his own field of vision for the limits of the world." It is possible because of this so many seem to live in a small, confined world.

Perhaps you do not ask enough of yourself. You are very conscious of your inadequacies. You know the things you cannot do. But have you ever taken stock of the things you can do? Not those easy, effortless things that everybody can do, but something demanding effort and concentration? You must not say "I cannot" until you have really tried. If you have tried and not succeeded, at least you have enriched your personality by your efforts. No real effort is ever wasted, for it has brought into play mental and "spiritual" muscles you never knew you possessed. Next time you attempt what is difficult you will be better equipped to deal with it.

Enlarge your life by attempting something difficult. Do not be afraid of problems. Such fear has destroyed many an embryo genius. It is far better to have tried and failed, than not to have tried at all.

The exciting aspect of this attitude is, that so often the thing you thought you could not do, you find you can do, thus you become mentally and spiritually alert for something even more difficult and a further broadening of the horizons of life.

AUTHOR UNKNOWN.

October 17th

KINDNESS IS ONE THING I CANNOT GIVE AWAY. IT ALWAYS COMES BACK, WHATEVER THEY SAY.

MAY every life that touches mine ... Be it the slightest contact ... Get therefrom some good ... Some little Grace, one kindly thought ... One aspiration yet unfelt ... One bit of courage for the darkening sky ... One gleam of faith to brave the thickening ills of life ... One glimpse of brighter skies beyond the gathering mist ... To make this life worthwhile ... And Heaven a surer heritage.

THE HUMAN TOUCH.

October 18th

I AM NOT AFRAID OF "THEY"; NOR DO I DESIRE TO BECOME A MAGPIE; THEN THE LAUGH WILL BE ON ME.

I HAD a wonderful father. I was his only child. In 1907 my father sent for me and said, "I'm going to die and I've nothing to leave you. You've got to go out into the world and make your own living. How are you going to do it? You're nothing much to look at, never will be. You have no name. You haven't any money. But I'm going to leave you a legacy. It's three simple rules.

"First, never be afraid of 'they'. People are more afraid of 'they' than anything else in the world. Strong generals with great armies will face courageously the most outrageous foes yet be terrified of what 'they' might say, 'they' might do, 'they' mightn't like.

"The second rule," he said, "is even more important. Never collect inanimate objects. You can't do it, for they collect you." So I thought the more you own the more you are possessed; therefore I own nothing but essentials. I'm free as air, and it's wonderful.

And the third thing he said, which suited me rather well, was, "Always laugh at yourself first. Everybody has a ridiculous side and the whole world loves to laugh at somebody else. You laugh at yourself first, and the laughter of others falls off harmlessly as if you were in golden armour." I have always followed that, too.

From an Elsa Maxwell CBS broadcast.

GIVE to the world the best you have,
and the best will come back to you.
Madeline Bridges.

October 19th

MY HOME LIFE IS ONE OF RICH JOY ... THE BOND BETWEEN MY DAUGHTER (SON) AND MYSELF IS THE PUREST PLEASURE I KNOW ... A MEMORY THAT NEVER FADES.

SOME memories never fade. They just get sweeter and more precious ... At just what seemed to be the busiest time of my day—household chores yet unfinished and dinner preparations not even started—I would feel the tug of little DeDe's hand on my skirt.

Sometimes in my busy-ness and impatience, my first impulse was to brush away her hand, but then I would look down into my daughter's eyes shining in anticipation.

"Mummy," she whispered, "it's time."

"Time for what?" I teased.

Throwing herself into my arms she replied, "Time for loving!"

Hugging her to me and then drawing her to my lap, the next few minutes would be spent in just "loving time."

Just loving time? Nonsense! How precious those minutes were! Those meals and chores, temporarily delayed or laid aside, have long since been forgotten, but those precious memories and beloved treasures of "loving time" will linger forever.

Just like those other special times when I would feel a tug at my heart and then a beckoning voice whisper, "Daughter, cannot the meals and chores be set aside for just a few minutes? How I long to spend some time with you!" Then I was reminded that for the Father and me, it was that special time—our loving time ...

My daughter, now grown and married with children to whom she is now passing along the legacy of "loving time", still touches my hand and with shining eyes whispers, "Grandma, it's time."

I smile and hug her close. My heart rejoices that big or little, young or old, we can make time for what's needed—loving time.

SANDY GOETZ,
in Sunshine Magazine.

October 20th

**DEEP INSIDE ME LIES A RARE TREASURE. THERE IS ONE THING IN THIS WORLD I CAN DO BETTER THAN ANYONE ELSE ...
I AM THE ONLY PERSON WHO CAN BEAM INTO THE LIFE OF ANOTHER THE LIGHT OF MY OWN SINGULAR TALENT.**

YOU say you have no talents? Now, you know that's not true. Experience and history have convinced us that people possessing the most meagre gifts have changed the world. What they lacked in brains, they made up with perseverance, grit, and the ability to see through some distasteful duty to the very end.

Gifts increase our power to give help. They make us more useful citizens. Are you talented in banking or economics? It is your duty to seek service on local government councils, and not leave the job to political opportunists with only half the qualifications.

Everybody has a talent. True, we might be quite independent now. Completely self-contained. Yet in a few years the situation may be different. Strength may fail, health break down through overwork or unwise food combinations. Wealth may disappear overnight as it did for thousands in the '29 depression. Friends may desert us. Even our much vaunted twentieth-century science may prove of no avail when confronted with the realities of life. In short we may be thrown upon the chance mercies of the world. We may need a second string to our bow.

Now is the day when you have the greatest power and opportunity to do a good turn to someone far too proud to request your aid. Do it while you may. Do it while you have strength and ability. Do it while your talents are still silvery and shining. Do it with those few shillings you have left over after your commitments to the Welfare State. What, only a few coppers left? Then you can buy stamps and paper on which to write chatty notes to pen-pals in hospitals, prisons and places of confinement. Your talent will be to make people laugh and to leave a trail of smiles in a lonely and thirsty land.

Are you a good mixer? That's a talent indeed. Put it to good use. Thousands of unhappy folk just haven't got it. Their lives will be a little livelier for an occasional squirt of the oil of cheerfulness that only YOU can inject into their social gearbox. Good mixing is an art. Many of us have to learn it. If you want to be good at anything you must keep practising it for years.

We may not all be endowed with the specialist skills of the artist, musician, financier or master-builder, but our talents with spade, pen, or even a pair of knitting needles may bring rare inner contentment and yield rich fruits, tenfold, twentyfold ... not to mention an ever-widening circle of friends.

THOMAS.

October 21st

I WILL BEAR IT PATIENTLY, AND GLADLY IF NEEDS BE. THE STORM THAT HAS ARISEN WILL SUBSIDE, AND PEACE WILL FOLLOW PAIN.

THERE lives no man on earth who may always have rest and peace without trouble, with whom things go always according to his will. There is always something to be suffered here, consider it as you will. Seek only that true peace of the heart, which none can take away from you, that you may overcome all adversity; the peace that breaks through all oppression, suffering, humiliation, and what more there may be of the like, so that a man may be full of joy and patience. Now if a man were now to give his whole diligence and might to it, he could very soon come to know that true agelong peace which is God Himself, as far as it is possible to a creature; insomuch that his heart would remain constantly unmoved and stable among the various circumstances of his existence.

THEOLOGIA GERMANICA.
A collection of works of great literary beauty on German mysticism in the 14th century.

October 22nd

YES, IN AN O.A.P.'S GARDEN GROW
FAR MORE THAN HERBS AND FLOWERS—
KIND THOUGHTS, CONTENTMENT, PEACE OF MIND,
AND JOY FOR WEARY HOURS.

Author Unknown.

GARDENS mean a lot of work, and contrary to popular opinion, it is the wife who usually does it. In London and the south-east at least, wives do more of the gardening than their husbands, and are keener on it than wives anywhere else in the country.

According to a national survey it appears that even in Scotland much of the toil of gardening is left to the woman. Only in Wales and the south-west is the garden a male domain.

And it is said that you catch the gardening habit around twenty-five and are apt to become addicted between thirty-five and forty-four. Husbands who haven't started gardening by the time they are thirty-five are likely to stay the way they are for ever, lolling in a chair and watching their wives hard at work.

"Time and Tide".

October 23rd

I NO LONGER RUN AWAY FROM MYSELF ... I INTEND TO KEEP ON LEARNING AND GROWING ... I DAILY WIDEN MY HORIZONS IN A PROCESS OF SELF-RENEWAL.

SELF-RENEWING individuals become versatile and adaptive. They avoid being trapped in the procedures and routines of the moment, or being wholly imprisoned by fixed habits and attitudes. As the years go by, most of us progressively narrow the scope and variety of our lives. Of all the interests we might pursue, we settle on a few. Of all the people with whom we might associate, we select only a small number. Our opinions harden. Our ideas congeal. This may be an inevitable part of living, but it is also a kind of imprisonment.

The selective narrowing of habits and attitudes extends to every area of life. We view our family surroundings with less and less attentiveness. That is why travel can be such a vivid experience. It shakes us out of our apathy, renews our freshness of perception, and we recapture in some measure the unspoiled awareness of children and artists.

Much education today is monumentally ineffective in teaching the art of self-renewal. All too often we give our young people cut flowers when we should teach them to grow their own plants. We stuff their heads with the products of earlier innovation rather than teach them to innovate.

JOHN GARDNER,
President of the Carnegie Corporation.

NOTHING of any consequence was ever achieved without enthusiasm.

October 24th

"I AM DETERMINED TO STICK IT OUT."

"LIFE'S richest rewards often follow, like day the night, after the tedious, arid periods when little progress is made, and when the most we seem to be able to do is to hold on. We can always hold on a little longer. At the Battle of Copenhagen, Nelson put his telescope to his blind eye in order not to be put-off by the difficulties ahead. It also had an encouraging influence upon those standing by. This, he did, before retiring to his quarters aboard the 'Victory' to make his last prayer. It can be a source of strength to you also.

"May the great God, whom I worship, grant to my country, and for the benefit of Europe in general, a great and glorious victory: May no misconduct in anyone tarnish it; and may humanity after the victory be the predominant feature in the British Fleet.

"For myself individually, I commit my life to Him that made me, and may His blessing alight on my endeavours for serving my country faithfully. To Him I resign myself and the just cause which is entrusted to me to defend."

NELSON'S PRAYER BEFORE TRAFALGAR.

Horatio Nelson (1758–1805). Entered the Navy at twelve. Lost one of his eyes in the siege of Calvi; Victor of the famous battle of Cape Saint Vincent. Skill and courage made him the victor in many dangerous campaigns throughout which he always acknowledged his indebtedness to Almighty God. It was at Trafalgar that he sent up the signal: "England expects every man to do his duty", October 21st, 1805.

October 25th

I CAN CHANGE MY LIFE BY CHANGING MY ATTITUDE ... I AM WELL. I EXPECT LITTLE ... I GIVE MUCH ... I KEEP MY HEART FREE FROM HATE, MY MIND FROM WORRY.

FEAR and worry and all kindred mental states are too expensive for any person, man, woman or child, to indulge in. Fear paralyzes healthy action, worry corrodes and pulls down the organism, and will finally tear it to pieces. Nothing is to be gained by it, but everything to be lost. Long-continued grief at any loss will do the same. Each brings its own peculiar type of ailment. An inordinate love of gain, a close-fisted hoarding disposition will have similar effects. Anger, jealousy, malice, continual fault-finding, has each its own peculiar corroding, weakening, tearing-down effects.

We shall find that not only are happiness and prosperity a part of right living—living in harmony with the higher laws, but bodily health as well. The great Hebrew seer described a wonderful chemistry of life when he said: "As rightness tendeth to life, so he who pursues evil, pursues it to his own death."

The time will come when it will be seen that this means far more than most people dare *even to think as yet*. "It rests with a man to say whether his soul shall be housed in a stately mansion of ever-growing splendour and beauty, or in a hovel of his own building—a hovel at last abandoned to decay."

There comes to mind at this moment a friend, a lady well on to eighty years of age. An old lady, some, most people in fact, would call her, especially those who measure age by the number of the seasons that have come and gone. But to call our friend old, would be to call black white. She is no older than a girl of twenty-five, and indeed younger, I am glad to say than many a girl of that age.

Seeking for the good in all people and in all things, she has found the good everywhere. The brightness of her disposition and the voice that is hers today, that attracts people to her, and that makes her beautifully attractive, has characterized her all through life. It has in turn carried brightness and hope and courage and strength to hundreds and thousands of people through all these years, and will continue to do so.

No fears, worry, hatreds, jealousies or grief have found entrance into her realm of thought. As a consequence her mind, free from these abnormal states has not reproduced in her body the various physical ailments that a great majority of people carry around with them ...

She has been wise enough to recognize the fact that there is one kingdom, at least, in which she is ruler—the kingdom of her mind. That is hers to dictate as to what shall and what shall not enter there ... It is a pleasure, as well as an inspiration, to see her as she goes here and there, to see her sunny disposition, her youthful step, to hear her joyous laughter. Shakespeare said: "It is the mind that makes the body rich."

RALPH WALDO TRINE.
"In Tune With the Infinite".

October 26th

THY GRACE IS SUFFICIENT FOR ALL MY NEEDS.

'GRACE' is the unmerited favour of God. We cannot earn it. In the book of Ephesians we read that 'we have been healed (saved) through faith for Grace. This is nothing to do with our efforts, lest anyone may be boasting. It is God's gift. For He is creating us after the pattern of Christ Jesus …' It is through faith. Therein we are raised to the sphere of Grace's operation. It is God's way of winning our favour. It comes from the Greek word 'charis' meaning 'joy'. It is an act of producing happiness; a benefit bestowed on one who deserves the opposite. It is sometimes translated 'favour'. Like all the best things in life—it's free!

A. E. KNOCH.
Los Angeles, U.S.A.

October 27th

IF I CAN'T BE THANKFUL FOR WHAT I RECEIVE … I'LL BE THANKFUL FOR WHAT I ESCAPE.

WE LIVE on a quiet, residential street with very little traffic, so when I crossed the street to visit my neighbour, I was absorbed in my thoughts and didn't look both ways. Noticing another neighbour sitting in his lawn chair, I started to wave to him when suddenly someone screamed, "Watch out! Watch out!"

I turned and to my horror saw a speeding car coming at me. I felt paralyzed as if my worst nightmare had come true. As a little girl I dreamt of a monster chasing me and not being able to run, but now the monster was a car.

Luckily, the car stopped two inches in front of me. The driver, visibly shaken, came over to me and asked if I was all right. "Yes," I said gratefully. "Thanks to you and my neighbour." I apologized to the woman because it was really my fault and she was very nice about it.

I went over to my neighbour to say how appreciative I was at his saving my life. He said, "You're welcome, but I was reading my book and didn't know you were in trouble."

Whose voice did I hear, I wondered? Then I knew it was God's voice warning me, loud and clear as a bell. I heard its urgency and knew He had saved me. Now I know I will always have God's protection in my time of need.

SUSAN L. WIENER,
in Sunshine Magazine.

October 28th

COURAGE IS ALL AROUND US ... TO FACE A CRISIS TAKES COURAGE ... BUT IT IS THE ONLY WAY TO LIVE.

I WAS on my way home from the forest, and was walking up the garden avenue. My dog was running on in front of me. Suddenly he slackened his pace, and began to steal forward as though he scented game ahead.

I looked along the avenue. I saw on the ground a young sparrow, its beak edged with yellow, and its head covered with soft down. It had fallen from the nest (a strong wind was blowing, and shaking the birches of the avenue). There it sat and never stirred, except to stretch out its little half-grown wings in a helpless flutter.

My dog was slowly approaching it, when suddenly, darting from the tree overhead, an old black-throated sparrow dropped like a stone right before his nose, and, all rumpled and flustered, with a plaintive desperate cry flung itself, once, twice, at his open jaws with their great teeth.

It would save its young one. It screened it with its own body. The tiny frame quivered with terror. The little cries grew wild and hoarse; it sank and died. It had sacrificed itself.

What a huge monster the dog must have seemed to it! And yet it could not stay up there on its safe bough. A power stronger than its own will tore it away.

My dog stood still, and then slunk back disconcerted. Plainly he too had to recognise that power. I called him to me; and a feeling of reverence came over me as I passed on.

Yes, it was really reverence I felt before that little heroic bird and the passionate outburst of its love.

Love, I thought, is verily stronger than death and the terror of death. By love, only by love, is life sustained and moved.

IVAN TURGENEV.

Russian novelist. Son of an army officer. His prolific pen helped bring about the abolition of serfdom.

October 29th

I LIVE EVERY MOMENT OF EVERY DAY IN EXPECTANCY OF THE GOOD WHICH GOD IS POURING INTO MY LIFE ... HEALTH, HAPPINESS, PEACE AND HARMONY ALL ARE MINE. AND SO IT IS!

I SAY to you: Take no thought for your life ... what you shall eat, or what you shall drink. Nor yet for the body, what you should wear. Is not the life more important than the meat, and the body than clothes?

Consider the birds of the air. They do not sow, neither do they reap, nor store into barns. Yet your heavenly Father feeds them. Are you not more important than they?

Why do you take thought for clothing? Consider the lilies of the field, how they grow. They do not labour, neither do they spin. Yet I say to you that Solomon in all his glory was not arrayed like one of these.

If God thus clothes the grass of the field, which today lives, but which tomorrow will be cast into the oven ... think of how much more He will clothe you, O you of little faith!

Therefore, take no thought, saying: What shall we eat? or What shall we drink? How shall we be clothed? Your Heavenly Father knows you have need of these things.

But seek first the kingdom of God, and His goodness, and all these things shall be added to you.

MATTHEW 6: 25–33.

A Quaker Wedding (Love and Loyalty)

In the purity and simplicity of this Quaker wedding of the early nineteenth century, there are revealed the chief characteristics of that deeply spitual religion. It was the mission of its founder, George Fox (1642-1691), to restore, as he said, the primitive simplicity of Christianity and free it from its corruptions. It was revealed to him that every soul could have direct access to God without human agency or ceremonial, and that inward illumination was the privilege of all. In this simple service we note the absence of priest, or ritual. A spirit of solemn reverence pervades the little company, each member of which is conscious of immediate communion with the Father. As the young couple pledge their love and loyalty to each other in simple words, a silent prayer goes up from those present that the blessing of heaven may guide them throughout life's adventurous journey. – *Bibby's Annual.*

O STAND STILL, look long, and hold yourself quiet.
                                   Ruth Pitter

October 30th

CONTENTMENT IS MY LIFE'S FULFILMENT. DAILY, I LEARN TO BE AT PEACE IN WHATEVER CIRCUMSTANCES I FIND MYSELF.

LIKE all men, I love and prefer the sunny uplands of experience, when health, happiness, and success abound; but I have learned far more about God and life and myself in the darkness of fear and failure than I have ever learned in the sunshine. The treasures one learns in the darkness, one possesses forever.

From a sermon by Leslie Weatherhead.

October 31st

I AM THANKFUL FOR THE UNDERSTANDING OF FAMILY AND FRIENDS. LORD, RENEW A RIGHT SPIRIT WITHIN ME.

ONE DAY, which happened to be a Jewish holiday, I was returning from Temple. At the time I was eleven. As I approached a corner four boys challenged my progress and after making harsh comments about my holiday suit and my holiday appearance, beat me up.

When I got to my feet I wrapped my torn garments around me and made a headlong flight home, feeling extraordinarily sorry for myself. Why had I been chosen for this unprovoked attack?

My mother comforted me and began to clean me up. The words she spoke to me then have stayed with me all my life and prevented me from becoming cynical, bitter or disillusioned when events went against me. Her words went something like this:

"Son, it's the beatings you do not deserve that are always the hardest to bear. When you do something wrong and you are punished, it does little good because you know you deserve the punishment. But when you take a beating for no reason at all, then you must be stronger and more patient because it is these beatings that will give you the understanding and strength to cope with life."

DORE SCHARY,
author and co-producer of 'Sunrise at Campobello'.

November 1st

THERE'S A RADIANCE ON THE DISTANT HILL ... A LONG NIGHT DRAWS TO ITS CLOSE ... THE PROMISE OF A NEW DAWN SPELLS HOPE FOR A BRIGHTER DAY.

WEARILY have the years passed, I know; wearily to the pale watcher on the hill who has been so long gazing for the daybreak; wearily to the anxious multitudes who have been waiting for his tidings below. Often has the cry gone up through the darkness, "Watcher, what of the night?" and often has the disappointing answer come, "It is night still; here the stars are clear above me, but they shine afar, and yonder, the clouds lower heavily, and the sad night winds blow."

But the time shall come, and perhaps sooner than we look for it, when the countenance of that pale watcher shall gather into intenser expectancy, and when the challenge shall be given, with the hopefulness of a nearer vision, "Watcher, what of the night?" and the answer will come, "The darkness is not so dense as it was; there are faint streaks on the horizon's verge; mist is in the valleys, but there is a radiance on the distant hill. It comes nearer—that promise of the day, the clouds roll rapidly away, and they are fringed with amber and gold. It is, it is the blest sunlight that I feel around me—Morning! It is morning!"

WILLIAM M. PUNSHON.
Sincere thanks to the author whose address we are unable to trace.

November 2nd

I WILL LOOK AT THE WORLD WITH THE EYES OF A CHILD, AND FIND JOY IN EACH NEW DAY.

KNOW you what it is to be a child? It is to be something very different from the man of today.

It is to have a spirit yet streaming from the waters of baptism, it is to believe in love, to believe in loveliness, to believe in belief. It is to be so little that the elves can reach to whisper in your ear. It is to turn pumpkins into coaches, and mice into horses, lowness into loftiness and nothing into everything—for each child has his fairy godmother in his own soul. It is to live in a nutshell and count yourself king of the infinite space.

FRANCIS THOMPSON.
British poet, 1859–1907.

November 3rd

THERE IS AN INMOST CENTRE IN US ALL, WHERE TRUTH ABIDES IN FULLNESS; AND TO KNOW, RATHER CONSISTS IN OPENING OUT A WAY WHENCE THE IMPRISONED SPLENDOUR MAY ESCAPE THAN IN EFFECTING ENTRY FOR A LIGHT SUPPOSED TO BE WITHOUT.

Browning.

ALL appeared new and strange at first, inexpressibly rare and delightful and beautiful. I was a little stranger which at my entrance into the world was saluted and surrounded with innumerable joys. My knowledge was Divine; I knew by intuition those things which since my apostasy I collected again by the highest reason. My very ignorance was advantageous. I seemed as one brought into the estate of innocence. All things were spotless and pure and glorious; and infinitely mine and joyful and precious . . . I was entertained like an angel with the works of God in their splendour and glory; I saw all in the peace of Eden; heaven and earth did sing my Creator's praises, and could not make more melody to Adam than to me. All Time was Eternity, and a perpetual Sabbath. Is it not strange that an infant should be heir of the whole world, and see those mysteries which the books of the learned never unfold?

THOMAS TRAHERNE,
"Centuries of Meditation".

November 4th

I OUGHT, THEREFORE I CAN.

I USED to let myself be shoved around willy-nilly by every little thing that happened to me. Then I decided that if we are, to a certain degree anyway, masters of our own fate, I master mine. So I started doing this as a daily practice. In the morning when I get up, I pick out the pleasantest parts of the day ahead, and concentrate on them; the nice folks I meet, the good breakfast and lunch and dinner I will enjoy, the little interludes of friendship I am sure to meet, a telephone conversation with an old friend, all the nice things that could happen. These always outnumber the ugly things like disappointments and frustrations, but we give precedence to those and forget entirely the good in our lives. I reversed the order. Now every day is a good day: I think myself into them.

AUTHOR UNKNOWN.

November 5th

ALIVE'S A LOVELY THING TO BE, GIVER OF LIFE—WE SAY—BLESS THEE!

TWO or three times a day our busy, separate lives come together for refreshment. The trouble with most of us is that we allow routine to dull these daily events. We take not only our food for granted, but the company in which we eat it. How different it is when you have been ill in bed, eating alone on trays, and at last come down for the first meal with the rest of the family. How willingly each puts his best foot forward to entertain. The meal is then a homecoming, a feast where is served not only food, but news, thoughtfulness and laughter. On such occasions the old truth seems beautifully new: Man cannot live by bread alone.

With a little thought a little effort, the simple necessary ritual of eating together can be raised from a monotonous habit to an art. Variety can spice our frame of mind as well as the food itself.

The meaning of the blessing can be preserved even without the saying of a formal grace—if only we will bring grace to the table, and be our best selves, not our pettiest, in the company of friends and family ...

... To the pleasure of dining well in good company each of us can add something. Just as one man, woman or child can sabotage the whole meal, so each of us can contribute a living share to the oldest and most cheerful of all human rituals.

AUTHOR UNKNOWN.

Thank You for the world so sweet,
Thank You for the food we eat.
Thank You for the birds that sing,
Thank You God for everything.

E. Rutter Latham.

November 6th

I WILL MAKE A LARGE PLACE IN MY LIFE FOR MUSIC, AND AWAIT THE PRICELESS REWARD IT BRINGS.

IN THE hour of work you will rejoice in the strength and energy good music gives.

In the hour of love music will enrich your heart and feelings that magnify the meaning of existence.

In the hour of high purpose music will summon the potentials of your soul and urge them forward to great and glorious achievement.

In the hour of rest music will uplift your spirit and give refreshment to every faculty of your being.

Such is the power of music. To this power open the doors of your soul, for there will enter into your life a greater fullness of all that makes for progress and joy.

HENRY GRAVES.

November 7th

THERE ARE MANY THINGS OF WHICH I AM AFRAID. IT IS BY ACTING AS IF I WERE NOT AFRAID THAT I GRADUALLY CEASE TO BE AFRAID.

HE SAT before the fireplace in the farmhouse listening to the old man's measured words. But already he knew what he must do.

"Son," the preacher said, "it's a hard thing to answer . . . Don't be bitter, son. You've had a run of bad luck. Why do the wicked prosper? Because God ain't interested in them. And they don't really prosper, unless you're fool enough to confuse material wealth with either happiness or peace of soul. And wealth is not that; most often it's a burden and a curse. You can buy a whole lot of hurtful things like soft living, hard liquor and easy women. But you can't buy health; you can't buy happiness; and you can't buy peace. And without those things, what do you have? Goodnight, son."

Riding home that moonlight November night, he was surprised at the feeling of peace he had. Nothing had changed; nothing had been solved; but he felt better about things—to face up even to writing his long-delayed letter to Jo.

FRANK YERBY.
"The Treasure of Pleasant Valley".

November 8th

I AM HOPEFUL, OPTIMISTIC, AND CONFIDENT THAT ALL EVENTS ARE ORDERED FOR THE BEST.

HOLIDAYS will soon be here, when it is time to spread goodwill and cheer . . . and produce lots of endorphines!

Endorphines? Yes. Researchers have found that the presence of endorphines—naturally-occurring substances that affect the receptor sites in the brain and spinal cord—are a dominating factor in our lives. They actually cause feelings of goodwill and happiness.

Studies on clinically depressed patients show a severe lack of endorphine chemical. This may be a breakthrough in understanding the origin of depression and joy. More importantly, researchers are learning that we can actually stimulate the production of endorphines through optimistic thoughts and a positive attitude. This may continue throughout every day of our lives.

Each one of us can learn to have positive attitudes and actions. People who are happy are successful in getting what they want from life. So try to radiate energy and goodwill, and spread around lots of endorphines during the approaching holiday season.

W. E. ADAMSON,
in "Sunshine" Magazine.

November 9th

I SHALL NOT FLAG OR FAIL. I SHALL GO ON TO THE END. THIS PRESENT ADVERSITY IS A GLORIOUS OPPORTUNITY— A STEPPING STONE TOWARDS FINAL VICTORY.

WE SHALL fight in France. We shall fight on the seas and oceans. We shall fight with growing confidence and growing strength in the air. We shall defend our island, whatever the cost may be. We shall fight on the beaches, we shall fight on the landing grounds, we shall fight in the fields and in the streets, we shall fight in the hills. *We shall never surrender.* And even if, which I do not for a moment believe, this island or a large part of it were subjugated and starving, then our Empire beyond the seas, armed and guarded by the British Fleet, would carry on the struggle until, in God's good time, the new world, with all its power and might, steps forth to the rescue and the liberation of the old.

WINSTON CHURCHILL,
From a speech in the House of Commons, June 4th, 1940.

November 10th

I WILL CULTIVATE THE POSITIVE HEART WHICH DOES GOOD LIKE MEDICINE.

WE CAN never gain health by contemplating disease, any more than we can reach perfection by dwelling upon imperfection, or harmony through discord. We should keep a high ideal of health and harmony constantly before the mind ...

Never affirm or repeat about your health what you do not wish to be true. Do not dwell upon your ailments, nor study your symptoms ... I would teach children early in life to build a barrier between themselves and disease, by healthy habits of thought, high thinking and purity of life. I would teach them to dispel all thoughts of death, all images of disease, all discordant emotions like hatred, malice, revenge, envy and sensuality, as they would banish a temptation to do evil. I would teach them that bad food, bad drink or bad air make bad blood; that bad blood makes bad tissue, and bad flesh makes bad morals ... I would teach the sick to have hope, confidence, cheer. Our thoughts and imaginations are the only real limits to our possibilities No man's success or health will ever reach beyond his own confidence. As a rule, we erect our own barriers.

The coming mother will teach her child to assuage the fever of anger, hatred, malice, with the great panacea of the world—Love. The coming physician will teach the people to cultivate cheerfulness, good-will, and noble deeds for a health tonic as well as a heart tonic. A merry heart doeth good like medicine.

RALPH WALDO TRINE.
In Tune with the Infinite.

November 11th

FATHER ... WHO HAS GIVEN US MUCH ... MERCIFULLY GRANT US ONE THING MORE ... A GRATEFUL HEART.

> HERE am I, with kitchen, stove, pots and pans,
> The wish to cook, and a pair of hands,
> Cupboards with all I want to take
> When busily making a home-made cake.
> Dear God, how kind you are,
> With thoughts of friends who will come to tea
> To eat the cakes which You made for me,
> So much to thank You for.

AUTHOR UNKNOWN.
Before making a Cake.

November 12th

> SUCCESS IS FAILURE INSIDE OUT:
> THE SILVER TINT ON A CLOUD OF DOUBT,
> I CAN NEVER TELL HOW CLOSE I AM.
> IT IS NEAREST WHEN I FEEL A HAM.
>
> *Author Unknown.*

SCARCELY a great man can be named who has not failed the first time. In such defeat no shame lies. The shame consists in not retrieving it. Lord Beaconsfield made, as everyone knows, a signal failure in his first speech in the House of Commons. But he was not discouraged by the derisive laughter which followed. With astonishing self-control and self-knowledge, he exclaimed, "I have begun several times many things, and have succeeded in them all at last. I shall sit down now; but the time will come when you will hear me."

The command of temper, mastery over self, which these words reveal, is almost sublime. The late Lord Lytton made many failures. His first novel was a failure. So was his first play. So was his first poem. But he would not yield to disappointment. He subdued his mortification, and resumed his pen, to earn the distinction of a top place among novelists. We should be disposed to define genius as the capacity for surviving failure. In self-control, at all events, it finds a powerful auxiliary and agent.

E. LUCAS.

November 13th

> WE BLESS THEE FOR OUR CREATION.
>
> *Book of Common Prayer.*

HEAR, O Israel: the Lord our God, the Lord is One.

And thou shalt love the Lord thy God with all thine heart, and with all thy soul, and with all thy might. And these words, which I command thee this day, shall be upon thine heart: and thou shalt teach them diligently unto thy children, and shalt talk of them when thou sittest in thine house, and when thou walkest by the way, and when thou liest down, and when thou risest up. And thou shalt bind them for a sign upon thine hand, and they shall be for frontlets between thine eyes. And thou shalt write them upon the door posts of thy house, and upon thy gates.

Deuteronomy (Shema Yisrael).

November 14th

WITH A SONG IN MY HEART, RESTLESSNESS IS FAR FROM ME ... MY THOUGHTS CENTRE AROUND A QUIET ACCEPTANCE OF ALL AROUND ME ... FOR MY PRESENT ENJOYMENT.

FOLLOWING a session with the psychiatrist and thinking over our conversation, I was still searching for an answer to the dilemma of the insistent feeling that my life is unproductive. Restlessness and discontent were still rife in my mind as I drove along.

The vision of one small white blossom, nodding to the rhythm of a mountain breeze, came to thought. At the time the little flower had come to my notice I was on a ski lift, nearing the top of Mt. Mansfield in Vermont. The expanse and majesty of the landscape had momentarily turned my thought to meditation.

The sight of this dainty flower on the mountainside brought a new, refreshing idea to mind. While those going up the lift might see it, it would have been there and bloomed all the same even if there had been no human eye to behold it. Therefore it was not there just for the pleasure of man because none would normally have seen it. It evidenced no demand to be seen and appreciated. This flower was fulfilling its appointed mission by being where and what it was.

I knew that, in one moment, I was understanding something beyond what my eyes beheld.

The memory of the mission of the tiny white mountain flower put to shame my demands that all my pursuits be productive. I remembered that God does not require tangible returns, only acceptance, from us for His great gifts. I thought of the colourful sunset, the deep blue sky, the sheer delight of the ever-changing clouds, the sweet smell of spring, the ripple of water over rocks of a mountain stream, and the bird songs of early morning. They are here for our enjoyment. How endless the list and how foolish my dilemma! It was no surprise that, at this point and with no effort on my part, I found a song in my heart.

MARY ELIZABETH CALDWELL,
in "Sunshine"

BOOK AT BEDTIME
Our sincere thanks to an unknown artist we have been unable to trace.

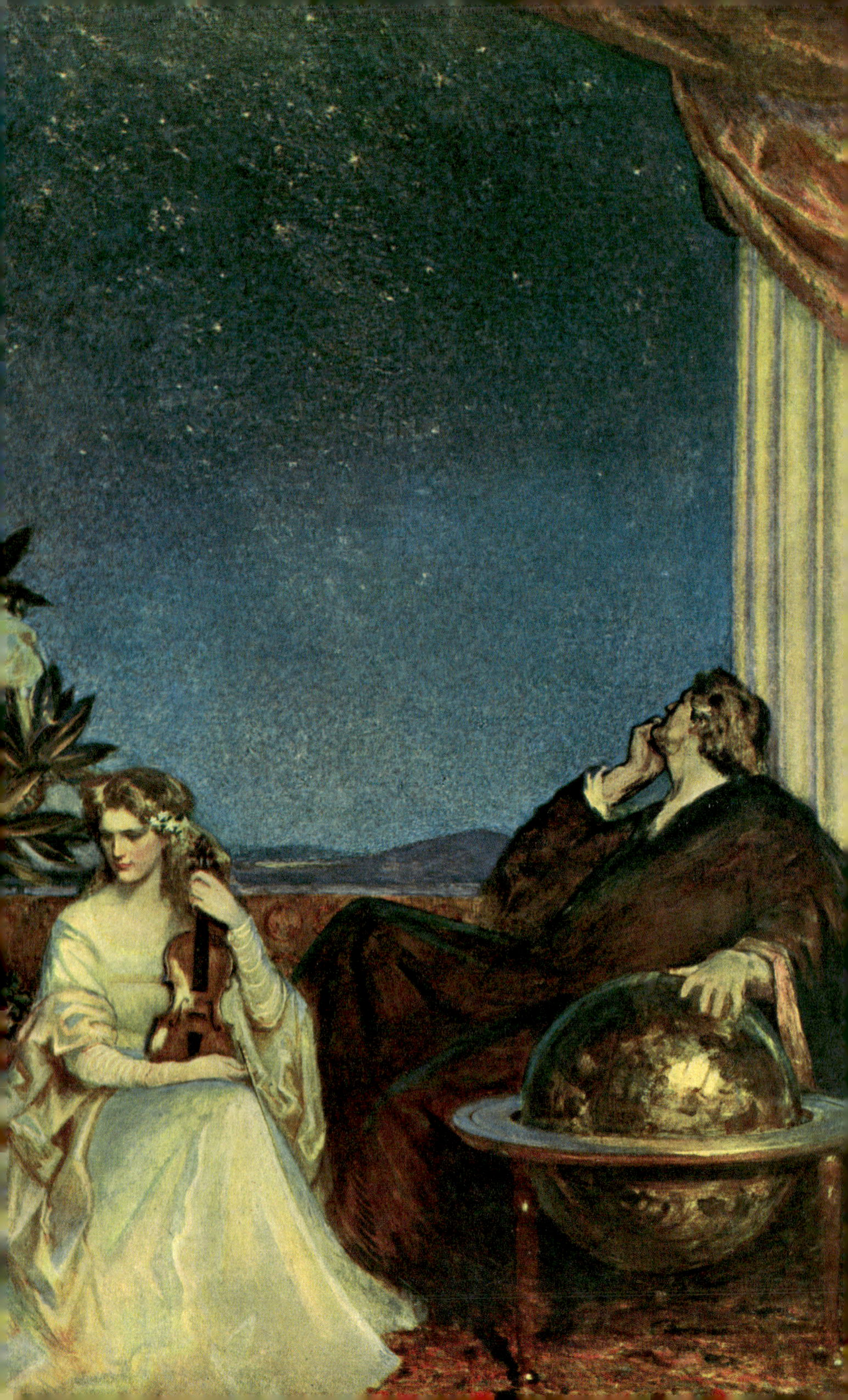

November 15th

TO KNOW THAT WHAT IS IMPENETRABLE TO US REALLY EXISTS, MANIFESTING ITSELF AS THE HIGHEST WISDOM AND THE MOST RADIANT BEAUTY ...
Albert Einstein.

WE LANDED on the Sea of Tranquillity, in cool of the early lunar morning, when the long shadows would aid our perception.

The sun was only ten degrees above the horizon, while the earth turned through nearly a full day during our stay, the sun at Tranquillity Base rose barely eleven degrees ... a small fraction of the month-long lunar day. There was a peculiar sensation of the duality of time ... the swift rush of events that characterizes all our lives ... and the ponderous parade which makes the ageing of the universe ...

In the next twenty centuries, the age of Aquarius of the great year, the age for which our young people have such high hopes, humanity may begin to understand its most baffling mystery ... where are we going? The earth is, in fact, travelling many thousands of miles per hour in the direction of the constellation Hercules ... to some unknown destination in the cosmos. Man must understand his universe in order of understand his destiny.

Mystery creates wonder and wonder is the basis for man's desire to understand. Who knows what mysteries will be solved in our lifetime, and what new riddles will become the challenge of the new generations? Science has not mastered prophesy. We predict too much for the next year and yet far too little for the next ten. Responding to challenge is one of democracy's great strengths. Our success in space leads us to hope that this strength can be used in the next decade in the solution to many of our planet's problems.

Reflections after returning from the Moon, by Neil A. Armstrong.
From Address to the American Congress, September 1969.

THE wise man looks into space and does not regard the small as too little, nor the great as too big; for he knows there is no limit to dimensions.

Lao-tse.

Sincere thanks to an unknown artist

November 16th

COURAGE PUTS A NEW FACE ON EVERYTHING ... IT MULTIPLIES THE CHANCES OF MY SUCCESS ... CALM AND COOL, I DO WHAT I HAVE TO DO.

PEOPLE often ask me if I have ever been afraid. They only make me smile. One Eastern philosopher said that any man who boasts that he has never been afraid has never put out a candle with his fingers. We are all afraid. Intelligent people, those with imagination, are the ones who know the most overpowering fears, and there is only one answer to fear—and that is faith. Unless we have something greater than ourselves to believe in, we are lost. We are prey to fears unless we can pray our fears away.

Talk about dauntless courage makes me smile. I knew what fear was every time I entered the ring. One night I shall never forget I was sound asleep and I woke up in the dark wondering what was wrong with my bed. It was shaking like a 1910 Ford. Then I suddenly realized that it wasn't the bed shaking at all. It was I who was shaking. I was trembling all over with fear. That was the night before my first meeting with Jack Dempsey, and even in my dreams I was thinking of what he was going to do to me the next day. Courage? ... It is not being fearless, it is finding the strength from God to do what you have to do—whether you are afraid or not.

GENE TUNNEY.

November 17th

I LOVE EACH PASSING DAY. THOUGH THEY BE SHORT, I MAKE THE MOST OF THEM. I HAVE EVERYTHING TO MAKE LIFE HAPPY.

YOU say that "this world to you seems drained of its sweets!" I don't know what you call sweet. Honey and the honeycomb, roses and violets, are yet in the earth. The sun and moon still reign in heaven, and the lesser lights keep up their pretty twinklings. Meats and drinks, sweet sights and sweet smells, a country walk, spring and autumn, follies and repentance, quarrels and reconcilements have all a sweetness by turns. Good humour and good nature, friends at home who love you, and friends abroad who miss you—you possess all these things, and more innumerable. These are all sweet things. You may extract honey from everything.

CHARLES LAMB, 1735–1834.
British essayist and critic. Born in London and educated at Christ's Hospital. Devoted his life to caring for his sister Mary who was mentally ill.

November 18th

I NEVER MINIMIZE MY ABILITY TO GROW A PERSONALITY
… I BELIEVE I HAVE ALL THE RESOURCES I NEED …
ALL I REALLY NEED IS IMAGINATION,
COMMON SENSE AND COURAGE.

THERE is no use in a round peg's imagining itself fitted in a square hole. As a matter of fact, many people flounder about pitifully before they discover the true direction of their lives. Whistler, the artist, started out to be a general and was dropped by the West Point Military Academy because he could not pass in chemistry. Sir Walter Scott wanted to be a poet and turned to novel writing only when Byron outshone him in his chosen field. Study yourself and use your head in picturing your goal. But whether with wisdom or without, pick a goal; don't drift.

Real personalities always have the kind of faith that produces courage. When his generation was against him, Richard Wagner had faith in his music, and it overcame the world. After centuries had borne unimpeachable testimony to the devastating virulence of yellow fever, a little group of American medical men in Cuba had faith that it could be conquered, and it was.

… Imagination, common sense and courage—even a moderate exercise of these will produce remarkable results. If a man is primarily after wealth, the world can beat him; if he is primarily after pleasure, the world can whip him; but if a man is primarily growing a personality, then he can capitalize anything that life does to him.

HARRY EMERSON FOSDICK.

November 19th

I PRACTISE FAITH—THE QUALITY THAT MAKES FOR SUCCESS.

THE world would have been deprived of knowing many great people if it had not been for the sacrifices of their mothers. There was, for example, a small boy working in a factory in Naples, Italy, years ago, who longed to be a singer. But this ten-year-old lad quickly was discouraged by his first singing teacher.

"You can't sing," the teacher said. "Your voice sounds like the wind in the shutters."

But the boy's mother did not agree. She encouraged her son to keep trying. She made all sorts of sacrifices, even going barefoot, in order to pay for his singing lessons.

This mother's faith was magnificently rewarded. Her son became one of the great singers of all time—Enrico Caruso.

THE CHRISTOPHERS.

November 20th

A SMILE DOESN'T COST ANYTHING YET PAYS DIVIDENDS ... NOT ONLY DOES IT MAKE YOU FEEL GOOD ... BUT IT MAKES EVERYONE ELSE FEEL BETTER TOO.
Author Unknown.

I WILL talk health instead of sickness;
I will talk prosperity instead of failure;
I will carry good news instead of bad news;
I will tell the cheerful tale instead of the sad tale;
I will mention blessings instead of my burdens;
I will speak of the sunshine instead of the clouds;
I will think of the cheerful things, not the gloomy, and my thoughts will shine in my face;
I will praise, whenever I can, those who are putting forth an honest effort to perform their tasks creditably;
I will always remember: a merry heart doeth good like a medicine.

AUTHOR UNKNOWN.

November 21st

I AM A SINGLE DROP, HOW CAN IT BE—THAT GOD, THE WHOLE OCEAN, FLOWS INTO ME?
Angelus Silesius.

WHEN prayer is habitual and really fervent, its influence becomes very clear. It is slightly comparable to that of an internal secretion gland, as for example the thyroid gland or the suprarenal gland. It consists of a kind of mental and organic transformation. This transformation operates in a progressive way. One might say that in the depths of consciousness a flame is kindled. Man sees himself as he is. He discovers his egoism, his stupidity, his errors of judgement, his pride. He bends himself to the accomplishment of moral duty. He endeavours to acquire intellectual humility. Thus there opens before him the kingdom of *Grace* ... little by little an inward appeasement is produced, a harmony of the nervous and moral activities, a greater endurance in regard to poverty, slander, worries, and the capacity for enduring without enfeeblement the loss of dear ones, pain, illness, death.

A doctor who sees a patient give himself to prayer, can indeed rejoice. The calm engendered by prayer is a powerful aid to healing.

DR. ALEXIS CARREL,
in 'Prayer'.

_{Sincere thanks to the author whose address we are unable to trace.}

November 22nd

AFTER MY SHATTERING EXPERIENCE, I FACE THE FUTURE WITH CONFIDENCE AND COURAGE. EACH DAY I AM INITIATED INTO THE DEEPER REALITY OF LIFE. NO MATTER WHAT COMES, I CAN TAKE IT.

A SHATTERING experience, if we have never before had one, we can hardly claim to be a real person. Most people look on suffering, from whatever quarter it comes, as an unrelieved evil. On the contrary, suffering is a part of the human condition and to over-cushion ourselves against it, is to deny ourselves a great maturing experience. You know how frustrating it is to try to share your troubles with someone who has never suffered. You get the feeling they have never really lived. AND, you would not be far wrong.

It is quite true some suffering is unnecessary and should be abolished forthwith. But as we mature and we get a grasp of the realities of our human condition, it becomes increasingly clear to us that it is neither possible nor desirable, to abolish the tragedy of life. To produce the complete human being some element of sorrow in life is essential. Indeed the very quality of our mature happiness is directly related to the quality of the suffering experienced. Suffering enables us to accept more and more the reality of Life.

R. J. LAWLESS.

I BASE my whole life on prayer. A hundred times a day my thoughts go to the one human life that so supremely influenced the world, and I renew my faith in my relationship with the Saviour of mankind. I have prayed silently during battles, during crises in the nursery, at glittering dinner tables and as a speaker on flag-draped platforms.

Gradually the miracle has been forced on me that no prayer goes unanswered. It may be answered by seeming disappointment, even humiliation. Often it is answered in a totally unexpected way, or when it has been forgotten even by the suppliant. The insufferable has disappeared, the unbearable has become precious and right, the heart-break has become heart's-ease.

KATHLEEN NORRIS.
Novelist.

November 23rd

I WILL GLORIFY GOD, AND ENJOY HIM ALL THE DAYS OF MY LIFE.

PRAISE, my soul, the King of heaven,
  To his feet thy tribute bring;
Ransomed, healed, restored, forgiven,
  Who like thee his praise should sing?
    Alleluia! Alleluia!
  Praise the everlasting King.

Praise him for his grace and favour
  To our fathers in distress;
Praise him still the same for ever,
  Slow to chide, and swift to bless,
    Alleluia! Alleluia!
  Glorious in his faithfulness.

Fatherlike he tends and spares us;
  Well our feeble frame he knows;
In his hands he gently bears us,
  Rescues us from all our foes;
    Alleluia! Alleluia!
  Widely yet his mercy flows.

JOHN GOSS, 1800–1880.

November 24th

I FILL MY HOURS WITH PATIENCE AND GLADNESS AND AM BLESSED WITH COURAGE AND CONFIDENCE.

IN SPITE of loneliness, poverty, and so many other causes of suffering, Christopher bore his lot patiently. He had never been so patient. He was surprised at himself. Illness is often a blessing. By ravaging the body it frees the soul and purifies it: during the nights and days of forced inaction thoughts arise which are fearful of the raw light of day, and are scorched by the sun of health. No man who has never been ill can have a thorough knowledge of himself.

ROMAIN ROLLAND,
from Jean-Christophe.

November 25th

LIFE IS EVERYTHING: LIFE IS GOD. EVERYTHING CHANGES AND MOVES TO AND FRO, AND THAT MOVEMENT IS GOD. AND WHILE THERE IS LIFE THERE IS JOY AND CONSCIOUSNESS OF THE FATHER-CREATOR. TO LOVE LIFE IS TO LOVE GOD.

Tolstoy.

WHEN I survey the scene of my past life as a whole, I have no doubt that I do not wish to live it over again. Happy, vivid, and full of interest as it has been, I do not seek to tread again the toilsome and dangerous path. Not even an opportunity of making a different set of mistakes and experiencing a different set of adventures and successes would lure me. How can I tell that the good fortune which has up to the present attended me with fair constancy would not be lacking at some critical moment in another chain of causation?

Let us be contented with what has happened to us and thankful for all we have been spared. Let us accept the natural order in which we move. Let us reconcile ourselves to the mysterious rhythm of our destinies, such as they must be in this world of space and time. Let us treasure our joys, but not bewail our sorrows. The glory of light cannot exist without its shadows. Life as whole, and good and ill must be accepted together.

Sir Winston Churchill.

November 26th

"DAY BY DAY I SLOWLY ATTAIN A STATE OF INWARD SECURITY REGARDLESS OF CIRCUMSTANCES."

"HOW can you live amicably amid the vexatious things, the irritating things, the multitude of little worries and frets, which be all along your way, and which you cannot evade? You cannot at present change your surroundings. Whatever kind of life you are to live, must be lived precisely amidst the experiences in which you are now moving.

"Here you must win your victories and sustain your defeats. No restlessness or discontent can change your lot. Others may have other circumstances surrounding them, but here are yours. You had better make up your mind to accept what you cannot alter. You CAN live a beautiful life in the midst of your present circumstances."

J. R. Miller.
Daily Strength for Daily Needs.

November 27th

> IT IS NOT THE WORK, BUT THE WORRY
> THAT MAKES THE WORLD GROW OLD,
> THAT SHORTENS THE YEARS OF MANY
> BEFORE HALF THEIR LIFE IS TOLD.
>
> *Author Unknown.*

NOBODY grows old merely by living a number of years. People grow old only by deserting their ideals. Years wrinkle the skin, but to give up enthusiasm wrinkles the soul. Worry, doubt, self-distrust, fear and despair, these are the long, long years that bow the head and turn the growing spirit back to dust.

Whether 70 or 17 there is in every being's heart the love of wonder, the sweet amazement of the stars, and starlike things and thoughts, the undaunted challenge of events, the unfailing child-like appetite for *what next* and the joy and game of life.

You are as young as your faith, as old as your doubt, as young as your self-confidence, as old as your fear, as young as your hope, as old as your despair.

While the central place of your heart receives messages of beauty, hope, cheer, courage, grandeur and power from the earth, from men, and from the Infinite, so long are you young.

AUTHOR UNKNOWN.

November 28th

> IT IS THE BEST OF GOOD THINGS FOR ME TO BE MYSELF.

IF YOU are criticized, you must have done something worthwhile; keep on! ... If your neighbour drives a better car than you do, that makes your old car no worse; and, who knows, maybe he has a bigger mortgage than you do too! ... If somebody calls you a fool, go into a huddle with yourself—he may have something there! ... If your competitor gets business by unfair means, don't worry; he can't keep it that way ... If the newspapers misquote you, think how much worse it might have been had they quoted you correctly ...

If you don't get everything you want, think of how many things you didn't get that you didn't want!... If the world laughs at you, laugh right back—they're as funny as you are ... If you have tried something and failed, just think how much better that is than not to have tried and succeeded ... So, keep your chin up and your eyes on the stars—they're always shining somewhere.

AUTHOR UNKNOWN.

November 29th

AT THE BACK OF THE CLOUD THERE'S A LINING —
AND IT'S GOLDEN AND SILVER AND BLUE —
FOR THE BRIGHTNESS OF HEAVEN IS SHINING
ON THE SIDE THAT IS HIDDEN FROM YOU.
Author Unknown.

IT IS the great mystery of human life that old grief passes gradually into quiet, tender joy. The mild serenity of age takes the place of the riotous blood of youth. I bless the rising sun each day, and, as before, my heart sings to meet it, but now I love even more its setting, its long slanting rays and the soft, tender, gentle memories that come with them, the dear images from the whole of my long, happy life—and over all the Divine Truth, softening, reconciling, forgiving! My life is ending, I know that well, but every day that is left me I feel how my earthly life is in touch with a new infinite, unknown, but approaching life, the nearness of which sets my soul quivering with rapture, my mind glowing and my heart weeping with joy.

DOSTOEVSKY.
From The Brothers Karamazov.

November 30th

O, GOD OUR HELP IN AGES PAST,
OUR HOPE FOR YEARS TO COME:
BE THOU OUR GUIDE WHILE TROUBLES LAST
AND OUR ETERNAL HOME.
I. Watts.

THE whole fury and might of the enemy must very soon be turned on us. Hitler knows that he will have to break us in this island or lose the war. If we can stand up to him, all Europe may be free and the life of the world may move forward into broad, sunlit uplands. But if we fail, then the whole world, including the United States, including all that we have known and cared for will sink into the abyss of a new Dark Age made more sinister, and perhaps more protracted, by the lights of perverted science. Let us therefore brace ourselves to our duties, and so bear ourselves that, if the British Empire and its Commonwealth last for a thousand years, men will still say, "This was their finest hour."

WINSTON CHURCHILL.
From a speech in the House of Commons, June 18th, 1940.

December 1st

A GOOD TURN IS NEVER LOST. WHO SOWS SINCERITY, REAPS FRIENDSHIP; AND WHO PLANTS KINDNESS, GATHERS LOVE.

I THOUGHT my heart would break the day after we took our four-year-old physically and mentally handicapped daughter to an institution. The morning dragged by. Every glimpse of a familiar object connected with Helen's care brought on a fresh siege of weeping. No one called; no neighbour stepped in.

After lunch I went out on to the porch to collect the mail. There, on the step, lay seven huge pink peonies. As I straightened up, my arms full of the blooms, I looked across the street at two small peony bushes, planted the fall before by my newest neighbour. They were stripped of their beauty. Thus, without words, my neighbour had spoken to my sorrow and, in that moment of warmth, my healing began.

ELIZABETH B. BAGLEY,
in "The Catholic Digest".

December 2nd

TO A MAN WHO HAS HAD A MOTHER, ALL WOMEN ARE SACRED FOR HER SAKE.
Jean Paul Richter.

A MOTHER can be almost any size or any age, but she won't admit to anything over thirty. A mother has soft hands and smells good. A mother likes new dresses, music, a clean house, her children's kisses, an automatic washer and Daddy.

A mother doesn't like having her children sick, muddy feet, temper tantrums, loud noise or bad school reports. A mother can read a thermometer (much to the amazement of Daddy) and like magic, can kiss a hurt away.

A mother can bake good cakes and pies but likes to see her children eat vegetables. A mother can stuff a fat baby into a snow suit in seconds and can kiss sad little faces and make them smile.

A mother is underpaid, has long hours and gets very little rest. She worries too much about her children but she says she doesn't mind at all. And no matter how old her children are, she still likes to think of them as her little babies.

She is the guardian angel of the family, the queen, the tender hand of love. A mother is the best friend anyone ever has. A mother is love.

From an unknown child.

December 3rd

EVEN THOUGH I AM ALONE WITH THE BEATING OF MY HEART, THE EARTH IS STILL FAIR AND FRUITFUL. ALL IS WELL.

ANOTHER time in a lowering and sad evening, being alone in the field, when all things were dead and quiet, a certain want and horror fell upon me, beyond imagination. The unprofitableness and silence of the place dissatisfied me. Its wideness terrified me. From the utmost ends of the earth fears surrounded me. How did I know but dangers might suddenly rise from the East, and invade me from the unknown regions beyond the seas? I was a weak and little child, and had forgotten there was a man alive on the earth. Yet something also of hope and expectation comforted me from every border. This taught me that I was concerned in all the world: and that in the remotest borders the causes of peace delight me, and the beauties of the earth when seen were made to entertain me. I was made to hold communion with the secrets of Divine Providence in all the world. A remembrance of all the joys I had from my birth ought always to be with me. The presence of Cities, Temples and Kingdoms ought to sustain me, and that to be alone in the world was to be desolate and miserable.

The comfort of houses and friends, the clear assurance of treasures everywhere, God's love and care, his goodness, wisdom, and power, his presence and watchfulness in all the ends of the earth, were my strength and assurance for ever. These things being absent to my eye, were my joys and consolations, as present to my understanding as the wideness and emptiness of the Universe which I saw before me.

THOMAS TRAHERNE.

December 4th

MY AGE HAS NOTHING TO DO WITH MY YEARS ... MY MIND IS CLEAR ... MY HEART IS YOUNG ... I HAVE A GOOD CHANCE OF REACHING A GREAT AGE ... AND ABLE TO ENJOY IT WHEN I GET THERE.

TO BE young is not a matter of years. Youth lives forever in a love for the beauty that is in the world, in the mountains, the sea, and sky, and in lovely faces through which shines the kindliness of the inner mind.

It is the tuning into the orchestra of living sound, the soughing of the wind in the trees, the whisper and flow of the tide on wide beaches, the pounding of surf on the rocks, the chattering of brooks over the stones, the pattering of rain on leaves, the song of the birds, and of peepers in the spring marches, and the joyous lilt of sweet laughter.

Youth lives without counting the years in a fluid mind which is open to new theories, fresh opinions, changing impressions, and in the willingness to make new beginnings.

What is it to stay young? It is the ability to hold fast to old friends, and to make new ones, to keep forever our beloved in dear remembrance, and to open our hearts quickly to a light knock on the door.

Youth is to remain faithful to our beliefs, to preserve our enthusiasms, to trust in ourselves, to believe in our own courage, and to follow where courage bids us go.

And, at last youth means that, like an unquestioning child, we place our hand without fear in the hand of the Gentle Guide, who will lead us through the little gate at the end of the winding road.

CORNELIA ROGERS.
Sincere thanks to the author whose address we are unable to trace.

I COUNT myself in nothing else so happy ... As in a soul remembering my good friends.

Shakespeare.

December 5th

I SENSE HARMONY IN EARTH'S MUSIC. I AM ONE OF THE STRINGS IN THE CONCERT OF ITS JOY.

Author Unknown.

LISTEN to earth's strong note, lie on the gorse spangled hill, ear pressed down to the ling, the mind untroubled and still ... D is the note of earth, singing for ever in space, lost in the city's din, unheard in the market place ... Only where land and sky commune in glad harmony, in tracts where no man dwells, is heard the resonant D ...

Stars in the galaxy, sing on with tone pure and clear, notes to mortals unknown, octaves are all earth can hear ... Not for eternity, shall the world groaning in strife, fail to hear the great chords, giving the universe life ... When the Word is fulfilled, reached is creation's desire, as love floods through the earth, O glorious the stellar choir.

(Mrs.) Gladys Cooper, Parkstone, Poole, Dorset.

December 6th

ALL WE ARE ASKED TO DO IS TO TRUST IN THE "ALL-PROVIDER" THAT ALL OUR NEEDS (NOT OUR WANTS) WILL BE SUPPLIED ... THIS IS THE LAW OF THE SPIRITUAL LIFE ... THE ONLY HINDRANCE TO THE WORKING OF THIS LAW, IS LACK OF FAITH.

EARLY in my father's ministry, there was no salary for pastors and the grocery list depended on the collection plate.

One blustery day when few people had been to church and the collection yielded only some coins, mother grumbled a little as she prepared a Sunday dinner. She scraped two cups of flour from the almost empty bin; at least there would be hot biscuits for Dad.

Dad's sermon that day had been on "Faith" and he assured mother now that the Lord would provide if they just believed.

"Vern Poole," mother said "can you stick your head in an empty flour bin and say 'Amen'?"

"I will," Dad answered, "if you will."

So, holding hands and giggling, they put their heads down into the flour bin and together said, "Amen."

Before the biscuits were in the oven, a church member came to the door. Their friend exclaimed: "For some reason my wife and I felt a little worried about you. We would like you to come over for dinner. Could you?"

From then on, mother's faith was as strong as Dad's. They both *knew* "the Lord would provide."

MURIEL VELTON.

December 7th

THE JOY THAT I CANNOT SHARE WITH OTHERS IS ONLY HALF ENJOYED.

TO LAUGH is to risk appearing a fool ... To weep is to risk appearing sentimental ... To reach out is to risk involvement ... To expose feelings is to risk exposing your true self ... To place your ideas and dreams before the crowd is to risk their regard ... To love is to risk not being loved in return ... To live is to risk dying ... To hope is to risk failure.

But the greatest hazard of life is to risk nothing ... The one who risks nothing and has nothing—and finally is nothing—may avoid sufferings and sorrow ... But he simply cannot learn, feel, change, grow and love ... Chained by his persuasion, he is a slave ... he has forfeited freedom. Only one who takes risks is free.

AUTHOR UNKNOWN.

December 8th

LET US, THEN, BE UP AND DOING ... WITH A HEART FOR ANY FATE ... STILL ACHIEVING, STILL PURSUING ... LEARNING TO LABOUR AND TO WAIT.

Longfellow.

JUST for today, I will try to live through this day only, and not tackle my whole life problem at once. I can do some things for twelve hours that would appal me if I felt I had to keep them up for a lifetime.

Just for today, I will be cheerful, though it break my heart. Happiness is from within; it is not a matter of externals.

Just for today, I will adjust myself to what is, and not try to adjust everything to my own desires.

Just for today, I will take care of my body. I will exercise it, care for it and nourish it, and not abuse it or neglect it.

Just for today, I will try to strengthen my mind. I will study. I will learn something useful. I will not be a mental loafer. I will read something that requires effort, thought, concentration.

Just for today, I will be agreeable. I will think of God, so as to get a little more perspective to my life. I will do somebody a good turn and not get found out.

Just for today, I will be unafraid. Especially, I will not be afraid to be happy, to enjoy what is beautiful, to love and to believe that those I love, love me.

DR FRANK CRANE,
in Sunshine, May 1931.

December 9th

I AM NOT CONCERNED WITH DISEASES, BUT WITH MISTAKES IN LIVING... I GET RID OF THE MISTAKES AND DISEASES TAKE CARE OF THEMSELVES.

I believe that you are as young as you look, feel, think, hope, believe and act. I believe the way you look, feel, think, hope, believe and act depends on three things:

1. *Good food.* 2. *A strong, vibrant body.* 3. *An adventurous spirit.*

In short, I believe you are as young as your diet. The world over, scientists studying the extension of life are finding more and more evidence that the fountain of youth is good nutrition. Dr. Henry C. Sherman of Columbia University is considered one of the world's outstanding authorities on nutrition. In a lecture given before the New York Academy of Medicine, Dr. Sherman stated that, given the right selection of foods, human life can be greatly extended. Furthermore, the later years can be lived in much fuller measure of usefulness.

What is meant by good nutrition? First it is adequate nutrition, giving the individual cells of the body not only the quantity but also the quality of nourishment they require. Second, it is balanced nutrition, supplying the body cells with vital nutrients in the proper proportion. Scientists are unanimous in agreeing that over-nutrition, through excess calories stored as fat, can contribute materially to physical deterioration and the ageing process.

As a simplified, perhaps crude, illustration, think of your body as a motor car. It is made of protein, inside and out. Arteries, glands, colon, connective tissue; muscles, skin, bones, hair, teeth, eyes: all contain protein and are maintained and rebuilt with protein. Fats and carbohydrates are your body's oil and petrol; they are burned together to produce energy. Vitamins and minerals are the sparking plugs, essential to the utilization of food and its assimilation into the blood stream.

It is a marvellous, sturdy motor car, this body of yours—marvellous in its ability to maintain and rebuild itself. Given care, consideration and respect, it will function smoothly, on and on. Provided that none of its important organs have been allowed to break down, it can and will heal and regenerate itself at any age. It cannot be neglected or abused. It must be fed and cared for faithfully.

GAYLORD HAUSER.
"Look Younger, Live Longer".
Reproduced by permission of Faber & Faber Ltd.

December 10th

ENTHUSIASM MAKES ORDINARY PEOPLE EXTRAORDINARY.

A MAN had died, and the whole city mourned his going. At a club we were discussing him, reminding ourselves of one characteristic and another that had endeared him to us.

Finally, a man whose name is famous spoke; "You know our friend hardly had a fair start," he said quietly. "Nature did not mean to let him be a big man. She equipped him with very ordinary talents.

"I can remember the first time I heard him speak. It was a very stumbling performance. Yet, in later years, we regarded him as one of the real orators of his generation.

"His mind was neither very original nor very profound, but he managed to build a great institution, and the imprint of his influence is on ten thousand lives."

The speaker stopped, and we urged him to go on.

"How then do you account for his success?" we asked.

"It is simple," he replied. "He merely forgot himself. When he spoke, his imperfections were lost in the glory of his enthusiasm. When he organized, the fire of his faith burned away all obstacles. He abandoned himself utterly to the task; and the task moulded him into greatness."

BRUCE BARTON.

Sincere thanks to the author whose address we are unable to trace.

December 11th

GOD IS THE FIRE IN ME. I AM THE GLOW IN HIM. THE UNIVERSE NEEDS ME. SOMEWHERE, SOMEONE AWAITS A WARMTH I ONLY CAN IMPART.

LITTLE do men perceive what solitude is, and how far it extends. For a crowd is not company, and talk is but a tinkling cymbal where there is no love. A principal part of Friendship is the ease and release of the fullness and swellings of the heart, which passions of all kinds cause and induce. We know that diseases of congestions and difficult breathing are among the most dangerous in the body. It is not much otherwise in the mind. You may take sarsaparilla for the liver ... vervain for the brain; but no recipe opens the heart like a true friend, to whom you may impart griefs, joys, fears, hopes, suspicions, counsels and whatsoever lies on the heart to oppress it, in a kind of confession ...

FRANCIS BACON,
Baron Verulam.

December 12th

I AM TOO BUSY TO WORRY DURING THE DAYTIME ... AND TOO SLEEPY TO WORRY AT NIGHT.

I THINK that human life is much like road life. You stand on a hill, and look down and across the valley, and another prodigious hill lifts itself upon the other side. The day is hot, your horse is weary, and you are tired. It seems to you that you cannot climb that long hill. But you had better trot down the hill you are on, and not trouble yourself about the other one. You find the valley pleasant and inspiring. When you get across it, you meet only a slight ascent, and begin to wonder where the steep hill is which you saw. You drive along briskly, and when you reach the highest point, you find that there has not been an inch of the hill over which you have not trotted. You see that it was illusory. The slight ascent looked almost like a perpendicular steep; but when you come to pass over it, step by step, you find it to be a good travelling road.

So it is with your troubles. Just in that way your anticipations of mischief hang before you. When you come to where they are, you find them to be all smooth turnpikes. Men ought to be ashamed, after they have done that two or three times, not to take the hint, and profit by it. Yet they will not. They will suffer from anticipated troubles just as much as though they had no such experience. They have not wit enough to make use of the lesson which their life is continually teaching them; namely, that a large majority of the troubles which they worry themselves about beforehand either never come or are easily borne. They form a habit of fretting about future troubles. It was not the old monks alone who wore sackcloth and hair shirts; you wear them as much as they did; only you wear them inside, while they wore them outside. You wear them in your heart, they wore them on their flesh. They were wiser than you are.

HENRY WARD BEECHER.

MAY the road rise with you,
May the wind be always at our back.
May the sun shine warm upon your face,
And the rains fall soft upon your fields.
And, until we meet again
May God keep you in the hollow of his hand.
Anonymous

The Mitherless Bairn, by T. Faed.
By courtesy of The Royal Pavilion Libraries & Museums, Brighton & Hove.

December 13th

I WILL REINSTATE THE PRACTICE OF SAYING "GRACE" WITH MY MEALS: AND AS HE BLESSED THE LOAVES AND THE FISHES, SO BLESS THIS FOOD WE FIND IN OUR DISHES.

I HAD now brought my state of life to be much easier in itself than it was at first, and much easier to my mind as well as to the body. I frequently sat down to my meals with thankfulness, and admired the hand of God's providence, which had thus spread my table. I learned to look more upon the bright side of my condition, and less upon the dark side, and to consider what I enjoyed, rather than what I wanted. This gave me sometimes such secret comforts, that I cannot express them. I take notice of them here, to put discontented people in mind of them—those, who cannot enjoy comfortably what God has given them, because they see and covet something that He has not given them.

All our discontents about what we want, appear to me to spring from the want of thankfulness for what we already have.

ROBINSON CRUSOE.

December 14th

YEA ... THOUGH I WALK THROUGH THE VALLEY OF THE SHADOW OF DEATH, I WILL FEAR NO EVIL; FOR THOU ART WITH ME.
Psalm 23.

THE story of the Battle of Britain I can never forget is of Mr Churchill going to the Headquarters of Air Vice-Marshal K. R. Parks, who was commanding the all-important No. 11 Group. On the radar screen the Prime Minister watched the advance of the German bombers. As each wave approached the Air Vice-Marshal gave his orders to put in the British fighter squadrons.

Calm, quiet and authoritative, the Air Marshal's voice showed no sign of emotion, and Mr Churchill, tense, his bulldog face set, watched in silence. Each attack was successfully repelled, but to the waves of German bombers there seemed to be no end. Wave after wave appeared, wave upon wave ...

At last Mr Churchill turned abruptly. "How many more have you got?"

The Air Marshal's voice didn't alter. "I am putting in my last."

Their eyes fixed on the screen, the two men waited for the next German wave. It never came. With tears in his eyes Winston Churchill got into his car. It was on his way back to London that he composed the immortal phrase: "Never in the field of human conflict has so much been owed by so many to so few."

DAME BARBARA CARTLAND.
"The Light of Love" (Sheldon Press).

December 15th

WHEN I FIND MYSELF BOGGED DOWN BY DEPRESSION—DOWN IN THE DUMPS—MY SURE SOLUTION IS TO GO OUT AND DO SOMETHING KIND FOR SOMEBODY ELSE.

AFTER the birth of my fourth child, the housework piled up, the children were unmanageable and I felt depressed. A kind neighbour began to appear regularly to mop my kitchen floor or iron or read to the children while I took a nap.

When her husband was transferred to another city, before moving she sent me a big box of clothespins and a note: "String this up in your back garden. Get out into God's sunshine and hang up your washing. I'll be thinking of you when I'm hanging up mine."

With my electric dryer so handy, it was hard to follow her advice. But I soon discovered the value of getting out into the wind and sun to put up a row of nappies across a line. I began to get acquainted with my neighbours. I waved to the postman, chatted to delivery boys and patted stray dogs. I even dug in the sandbox with my sons, aged three and four. They in turn helped me fold the nappies. I spent less time on housework, but it no longer seemed so important. I was learning to separate the wheat from the chaff.

The summer passed and with it my weariness and depression.

Mrs. K. J. Baker,
in "Catholic Digest".

December 16th

IN THIS CERTAIN PROMISE, I CAN SAFELY REST: ALL THINGS WORK TOGETHER ALWAYS FOR THE BEST.

I ASKED for strength that I might achieve ... He made me weak that I might obey ... I asked for health that I might do greater things ... I was given Grace that I might do better things ... I asked for riches that I might be happy ... I was given poverty that I might be wise.

I asked for power that I might have the praise of men ... I was given weakness that I might feel the need of God ... I asked for all things that I might enjoy life ... I was given life that I might enjoy all things.

I received nothing I asked for, but all things hoped for. From experience I know this to be true.

Author Unknown.

December 17th

> I THOUGHT IT ONLY HAPPENED SO,
> BUT TIME THIS TRUTH HAS TAUGHT ME;
> GOD NEVER TAKES ONE THING AWAY, BUT
> SOMETHING ELSE IS BROUGHT ME.
>
> *Anonymous.*

WE KNOW a great deal about grief, thanks to the work of social scientists, behavioural specialists, and the medical profession.

For some it is a constant, numbing experience that takes years to surmount. For others it is a temporary pain to be handled as well as possible but destined to pass.

People who deal with the grief-stricken speak of stages of grief. Some have identified as many as 10 such stages. Others, like Rita Barclay, a Long Island widow who founded a group to help widows, reduce the stages of grief to three: the initial shock, a period of suffering, and recovery.

The grieving person may experience anger, guilt, depression, denial, withdrawal, loneliness or yearning. There may also be disorientation, restlessness, loss of energy, anxiety, panic, hostility or a combination of these and other emotions.

No two people experience grief the same way. Children may mourn longer than others because they are beset by uncertainty. The unhappily married who lose a mate sometimes mourn longer because of guilt.

Men frequently find it more difficult to handle grief than women, having been taught to suppress emotion. Many women grieve when a child is stillborn, having already begun to love the baby.

Genevieve M. McClelland of Missouri, whose detective son was killed in the line of duty, spoke for many in describing her grief on visiting his grave.

"The dullness creeps over you and you recognize it instantly. The creeping lethargy—then the sudden, tearing, agonizing ache. The agony of loss. For this is what it is like when you become a citizen of two worlds. The real world—and that other, just as real, the silent, lonely world of grief."

Yet grief has its positive aspects. An old Chinese proverb has it that "Without sorrows no one becomes a saint." The Englishman Edward Markham wrote, "only the soul that knows the mighty grief can know the mighty rapture."

THE CHRISTOPHERS.

December 18th

    I NEED THY PRESENCE EVERY PASSING HOUR;
WHAT BUT THY GRACE CAN FOIL THE TEMPTER'S POWER?
WHO LIKE THYSELF MY GUIDE AND STAY CAN BE?
THROUGH CLOUD AND SUNSHINE, O ABIDE WITH ME.

    ABIDE with me: fast falls the eventide;
The darkness deepens; Lord, with me abide:
When other helpers fail and comforts flee,
Help of the helpless, O abide with me.

Swift to its close ebbs out life's little day;
Earth's joys grow dim, its glories pass away;
Change and decay in all around I see;
O thou, who changest not, abide with me.

I need thy presence every passing hour;
What but thy grace can foil the tempter's power?
Who like thyself my guide and stay can be?
Through cloud and sunshine, O abide with me.

I fear no foe, with thee at hand to bless;
Ills have no weight and tears no bitterness;
Where is death's sting? Where, grave, thy victory?
I triumph still, if thou abide with me.

Hold thou thy cross before my closing eyes;
Shine through the gloom and point me to the skies;
Heaven's morning breaks and earth's vain shadows flee;
In life, in death, O Lord, abide with me.

                                    H. F. Lyte, 1793–1847.

December 19th

WONDROUS PROMISE FROM ABOVE. FROM A FATHER'S HEART OF LOVE: IN ITS FULLNESS SENT TO ME, AS MY DAYS, MY STRENGTH SHALL BE.

NOT to love is not to live, or it is to live a living death. The love that goes out in love to all is the life that is full, and rich, and continually expanding in beauty and in power. This is the life that becomes ever more inclusive, and hence larger in its scope and influence. The larger the man or the woman, the more inclusive they are in their love and their friendships. The smaller the man or the woman, the more dwarfed and dwindling their natures, the more they pride themselves upon their "exclusiveness".

Anyone can be exclusive. It comes easy. It takes and it signifies a large nature to be universal, to be inclusive. Only the man or the woman of a small, personal, self-centred, self-seeking nature is exclusive. The man or the woman of a large, royal, unself-centred nature never is. The small nature is one that continually strives for effect. The large nature never does.

One goes here and there in order to gain recognition, in order to attach himself to the world. The other stays at home and draws the world to him. The one loves merely himself. The other loves all the world: but in his larger love for all the world he finds himself included. The more one loves the nearer he approaches to God, for God is the spirit of infinite love.

RALPH WALDO TRINE.
"In Tune with the Infinite".

December 20th

HOME IS WHERE THE CARES OF THE WORLD ARE SHUT OUT ... I BELIEVE IN THE FAMILY ... I SHARE IN ITS FUN, PEACE AND HAPPINESS.

WHEN I first saw her I never dreamed she would become so special to me. She isn't a person you'd notice in a crowd. If you examine her, feature by feature, you would soon conclude that Susan is plain looking. Except for her eyes, that is. They are large and expressive and the brilliant blue of a summer sky. And, of course, her smile. It lights up her plain face and has a wistful quality as if she were pleading for approval. And her heart—some people laugh and say: "One can't see a heart," but you can Susan's. She is kind and gentle and when we're together all my cares and worries cease.

She loves pretty clothes and enjoys dressing up to please me. She has chosen me as her future husband! She certainly loves me. She shows it in her enthusiastic hugs and soft kisses. And I do love her, very much.

Of course, she's too good to be true; but isn't any 6-year-old girl as seen through the eyes of her father?

DOROTHY LABELLE.
Sunshine Magazine.

December 21st

I AM RESOLVED THAT, AS LONG AS MY DAY LASTS, TO FIND STAMINA AND STRENGTH RISING FROM THE HEART OF EVERY CRISIS.

JUNE 1940. Brigadier Bishop described to us a meeting of the War Cabinet that he had witnessed, at which Winston Churchill, who had just returned from Tours, had announced to his dismayed ministers that France was on the verge of asking Hitler for terms. The Prime Minister had painted the situation in the grimmest possible colours. He had reviewed the desperate military outlook, the desperate political outlook. Coming to his conclusion, he had said in a low, firm voice: "We are now facing Germany completely isolated. We are alone."

"Then," said Brigadier Bishop, "there was a dead silence that I shall never forget. We saw Churchill proudly lifting his head. Looking defiantly at us all, he simply said: 'I find it rather inspiring'."

EVE CURIE,
From *"Journey Among Warriors".*

December 22nd

MY SUCCESS IN THE BIG THINGS IS THE SUM TOTAL OF EFFORTS TO MASTER THE LITTLE THINGS. I AM GLAD OF LIFE BECAUSE IT GIVES ME THE CHANCE TO MAKE A GOOD JOB OF THE MATTER IN HAND.

AFTER a concert Paderewski, the well-known pianist, was asked: "To what do we owe your breathtaking ability on the keyboard?"

Hesitatingly, he replied: "I am not sure. I suppose music was born in me. If I can take any credit at all for being able to play the piano it is perhaps because every day I practice scales for hours on end."

"Scales?" echoed a surprised admirer. "Just scales?"

"Yes, just scales," said the artist. "If I cannot do the little things simply and easily, how am I to do the bigger things?"

Do you not think that so many of us miss the main point of living because we are ever striving for the big things? We envy those who hit the headlines, board their weekend rivercraft, recline in a luxury flat possessing the latest stereophonic "sound" for their background music. We grow impatient when we cannot sing like Joan Sutherland after a few months' tuition, or "put-together" some fabulous flower arrangement after six easy lessons.

Not all of us have been ordained to fame. Let us not waste our powers in vain regrets hankering after the impossible. We cannot all become stars. But we can all shine in our part of the sky. It is when we do the daily humdrum things to perfection that we give our gala performance, bringing help and pleasure to those whose lives touch ours.

THOMAS.

December 23rd

TO SEE A WORLD IN A GRAIN OF SAND, AND HEAVEN IN A WILD FLOWER: HOLD INFINITY IN THE PALM OF YOUR HAND AND ETERNITY IN AN HOUR.

William Blake, 1757–1827.

EVERYONE loves flowers. They make us happy, they make us smile. And the fact that they arrive without fail each spring, peeping through the dark earth, makes even a hardened pessimist believe in the wisdom of nature.

And yet working in the garden on a clear summer day—the air sweet with fragrance, a soft wind rustling through the trees, and the sun shining on all the little masterpieces we call flowers—makes one stop to think how truly fragile all this is.

BARBARA MILE OHRBACH.
From: "A Bouquet of Flowers".

December 24th

FOR UNTO US A CHILD IS BORN, UNTO US A SON IS GIVEN, AND THE GOVERNMENT SHALL BE UPON HIS SHOULDER, AND HIS NAME SHALL BE CALLED WONDERFUL, COUNSELLOR, THE MIGHTY GOD, THE EVERLASTING FATHER, THE PRINCE OF PEACE.

Isaiah 9:2,6.

AND there were in the same country shepherds abiding in the field, keeping watch over their flock by night.

And, lo, the angel of the Lord came upon them, and the glory of the Lord shone round about them: and they were sore afraid.

And the angel said unto them, Fear not: for, behold I bring you good tidings of great joy, which shall be to all people.

For unto you is born this day in the city of David a Saviour, who is Christ the Lord.

And this shall be a sign unto you: Ye shall find the babe wrapped in swaddling clothes, lying in a manger.

And suddenly there was with the angel a multitude of the heavenly host praising God, and saying,

"Glory to God in the highest, and on earth, peace, good will toward men."

Luke 2: 8–14.

December 25th

> LOVE CAME DOWN AT CHRISTMAS,
> LOVE ALL LOVELY, LOVE DIVINE;
> LOVE WAS BORN AT CHRISTMAS,
> STAR AND ANGELS GAVE THE SIGN.
>
> *Traditional Carol.*

ACROSS the gulf of centuries—the angel music comes—above the thunders of the earth—the tumult and the drums—the distant choirs that sing the promise of the golden years—when men shall see a vision through the mist of human tears ... When Peace shall reign upon the earth, and Love be understood—and nations be united in a happy brotherhood ... He came to earth and gave the world His great divine command—"Love one another"—Simple words—when shall we understand? ... The world seems dark and evil, men still doubt, hate and condemn—yet here our eyes may see the glory of a Bethlehem—each time we rise above the mere desire for selfish gain—each time Love triumphs over hate, the Christ is born again.

Patience Strong.
"Quiet Thoughts", Copyright: Rupert Crew Ltd, London.

December 26th

MY PURPOSE SHALL BE TO REACH THE STARS, NOT THAT I ALONE SHALL ENJOY THE SPLENDOUR OF THE HEIGHTS BUT THAT OTHERS MAY FIND THE WAY.

THE words of the beautiful carol "Silent Night" were born, over a hundred years ago, in the village of Arnsdorf, Austria. It happened on the night before Christmas Eve. The parish priest, Father Josef Mohr, was troubled. The old organ in the little church was broken. He thought of the Christmas Eve service. If only there could be some special music!

Coming home from a visit to a parishioner, Father Mohr found himself beneath the stars, on the heights overlooking the little village where a few lights glimmered in the silent darkness. So it must have been in Bethlehem on that silent, holy night when Christ was born. Silent night, holy night! Words came to him. He hastened home and put them down. The next day he showed them to his organist, Franz Gruber. As he read the words, Franz Gruber felt the beauty of that first holy night. He began to sing, and those who listened knew the song would be immortal.

There was no organ music in the church on Christmas Eve. But, as Father Mohr sang, with Franz Gruber accompanying him on the guitar, the congregation listened in wonder to the first rendition of a song that was to be a Christmas gift to all the world—"Silent Night".

AUTHOR UNKNOWN.

HOW GREAT is the wonder of heavenly and earthly things.
Cicero.

December 27th

> SOMEHOW, NOT ONLY FOR CHRISTMAS
> BUT ALL THE LONG YEAR THROUGH
> THE JOY THAT YOU GIVE TO OTHERS
> IS THE JOY THAT COMES BACK TO YOU.

John G. Whittier.
American poet born in Massachusetts.
Always in poor health from overstraining himself by work on the farm. Found strength to communicate hope and inspiration. Was colour blind, deaf and endured hardships before he won through to an inner peace reflected in his poetry.

I SALUTE you. I am your friend, and my love for you goes deep. There is nothing I can give you which you have not already; but there is much, very much, which though I cannot give it, you can take. No heaven can come to us unless our hearts find rest in today. Take heaven. No peace lies in the future which is not hidden in this precious little instant. Take peace. The gloom of the world is but a shadow. Behind it, yet within our reach, is joy. There is radiance and courage in the darkness could we but see; and to see, we have only to look. Life is so generous a giver, but we, judging its gifts by their coverings, cast them away as ugly or heavy or hard. Remove the covering, and you will find beneath it a living splendour, woven of love, and wisdom, and power. Welcome it, greet it, and you touch the angel's hand that brings it.

Everything we call a trial, a sorrow, a duty, believe me, that angel's hand is there, the gift is there, and the wonder of an overshadowing Presence. Our joys, too, be not content with them as joys. They, too, conceal diviner gifts. Life is so full of meaning and purpose, so full of beauty beneath its covering, that you will find earth but cloaks your heaven. Courage, then, to claim it, that is all! But courage you have, and the knowledge that we are pilgrims wending through unknown country our way home.

And so, at this Christmas time, I greet you my friend, not quite as the world sends greetings, but with profound love now and forever.

Yours till the day breaks and the shadows flee away.

GIOVANNI DA FIEOLE,
(Fra Angelico) (1387–1455).

December 28th

FROM NOW ON, I'M GOING TO INVEST IN REAL ASSETS. I NO LONGER RACE. I ENJOY EVERY SECOND, AND PILE UP A BANK OF RICH SIMPLE JOYS. YESTERDAY IS GONE, TOMORROW NEVER COMES. I LIVE IN THE FUN AND THRILL OF TODAY.

IT ISN'T the great big treasures that count the most; it's making a great deal out of the little ones—I've discovered the true secret of happiness, Daddy, and that is to live in the *now*. Not to be for ever regretting the past, or anticipating the future; but to get the most you can out of this very instant. It's like farming. You can have extensive farming and intensive farming. Well, I'm going to have intensive living after this. I'm going to enjoy every second, and I'm going to *know* I'm enjoying it while I'm enjoying it.

Most people don't live. They just race. They are trying to reach some goal far away on the horizon, and in the heat of the going they get so breathless and panting that they lose all sight of the beautiful, tranquil country they are passing through. Then the first thing they know, they are old and worn out, and it doesn't make any difference whether they've reached the goal or not. I've decided to sit down by the way and pile up a lot of little happinesses, even if I never become a great author.

Yours ever, Judy.
JEAN WEBSTER.
"Daddy Long Legs".

Nothing great was ever achieved without enthusiasm.
Ralph Waldo Emerson.

December 29th

BLESSED ARE THE PEACEMAKERS, FOR THEY SHALL BE CALLED THE CHILDREN OF GOD.

Matt: 5.

PEACE is *heavenly*. It is a precious gift of God.

Peace is *beauty*. Nothing can be beautiful without peace. It is not easy to obtain unless one finds peace in his heart first. Without peace everything is ugly.

Peace is *love*. Wherever there is love, there is peace. War never brings love, only hatred and destruction. From love comes friendship and freedom. Peace is like a cup of cool water to the thirsty.

Peace is *blessed*, for those who give it and receive it. "Blessed are the peacemakers," Christ said, "for they shall be called the children of God."

HERMINE YAKOVBIAN *(aged 8)*.
Kokkinis, Greece.

December 30th

BEHOLD THIS, AND ALWAYS LOVE IT ... THE WHOLE OF CREATION IS VERY SACRED ... AND YOU MUST TREAT IT AS SUCH.

Sioux Indian.

... LOVE will teach us all things, but we must learn how to win love; it is got with difficulty: it is a possession dearly bought with much labour and in a long time; for one must love not sometimes only, for a passing moment, but always. There is no man who doth not sometimes love; even the wicked can do that.

And let not men's sin dishearten thee: love a man even in his sin, for that love is a likeness of the divine love, and is the summit of love on earth. Love all God's creation, both the whole and every grain of sand. Love every leaf, every ray of light. Love the animals, love the plants, love each separate thing. If thou love each thing thou wilt perceive the mystery of God in all; and when once thou perceive this, thou wilt thenceforward grow every day to a fuller understanding of it: until thou come at last to love the whole world with a love that will then be all-embracing and universal.

DOSTOEVSKY.
From Father Zossima's discourse in "The Brothers Karamazof".

December 31st

I AM NOT ALONE ... ALL THAT I HAVE SEEN TEACHES ME TO TRUST THE INVISIBLE FOR WHAT I HAVE NOT SEEN.
Author Unknown.

I FEEL within me the future life. I am like a forest that has been razed; the new shoots are stronger and brisker. I shall most certainly rise forward toward the heavens. The sun's rays bathe my head. The earth gives me its generous sap, but the heavens illuminate me with the reflection of—of worlds unknown. Some say the soul results merely from bodily powers. Why, then, does my soul become brighter when my bodily powers begin to waste away? Winter is above me, but eternal spring is within my heart.

I inhale even now the fragrance of lilacs, violets, and roses, just as I did when I was twenty.

The nearer my approach to the end, the plainer is the sound of immortal symphonies of worlds which invite me. It is wonderful yet simple. It is a fairy tale; it is history.

For half a century I have been translating my thoughts into prose and verse; history, philosophy, drama, romance, tradition, satire, ode and song. All these I have tried. But I feel I haven't given utterance to the thousandth part of what lies within me. When I go to the grave I can say as others have said, "My day's work is done." But I cannot say, "My life is done".

Victor Hugo, 1802–1885.
French novelist-poet. Much travelled during his childhood, his father being a general under Napoleon Bonaparte. Married his childhood sweetheart and introduced the new romantic movement in literature, writing his famous novel "Les Misérables" on Guernsey, Channel Islands.

✳